THE
AMISH
QUILT

Split Bars
Sugarcreek, Holmes County, Ohio, circa 1910–20
Cotton sateen, plain-weave cotton percale • 71 × 86½ • Darwin D. Bearley collection

THE AMISH QUILT

Eve Wheatcroft Granick

Good Books
Intercourse, Pennsylvania 17534

Acknowledgements

In researching and preparing this book there were many individuals who generously offered information, assistance, insight and encouragement. I would particularly like to thank the following people for their efforts: Darwin Bearley, David Pottinger, Jonathan Holstein, Gail van der Hoof, Kate and Joel Kopp, Julie Silber, Stephen Evans, Don and Patricia Herr, David Luthy, Michael Oruch, Rebecca Haarer, Joyce Brown and William Greenburg.

Grateful acknowledgement also goes to John A. Hostetler, Frederick Weiser, Marilyn Woodin, Connie Hayes, Scott and Cindy Albright, Daniel and Kathryn McCauley, Michael Kile, Roderick Kiracofe, John Wheatcroft, Quica Ostrander and Lydia Ann Nolt.

I would like to thank the following institutions and their staff members for making valuable research materials available for study and reproduction: Philadelphia College of Textile and Design, Philadelphia, Pennsylvania; *The Sugarcreek Budget,* Sugarcreek, Ohio; Goshen College Library and Archives, Goshen, Indiana; Sears Archives, Chicago, Illinois; New York City Public Library, New York, New York; ESPIRIT collection, San Francisco, California; and the county courthouse offices of Records, Wills and Deeds in Mifflin, Lancaster, Somerset and Union counties, Pennsylvania; Wayne, Holmes and Geauga counties, Ohio; Elkhart and LaGrange counties, Indiana; and Johnson County, Iowa.

Special mention must be made to the many women and men who would prefer to remain anonymous in Amish communities throughout the United States. I would like to thank all of those who spoke willingly, with great enthusiasm and often in great detail about their lives and their quilts. Many of the women who were interviewed in the course of my research have since passed away. We are fortunate that they helped us to preserve their oral histories. We are grateful for their time and efforts. Above all, I would like to thank my husband, David Wheatcroft. This book is the result of his assistance in gathering information, his insights and knowledge of the Amish and their quilts and, finally, and most importantly, his constant support and encouragement.

All photography by Jonathan Charles except: pages 39, 87, 102, 152, ESPRIT collection, San Francisco; pages 31, 82, 90, 118, 143, 144, 161, 162, 163, 164, 165, America Hurrah Antiques, N.Y.C.; page 141, Harvey Pranian; page 31, Indiana State Museum; page 141, Kelter-Malcé. Reprints on page 59 courtesy of *The Sugarcreek Budget,* page 62 Goshen College Library, and pages 65, 66, 67, 68, 69, 70, 71 courtesy of Sears Archives.

Design by Cheryl A. Benner
The Amish Quilt
© 1989 by Good Books, Intercourse, PA 17534
International Standard Book Number: 0-934672-74-1
Library of Congress Catalog Card Number: 89-39987

Library of Congress Cataloging-in-Publication Data

Granick, Eve Wheatcroft, 1954-
  The Amish Quilt / Eve Wheatcroft Granick.

    p.   cm.
  Includes bibliographical references.
  ISBN 0-934672-74-1 ; $45.00
  1. Quilts, Amish—History 2. Amish—Social life
  and customs.
I. Title.
NK9112.G7 1989   89-39987
746.9'7'088287—dc20   CIP

Crazy Quilt
Arthur, Illinois, circa 1910–20 • Made by Mattie Mast Kauffman.
Plain- and twill-weave cottons • 71 × 80 • Eve Granick and David Wheatcroft

Preface

Much has been written about the Amish and their quilts in recent years. Quilts have been collected, photographed, displayed, bought and sold for some time now. Today there are only a few old quilts left in the homes of Amish families. Many Amish have sold their quilts to pickers and antique dealers who have filled the marketplace with Amish quilts of all ages, sizes and descriptions. In the rush to gather these quilts for sale, often little attention has been paid to the oral and written histories that accompany these textiles.

The **Amish Quilt** draws together the body of available information about the Amish and their textile traditions. Much of what is presented here comes from interviews and conversations with Amish families and with people whose lives have touched the Amish community. Research in county courthouse records and public libraries provided other valuable data and insight. Finally, there is the information based on seeing these quilts in Amish homes, watching them come out of blanket chests or off beds. When women were asked about the age or history of their quilts they had much to say. By listening to their stories, handling thousands of quilts, examining fabrics and comparing quilts made in different communities, we can begin to develop a larger sense of the Amish and their quilts.

— *Eve Wheatcroft Granick*
April 1989

Stripes
Kansas, circa 1910–20 • Plain-weave cotton percale, cotton sateen, plain-weave wool
37 × 45 • Michael Oruch

Introduction

The quilts made by Amish women in the years between the last quarter of the 19th century and the midpoint of the 20th century represent a unique achievement in American quiltmaking. The work of a small and relatively insulated group of women, these textiles are an expression of both personal and group sensibilities about the use of color and design. Their creation and use in the home are part of a way of life that centers on simplicity and places a high value on symbolism.

Textiles provide visual clues about the interests and concerns of any cultural group. They offer a subtle reflection of the emotional make-up of a group, as well as its individual members. The motifs, colors and designs in the quilts made by Amish women also reflect the group's history and its collective outlook on life.

As a society committed to simplicity and humility, the Amish place certain restrictions on the practice of the decorative arts. Rather than being vehicles for bold self-expression or individual achievement, Amish quilts must serve a utilitarian purpose while remaining within a seemingly narrow set of aesthetic boundaries.

The Amish are not ascetics; they do value well made objects and find great satisfaction in the creation of useful and decorative works. They do believe, however, that their enjoyment of the material world must be weighed against the larger claims of their religious faith. The tensions that arise out of the effort to maintain a proper balance between pride and humility, and between simplicity and more complex, "worldly" choices are well expressed in Amish quilts.

We enjoy these quilts for their decorative or visual impact and marvel at their surprising similarity to works of modern art. Their appeal is immediate and apparent to even the most casual viewer. If, however, we limit our interest solely to what we see, we lose a large measure of the meaning of these textiles. By examining Amish quilts in the light of their particular cultural and historical background, we can understand and appreciate both the objects themselves and the unique society that has created them.

As a group that has chosen to live apart from the ways of the world, the Amish must be both aware of and sensitive to that world which they strive to avoid. Amish quilts reflect both the interaction with and the avoidance of "English" culture, which the group has practiced successfully for two and a half centuries. These quilts bridge two worlds, enriching our vision of the Amish community and illuminating the larger world of American quiltmaking and textile arts.

Streak of Lightning
Indiana, dated "1927" • Plain-weave cotton percale, cotton sateen • 73 × 85
Eve Granick and David Wheatcroft

10

The Amish Church Community: Its Beginnings

Anabaptism and the Amish

The Amish are a small and highly conservative branch of the larger religious movement known as Anabaptism. The origins of this movement and of the "plain sects" which include the Amish were an outgrowth of the Protestant Reformation of 16th century Europe. In an era of dramatic and drastic changes in all aspects of European life, Anabaptism called for a purification of both the individual and the church.

Anabaptism was considered by the church and state to be a particularly dangerous ideology. The very word *Anabaptist* springs from the legal language of the Roman Catholic church, describing an individual who has challenged the authority of the clergy by practicing the punishable heresy of rebaptism. Members of the new movement called themselves "Brethren." Later they were nicknamed "Mennonites," after Menno Simons, a prominent leader from the Netherlands.

The concerns of the state and church officials were perhaps well founded, for Anabaptism was a radical departure from the established order. Anabaptists sought a more complete reformation of spiritual life than either Luther's Protestant movement or Zwingli's Swiss Reformed church. Protestant doctrine still considered all citizens as automatic members of the state church. For Protestants, infant baptism symbolized the entry of an individual into that community. For the Anabaptists, on the other hand, a voluntary commitment of faith could only by made by those with adult understanding. They considered infant baptism as invalid and their admission into the spiritual community not as a rebaptism, but as the only true baptism.

Anabaptism has no single founder as the Lutherans, for example, had. Several leaders did emerge, however, giving their names to various expressions of the movement: Menno Simons (Mennonites), Jacob Amman (Amish) and Jacob Hutter (Hutterites). Though Anabaptism was never a unified or well organized movement, there were a number of conferences and meetings held in the 16th and 17th centuries to formulate doctrines of faith.[1] Despite the efforts of the church and state authorities to suppress them, the ideas agreed upon at these meetings captured the imagination of enough people that Anabaptist congregations grew rapidly throughout the Palatinate in southern Germany, in the Netherlands and throughout Switzerland. However enthusiastic they were, these groups were unorganized and persecuted relentlessly by state authorities. Many of the groups flourished for brief periods and then, unable to withstand the persecution, disappeared.

The history of this time is recounted vividly in the *Martyrs Mirror*, a book found in most Amish homes today. The memory of persecution and the sentiment of estrangement from the larger society are pervasive concepts in Anabaptism.

The development and growth of the Anabaptist movement in Europe was a remarkable, if relatively small, event achieved at great cost in human lives and suffering. While the initial concepts were the work of a small group of radical intellectuals, the growth and spread of this faith speaks of the power behind the message. In an age of great concern about matters of the spirit, people from all levels of the European population were drawn into the movement, expressing their faith in the face of great odds.

Of the extensive variety of sects that sprang up during the early years of Anabaptism, three primary ones have survived to the present day: the Mennonites, the Amish and the Hutterites.

Beginning of the Amish Church

The history of the Swiss Brethren or Mennonites, as the early followers of Anabaptism were often called during the 200 years before their emigration to America, is a long and complex story of growth, persecution and innumerable migrations within the European continent.

The schism which led to the formation of the Amish as a separate group did not occur until the 1690s, more than 150 years after the beginning of the Anabaptist movement. Sociologist John Hostetler has described this split as "merely a family squabble" when compared to the major religious upheavals of the period. He also suggests that, although the struggle for leadership among the Swiss Brethren (Mennonites) had much to do with the personalities and personal ambitions of several leaders, the tensions created by the differences in experience between the original "mother" community in Switzerland and the "daughter" community where Jacob Amman was bishop may have been equally important.[2]

Jacob Amman was a Mennonite bishop living in the Alsace region of the Rhine Valley. Many of the Alsatian Brethren were immigrants from Switzerland, where they had suffered severely under the state-run program of persecution during much of the 1600s. When they were permitted to leave Switzerland and move to the Alsace region, they achieved a small measure of security and found land and livelihoods under the auspices of local princes to whom they felt gratitude and a certain degree of loyalty. The Alsace area was, in those years, a haven from religious persecution; several other minority groups also settled in the region. In this atmosphere of general peace there were social and even religious associations that developed between the Brethren and their neighbors. The ambivalence created in this atmosphere of liberalized attitudes greatly concerned Amman. He feared that these sentiments were leading the group into compromises that were unacceptable in religious terms and dangerous to the social unity of the group.

Amman sought a stricter discipline of the membership than was practiced by Swiss Brethren groups in other areas. Concerned that the church maintain its purity, he supported the Dutch Mennonite practices detailed in the Dordrecht Confession and urged the use of shunning and the ban when members digressed. The practice was intended as a disciplinary measure that would eventually draw transgressors back to the group. In addition, Amman emphasized the practice of footwashing as Jesus did for his disciples immediately prior to his death. He also advocated simplicity in clothing and appearance. Amman's intent was to strengthen both the resolve and identity of the Mennonites so they would not lose their faithfulness and distinguishing qualities. Although some of his fellow ministers found his ideas too harsh and confining and his personality somewhat strident, Amman maintained his convictions.

In 1693 Amman confronted the leadership of the Swiss Mennonites in Switzerland, the Alsace and Germany. Of the 69 ministers in the area of the Rhine Valley, 26 sided with Amman. Twenty of these were ministers from the Alsace region. They, along with one group in Switzerland and five in Germany, followed Amman. These congregations came to be known as "Amish." Although there were some attempts in the early 1700s to resolve the differences between the two factions, they could not reach an agreement, and the separation continued.[3]

The Amish concern for a strong and visible faith community, supported by a discipline that separates them from the secular world, has been a key element in their survival in North America. Today the Amish regard themselves as the most conservative branch of Mennonites. They live in close proximity to a variety of Mennonites groups with whom, despite their differences, they feel a special affinity.

The Principles of Faith

During the course of two and a half centuries in America, the Amish have evolved from a handful of isolated immigrants into a culture whose endurance, strength and symbolism offers a dynamic social message. Resisting attempts to force them into the mainstream of American life, they have survived the stress of wars and the equally disruptive effects of the industrial revolution. They have also withstood the frantic pace of social change, urban sprawl and technological growth which has so radically altered American culture over the past two centuries. However, despite their concerted effort to remain unchanged, the Amish today are different from their ancestors who arrived in Pennsylvania in the 18th century. They are even substantially different from their more immediate forebears of the late 19th and early 20th centuries.

While successfully maintaining many aspects of pre-industrial American and European culture, they have also selectively accepted changes that were necessary to ensure their survival as a group. While absorbing some of American culture, they have remained staunchly committed to certain basic principles. This combination of adaptation and persistence has created a society capable of straddling two worlds. The Amish adhere to a social order emphasizing strong family and community life, they maintain a link to their historical past and they integrate their religious faith with all aspects of everyday life. Consequently, they have survived and even thrived as a group. By examining their principles and expressions of faith we can gain insight into both Amish culture and the objects created by these people.

Flying Geese
Indiana, circa 1920 – 30 • Plain-weave cotton percale, broadcloth, cotton sateen
61 × 74 • Kelter-Malcé Antiques, New York City

13

Gemeinde

The Amish use a single word, *Gemee,* to describe one of the most important aspects of their daily and religious life. *Gemee* is a dialect form of the German word, *Gemeinde,* meaning community, communion and fellowship of all members of a faith.[4] This strong sense of community and spiritual unity and the sense of the group's importance over the individual is intrinsic to Amish life.

Nearly all Amish members can trace their family lines back to a handful of European immigrants. Moreover, during two and a half centuries they have consistently intermarried and experienced little influx of "outsiders" into their group. Consequently, most Amish are at least indirectly related to one another. In addition to an historical group solidarity, the Amish strive to maintain a quality of smallness in their communities. This is a basic principle of organization, and each settlement is divided into church districts of no more than about 20 to 30 families. Even among the largest settlements, the Amish community is organized and experienced as a family and friendship group.

The sense of community, unified by bonds of faith, is a significant part of each member's experience of spiritual salvation. It is not possible, within this framework, to separate how one lives from what one believes, nor is it possible to be separate from the community if one is obedient. Fundamentalist Christians find salvation and "grace through faith alone," while the Amish also rely upon the discipline and support of their faith community. Faith and good intentions are not enough. Only by also practicing self-denial and obedience, living in "full fellowship" and living apart from the world may the Amish hope for salvation.

Responsibility to the group and separation from the rest of the world are principles based on very literal interpretations of biblical injunc-

tions, such as:

> . . . Be not conformed to this world: but be ye transformed by the renewing of your mind, that ye may prove what is that good, and acceptable, and perfect will of God. (Romans 12:2)
>
> Be ye not unequally yoked together with unbelievers: . . . what communion hath light with darkness? (II Corinthians 6:14)

These definitions and conception of the church are the ideals to which the community strives. They are difficult standards and the individuals in the community are humans who must cope with pride and desire. The rewards of the struggle are a rich and sustaining family and community life. Consequently, the world outside the tight sphere of community, church and family is of little concern for the Amish person.[5]

The *Ordnung*

Gemee is the sentiment that binds the Amish together emotionally. It is the *Ordnung* (pronounced "ott-ning") that provides the rules for their social order.

The *Ordnung* consists of two separate sets of instructions to the membership. The first part is written and includes the articles of faith which were developed at conferences held in the early 16th century and adapted since then. The articles of faith from the Dordrecht Confession of 1660 are printed and accepted by the Amish church, as well as by many Mennonite groups. Included are such basic doctrines as non-resistance and non-violence, what constitutes apostasy, and guidelines for the correction or shunning of wayward members.

The *Ordnung* and disciplines of the 19th century added more specific and restrictive statements. These reflect the tensions and uncertainties of that period and the need to clarify for the membership what was not acceptable in the face of expanding choices. The following two examples speak specifically about the use of decoration in the home and style of clothing:

> Decided that there shall be no display in houses, namely when the houses are built or painted, with various colors or filled with showy furniture, namely with wood, porcelain or glass dishes and having cupboards and mirrors hung on the wall and such things . . . the cabinet makers are not to make such proud kinds of furniture and not to decorate them with such loud or gay colors. (Discipline of 1837, Somerset County)

> Likewise, decided not to allow gayly colored, stripped or flowered clothing made according to the fashions of the world . . . also it is considered improper to decorate the house with all sorts of unnecessary and luxurious things such as gayly colored walls, window curtains, large mirrors and such.[6] (Discipline of 1865, Holmes County)

This *Ordnung,* written in the 1950s, explains in even greater detail what is and is not considered correct:

> No ornamental, bright, showy, form fitting, immodest or silk like clothing of any kind. Colors such as bright red, orange, yellow, pink are not allowed. Amish form of dress to be followed. Costly Sunday clothing to be discouraged. Dresses not shorter than half way between knees and floor. Longer advisable. Clothing in every way modest, serviceable and as simple as scripturally possible. Only outside pockets allowed are one on work *eberhern* or *vomas* and pockets on large overcoats. Dress coats, if any, to be plain black only. No high heels or pump slippers. Dress socks to be black except for foot hygiene for both sexes.

> Hat to be black, no pressed trousers, no sweaters. Prayer covering to be simple. To be worn wherever possible. Young children to dress according to the word as well as parents. No pink or fancy baby shawls, bonnets or caps. Women to wear shawls, bonnets and caps in public. Apron to be worn at all times. No decoration of any kind in buildings, inside or out. No fancy yard fences. Linoleum, oilcloth shelf and wall paper to be plain and unshowy. No large mirrors, statues or wall pictures for decorations. Curtains either dark green rollers or black. No boughten dolls. Not bottle gas or high line electrical. Stoves to be blackened if bought new. Weddings should be simple and without decoration.[7]

The first part of the *Ordnung* is written and includes both basic doctrines and specific rules. The second part is generally unwritten and represents the current thinking of the church leaders and community members in each particular church district. Here are described what the community regards as worldly, what practices are to be maintained and what changes are acceptable to the group. Despite their specific nature, these guidelines are usually preserved only orally, since each member understands what is being stated, or even implied. This group knowledge is a mixture of biblically inspired rules and time tested customs, supported by a tradition of respect for *Das Alt Gebrach* (the old way).[8]

It is the unwritten portion of the *Ordnung* that most often applies specifically to quiltmaking. Rather than rules, these are generally held perceptions about the proper way to make a quilt. In fact, when Amish women were asked

Split Bars
Ohio, circa 1920 – 30
Cotton sateen • 69 × 76 • Jonathan Holstein and Gail Van der Hoof
These two quilts were made in Ohio by a woman who moved there from Lancaster.

16

what guidelines affected the design or colors of their quilts, most responded, "There aren't any rules really; certain things just look better."[9] A few women did mention color restrictions or the required use of only solid colored materials, but in most communities there seemed to be no stated or specific rules.

This variety of both written and understood rules that govern the details of daily life in different communities is an example of the adaptive process permitted by the Amish church. Conformity is more easily attained and maintained when practices are agreed upon by a relatively small group of friends and family members. Consequently, a variety of details in custom and discipline can exist between one church district and the next, although there is general unity within a whole community on the most basic issues. Within each congregation members strive to agree on how to be different from the world, and how to live faithfully according to their understanding of the scriptures.

In the large Amish communities in Indiana and Ohio, Amish families living as neighbors on the same road may belong to different church districts or different church groups, which are distinguished as "higher" or "lower" in their interpretation of the basic rules. One farm family may use a gas-run refrigerator, while their next-door neighbors have a traditional oak ice box. The objects found in the home of a Nebraska Amish family in Mifflin County are considerably less advanced technically than those of their Renno (Peachey) Amish neighbors, who belong to a less conservative or "higher" group.[10] A quilt made while living in one community might be put away and never used again if the family moves to another settlement where the rules are more restrictive. In some communities, using a particular color in quilts or clothing may be unacceptable, whereas another community will have no restrictions on its use.

Bow Tie
Ohio, circa 1920–30
Cotton sateen • 67 × 88 • Jonathan Holstein and Gail Van der Hoof

In the end, the rules themselves are not as important as the members' willing obedience to the group's decision. The Amish value the community voice more highly than individual preference. In exchange, the group offers support and security to those who belong.

One man who is a member of a fairly strict group in Indiana explained his reluctance to suggest changes, despite his desire to do so. "It's true we'd like to have a gas refrigerator. But no one wants to bring up changes, for these little things can lead to a big argument."[11] This effort to avoid disagreements leads to considerable harmony. Agreement among members is reinforced by the biannual communion and footwashing, prior to which members are asked to state their peace with the *Ordnung* and their "fellow men." Thus the impetus toward change is held in check, and the "old way" is preserved, or its erosion is at least slowed.

The Amish and Other Pennsylvania Germans Settle in America

The Amish who came to Pennsylvania during the colonial period were part of a small group of Anabaptists that included the Mennonites and other "plain" groups. The Amish also belonged to a larger community, known as the Pennsylvania Dutch or Pennsylvania Germans. The Amish, along with thousands of other German-speaking immigrants, came from the area of southern Germany along the upper and middle Rhine known as the Palatinate (or Palatine), and from the French Alsace region.

Through much of the 16th, 17th and 18th centuries the Palatinate was fragmented by political and religious warfare. During the 16th century alone, the population was compelled by law to change its religion five times to match the faiths of an ever changing succession of rulers.[12]

These events affected a wide spectrum of citizens, including Lutherans, Reformed, Schwenkfelders, Dunkards, Moravians and Mennonites. Years of intermittent warfare, religious persecution and the devastation of the agricultural and urban life of the Palatinate during much of the 17th century helped to foster the atmosphere that led many to consider emigration to Pennsylvania. All of these groups, who shared the dialect known today as Pennsylvania Dutch and the cultural, social and artistic traditions of the Rhineland and Palatine, joined in the movement to the New World in search of a more secure economic future and greater religious freedom.

Beginning in the 1680s with the arrival of Francis Pastorius and his "German Quakers," Germans began to come to Pennsylvania in great numbers.[13] The emigration grew to massive proportions by the end of the 18th century. The total number of Germanic immigrants who arrived in America between 1683 and 1820 approached 75,000 people and is a part of what historians consider a major demographic shift.[14] In the 70 years between 1720 and 1790, the Commonwealth of Pennsylvania saw its population grow from 30,692 to 434,000 people. The newcomers included Europeans of every nationality, but the Germans constituted a particularly large percentage and accounted for 33 percent of the total Pennsylvania population by 1790.[15]

Although there were thousands of Pennsylvania German immigrants, the Anabaptist groups made up only a small percentage of the total. Among those, the Amish represented a fractional number. Both Hostetler and historian C. Henry Smith estimate that no more than 500 Amish came to America during the colonial period, and they believe that an even smaller figure may be more accurate.[16] These numbers are important to remember when considering the lives of the colonial Amish. Although they maintained strict attitudes of separation, their small numbers would suggest that they were at least minimally linked to the rest of the Pennsylvania German community. We should keep in mind that, however different the Amish appeared, they were still a part of the larger cultural group of Pennsylvania Germans.

The majority of German immigrants to Pennsylvania were members of the Lutheran and Reformed churches; most were drawn from the German middle class. Their migration to the New World seemed less the result of religious persecution and more likely the quest for economic security. Seeking a sort of "upward mobility" they anglicized their names and lifestyles, learned English quickly and educated their children in the prevalent English culture of the day. Within a generation, most of these people were absorbed into the mainstream.[17]

Others, particularly the later arrivals who settled farther away from Philadelphia, as well as those belonging to sectarian groups, strove to maintain the language and cultural heritage of their homeland. Between 1740 and 1840, the production of distinctive Pennsylvania German furniture, tools, pottery, painting, textiles and household objects flourished among these immigrants.

Among the Palatinates, the Amish were relatively late arrivals to Pennsylvania, although the exact date of their coming to America is unknown. A few individuals or single families may have immigrated as early as the mid-1720s, but without the support of their church community these people likely joined the Mennonites or another religious group already established in the New World.[18]

In 1727, the Provincial Council of Pennsylvania began to require all incoming vessels to submit complete ship lists and each adult male was required to swear a declaration of allegiance to the English crown.[19] It is from these ship lists that genealogists and historians have been able

to determine the pattern and dates of the arrival of the Amish in America.

There are some individual passengers with typically Amish names listed on a few ships which came between 1727 and 1737, but it was not until the arrival of the *Charming Nancy* in October 1737 that a group of families who were clearly Amish appeared.[20] Smith and Hostetler note that organized Amish church life in the New World probably did not begin before this point.[21]

Other arrivals followed in September of 1742 on the ships *Francis* and *Elizabeth,* in 1749 on the *St. Andrew* and in 1750 on the *Brotherhood.* Several individuals arrived between 1750 and 1754 and a few were named on ship logs as late as 1765 and 1766. The major movement of Amish immigration in the 18th century is con-

Sewing Pockets and Pincushions • Mifflin County, Pennsylvania, 1820s, 1830s, 1840s
The People's Place Quilt Museum • Eve Granick and David Wheatcroft
The group of pockets, pincushions and the bird were hung by the string under the lid of a blanket chest. The printed fabrics and family histories help to date these items to the 1820s.

sidered to have been virtually complete by 1754.

Though they numbered less than 500 people, they were noticed, and there are reports on the group as early as 1737. Durst Thomme, in a letter to friends in Switzerland, wrote:

> There are a variety of sects here, Mennonite, Pietists, Lutheran, Amish, Seven Day Adventist, Catholics. All different nationalities are very friendly to one another.[22]

In 1742 Hans Burchalter in a letter to the Amsterdam Mennonite Relief Committee reported that "a number of Amisch in the Palatine are preparing to leave for Penncylfania."[23] In that same year, the Amish living in Pennsylvania petitioned the Provincial Assembly for exemption from taking an oath of allegiance when becoming naturalized. In a letter written in 1773 to colleagues in Europe, a Mennonite leader in Philadelphia wrote:

> As to the Amisch, they are many in number but they are not here near us and we can give no further information concerning them except this, that they hold very fast to the outward and ancient institution . . . concerning the question as to how many communities they have, we . . . are not in a situation to give definitely a number of even our own: and as for the Amisch, we also do not know in what places they dwell among us.[24]

After arriving in Pennsylvania, the Amish quickly moved away from areas populated by Mennonites and other religious groups, and sought farmland in both Lancaster and Berks counties. By 1740 there was a congregation of Amish families living near Hamburg in Berks County and a second settlement near Old Conestoga (Manheim and Upper Leacock townships) in Lancaster. These two settlements are regarded as the first in America. Land records show that these families selected contiguous farm sites, creating Amish neighborhoods. Many of the land grants list Amish names as the original title owners. Wills, estate records, tax lists and church alms books indicate that these farmers had small holdings and practiced diversified and largely self-sufficient farming operations. Their farms and homes appear to have been generally equivalent in size and holdings to their non-Amish neighbors in the largely Germanic communities near them.[25]

In 1760 a new settlement was established on the border of Lancaster, Chester and Berks counties. By 1767 several families had headed further west into Somerset County, and, in the last decade of the 18th century, families from Lancaster and Berks counties moved into the Kishacoquillas valley of Mifflin County. At the beginning of the 19th century the total American Amish population resided in Lancaster, Berks, Somerset, Chester and Mifflin counties in Pennsylvania and probably did not exceed a total of 1200 men, women and children. A large number of the Old Order Amish population in the United States today are the direct descendants of these few early families.

The Lives of the Colonial Amish

Their first years in Pennsylvania were difficult, filled with great uncertainty and disorganization. Unlike the Mennonites who arrived in larger numbers, the Amish were a comparatively small group, beset with many problems. That they survived these early struggles in a frontier environment attests to their strength and tenacity.

Facing the Amish leadership were spiritual, social, physical and economic difficulties. These issues forced the Amish to regroup several times and seek out new areas for communities. Some settlements were more successful

Bars
Lancaster County, Pennsylvania • circa 1910–25
Twill- and plain-weave wools • 72 × 83 • Jonathan Holstein and Gail Van der Hoof

than others, depending on a combination of such factors as geography and the charismatic powers of certain individuals who helped hold the group together.

The organization and structure of Amish community life as it exists today was unknown in the 18th century. Families were scattered over a wide geographic area, which sometimes made a sense of community almost impossible. Although the Amish were a rather distinctive group, in the early years a standardized way of life was not clearly defined and families often maintained a fair degree of autonomy.[26] The standards of color and form in dress, transportation, household goods and decorative arts, those objects which today symbolize the Amish, were relatively undefined in the 18th century.

Proselytizing by active religious groups was perhaps one of the largest threats to early Amish settlers in North America. The Amish church was not highly organized at that time; a few bishops traveled from one area to another offering only infrequent services and performing ceremonial rites of baptism, marriage and death. Consequently, the pull of more organized groups was strong. Furthermore, the small size of the Amish community led to many young people marrying outside the Amish church. Throughout the 18th century, some Amish families joined either the Dunkards, United Brethren or Lutherans.[27]

Much of Amish history in America has been shaped by their constant need for good land at affordable prices. Historian Richard K. MacMaster suggests that the Amish who cleared land in Pennsylvania's Berks County region were an example of those who settled in "fringe areas in order to afford viable-sized farms. Since the soil in those areas was thinner, they seem to have found a new reason to move on to new frontiers: soil depletion."[28] Indian raids threatened also, especially in the more isolated, outlying areas, but most families survived those.

Their greater problem was poor soil. This theory is supported by the fact that, whereas the most deadly Indian attacks occured in 1757, the Northkill community remained, as late as 1785, the strongest Amish settlement in America. During the colonial period, as well as today, Amish families needed land of sufficient quantity and quality to sustain themselves and their community. Moving for the purpose of assuring their economic survival has been one of the most commonly cited reasons in Amish history for abandoning a settlement to begin another.

Economic conditions and religious purity were variables that the Amish could control to a degree by moving on to form new settlements. But the Revolutionary War engulfed all Pennsylvanians, and the Amish community was not exempt from the anguish. Along with the members of other traditional "peace churches," the Amish were subjected to fines, imprisonment, double and triple taxes and confiscation of their property.

Although the Revolutionary War was a difficult time, it also strengthened the Amish and other sectarian groups as well. In the colonial period before the Revolution, religious practices were less clearly defined. Settlers were preoccupied with physical survival and the church had not yet established a clear identity in the New World. Joseph F. Beiler writes that in those years "most of our ancestors' families have not raised more than one son to remain in the old faith. Some have not kept any and some have kept a few."[29] The Revolution and the official persecution that the sectarians suffered during the 1770s and 1780s helped to foster their renewed feelings of separation and alienation from the larger society. In the years following the War, new standards for membership were established within these churches and a tightening of the ranks occurred. Ironically, what reformers of the church had been unable to effect, the government did for them.[30]

The 19th Century and Changing Lifestyles

By the beginning of the 19th century, the Amish, a group of perhaps 1200 to 1500 people, had settled into communities in various Pennsylvania counties. There is no evidence that these early families made or used quilts. Only a handful of objects have survived from the early 19th century; given the relatively small number of people and the Amish tendency toward pragmatism, this lack of carefully preserved heirlooms is not surprising.

The written record, however, in the form of wills, tax records, estate inventories and a few contemporary reports, does provide much information about the possessions of these people. It appears that early 19th century Amish families had little material wealth. The transatlantic trip was costly and many arrived in America without funds and only a few possessions. Some were forced to work as redemptioneers for a period of time. Others started out by leasing land or working as tenant farmers until they could save enough to purchase their own farms. David Beiler, the great-grandson of Jacob Beiler who emigrated in 1737, wrote of his forebears' lives:

> Nearly all our ancestors came to this land poor and had to manage with scanty food and clothes . . . and live almost in huts. I have been told that [an Amish man named] Kurtz and his wife had no table for a time. They held the dish with their food in their lap.[31]

As is the practice today, the early Amish aided one another financially. It was fairly common for them to make a joint purchase of land. Their religious understandings encouraged their working together and even pooling their resources, so that they were able to purchase land only a few years after their arrival and then to prosper relatively quickly.[32] Those who achieved comparative prosperity contributed to the stability of the church, since poorer members were often forced to become laborers in settings where they were more influenced by outside forces.[33]

Amish families' estate records from this period mention a variety of simple household goods, roughly equivalent to those found in most other Pennsylvania German homes of the time. The tax lists of Amish farmers in Berks County show small holdings of livestock, generally two horses and two cows.[34] Jacob Beiler's will, dated July 19, 1765, listed a stable, the old house, cherry trees, a meadow hemp patch and orchard, crops of wheat, rye, flax and straw. He left his wife two cows and a hog. He also instructed his heirs, in great detail, about the care of his widow and the management of the farm.[35]

Other Amish farmers' wills mentioned furniture, beds and bedsteads, farm animals, tools, grain and fruit trees. The bed, bedstead and textiles are all given significant value in these documents, and the description of these articles is no different from those described in the inventories and wills of other rural Pennsylvania German families in that period.

Contemporary reports provide some insight into the domestic life of these early Pennsylvanians. Benjamin Rush in his treatise on Pennsylvania German life wrote:

> . . . the first dwelling house upon the farm is small and built of logs. The German farmers live frugally in their families in respect to diet, furniture and apparel. The furniture in their house is plain and useful . . . they cover themselves in winter with light feather beds instead of blankets. The apparel of German families is usually home spun.[36]

In addition to the public record and accounts by observers, an invaluable essay, written in 1864 by a prominent Old Order bishop named David Beiler, describes life among the Amish at the beginning of the 19th century. Born in 1786, Beiler was 76 years old when he wrote this document for his children. An advocate of maintaining the old ways, Beiler let his writing reflect his personal concerns, but the differences in the inventories from the beginning of the century to the mid-1800s do support his contention that life among the Amish had changed. A general growing prosperity had affected the types and quantity of objects owned by many Amish families. David Beiler wrote in 1864:

> Now I will also tell of the great changes during these sixty years . . . Whoever has not experienced it himself can scarcely believe it. It seems to me that both the people and the weather have changed. I still remember well that it was customary to go to church on foot especially the young people and bare-footed. There was no talk of fine shoes and boots nor did one know anything of light pleasure vehicles in our congregation. Sixty years ago, among us, fine Sunday shirts or bosom shirts were not in use according to the fashion of the world as is the rage now, nor the wearing of all kinds of strange colored fine store clothes. One was satisfied with and delighted in home-made stuff. The wives and daughters spent the winter spinning. The flax seed was sown in the spring, and in the fall it had to be pulled, broken and hackled. That was work mostly for the wives and daughters. It was customary to hear the spinning wheel hum or sing in almost every farm house, and where this was not the case people remarked about it as of people who did not do their duty. The large amount of imported goods with which our country is flooded, as also the domestic cotton goods which

are to be had at such a low price, have almost displaced the home-made materials so that the daughters who now grow up no longer learn to spin.

> At that time young people were kept at home more, at work. One did not go to school every winter for months at a time. One was satisfied with learning to read and write. It was considered that for the humble state or for the common man more was not necessary. At that time there were not such splendid houses and barns, according to the custom of the world, as at present. One was satisfied with dwellings providing for pressing needs.

> At that time there was not so much time consumed in sweeping and decorating houses and much simpler house furnishings were sufficient. Spotted dishes were scarce. The spotted and flowered dishes were in the more pretentious houses and were not to be found with those who kept themselves among the lowly. Sofas and writing desks and bureaus there were none, or rag carpets. I still remember the wooden shoes very well. Leather shoes were considered too expensive. Clothing was much more simple. I verily believe that, sixty years and more ago, if anyone who wished to be a member of the church and would have dressed and conducted himself in the high fashion as is too much the case today . . . he would have had to be put out of the church as a disobedient person.[37]

There was likely little time for quiltmaking in an era when winter months were consumed by spinning. Furthermore, the production of flax and other household materials, as well as gardening and food preparation, were nearly all-absorbing for women of the time. We can only imagine Beiler's opinion about something as decorative and time-intensive as quiltmaking. The items related to the bed and bed textiles in his estate inventory of 1871 include only a bedstead, featherbed and bolster and some comforts.[38]

Beiler's account of the changes in textile production are supported by the testimony of some of the oldest Amish women living today. Although a few can remember seeing spinning wheels and looms among their family belongings, none can recall seeing their grandmothers use these tools. Nor do any remember wearing homespun goods. A few of the oldest women had heard their grandmothers talk about spinning and weaving, but it seems evident that by the late 1860s, these handicrafts were lost arts, even among the Amish. The accounts of two elderly Amish women, one from Ohio, the other from Iowa, provide valuable documentation of these changes.[39]

Lizzie Miller was born in 1894 in Millersburg, Ohio. Her mother was born in 1855 in Holmes County, Ohio, and married in 1882. She lived on the same farm almost her entire life. Lizzie recalled that her mother talked about spinning wheels but said that she never used one. Lizzie also remembered that when she was a child they often took goods to a woolen mill, Ailing Brothers near Charm, Ohio, where they would make a plain-weave, all wool, smooth fabric which the family used for clothing. When asked what she knew about the use of natural dyes in those days, Mrs. Miller noted that her mother spoke occasionally about the use of indigo blue for dyeing.

Lena Yoder was born in Kalona, Iowa, in 1891. Her mother was born in the mid-1850s in Cambria (Somerset County), Pennsylvania, and her father was from Holmes County, Ohio. They were married in the early 1870s. Mrs. Yoder said that her mother learned to spin as a child, but she did that only as a very young girl.

Lena's grandmother, who was born in Cambria, Pennsylvania, in the 1830s, did use a spinning wheel and did make her own fabrics.

Of the many women interviewed, only these two, both in their 90s, had any concrete memory of the production and use of homemade goods, and then only in the early years of their mothers' and grandmothers' lives.

These accounts are also consistent with information found in the public record. A comparison of the estate inventories of Amish families, Pennsylvania Germans and non-German families during various periods of the 18th and 19th centuries reveals definite trends in the ownership and production of textiles, including quilts. Items in Amish and Pennsylvania German inventories during the early 1800s are fairly equivalent and contrast noticeably with non-German inventories. The Amish, as well as other Pennsylvania Germans, typically owned such things as bed wallets and cases, bed ticks, bolster and bolster cases, bed curtains, sheets, chaff beds, haps, coverlets, feather beds, pillows and slips and "bed close" (bed clothes). Flax-working tools, weaving and spinning implements and a variety of looms are commonly listed in Amish inventories, as are extensive yardages of linen and flax.

The earliest known listings of quilts among the Amish are in the 1831 inventory of Abraham Kurtz of Wayne County, Ohio, and in the 1836 inventory of John Hartzler of Mifflin County, Pennsylvania. Haps, coverlets, comforts, blankets and chaff beds appear to have been the predominant form of bed coverings, rather than quilts. Of the nearly 100 Amish inventories checked, the earliest mention of quilts in Mifflin County, Pennsylvania, is the 1836 listing. Others appear in 1847 and 1849. There are two or three listings in the 1850s and a few in the 1860s.

Quilts appear with equal infrequency in inventories in Lancaster and Somerset counties in

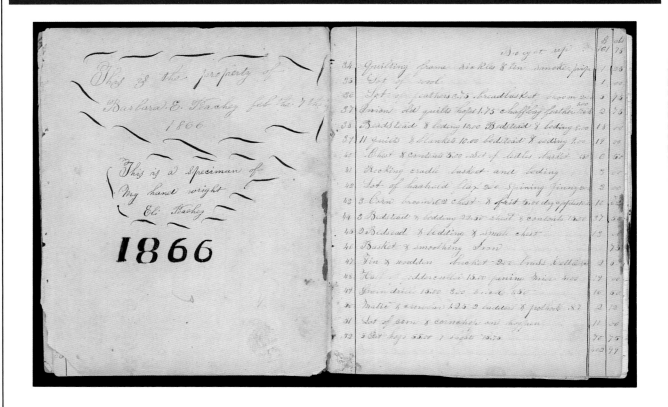

Pennsylvania during the years before the 1870s. The Amish of Pennsylvania and those who moved into the frontier areas of Ohio and Indiana seem to have clung to the use of traditional German bedding. Commonly listed in all of the inventories examined are bedsteads, chaff beds, bolsters, feather bags or coverlets. Quilts are rarely mentioned, even in inventories well into the 1880s. The fact that all of these inventories include coverlets and blankets, as well as large amounts of wool, linen, flax and flax-working implements, indicates that the Amish maintained the most traditional forms of bedding even after they had been abandoned by other Germans.

Throughout Pennsylvania, Ohio and Indiana, their Germanic neighbors seem to have adopted the quilt at least a decade earlier than the Amish. The inventories of Irish, Welsh and English families in many counties indicate that these groups made and owned quilts even before the beginning of the 19th century, several decades ahead of the Germans.

In all families — Amish, Pennsylvania Ger-man and those from the British Isles — ownership of textiles is most noticeable in the inventories of women. In their accounts, clothing, bedding, linen and unused yardage of goods are often the major, and occasionally the only, type of entry listed. In a society where women had little independent legal status and few possessions of their own, many were concerned with leaving specific instructions about the division of their few worldly goods. These two examples are typical of such expressions:

Rosina Schlabaugh 1839 I give and bequeath unto my four daughters, Elizabeth, Mary, Rosina and Salome, all my clothing as well as my old bedding to be divided amongst them without sale. Elizabeth to have one of my best gowns and one of the best handkerchiefs.[40]

Nancy Hartzler 1849 I give and bequeath to my son Adam Hertzler's two daughters, Nancy and Mary, all my wearing apparel.[41]

Inventory Book • Mifflin County, Pennsylvania, inscribed, "This is the property of Barbara E. Peachey Feb the 7th 1866. This is a specimen of my hand wright. Eli Peachey 1866." A listing of items sold at sale including "old quilt" and other bedding items.

Woman's Shift
Lancaster County, Pennsylvania • "F. K. 1848" (Fanny King)
Plain-weave cotton, cross-stitch worked in red cotton thread
Dr. and Mrs. Donald M. Herr
Woman's Shift
Lancaster County, Pennsylvania • "S.E." (S. Ebersol)
Plain-weave cotton, cross-stitch worked in red cotton thread
Eve Granick and David Wheatcroft

Woman's Bonnet and Scoop Hat
Indiana; Mifflin County, Pennsylvania
The People's Place Quilt Museum
The bonnet/straw hat made of twill-weave wool is typical of the head covering worn by Amish
women in nearly all Amish communities. Each community has small stylistic differences but
the general form is the same. The straw scoop hat is the only type of outdoor headgear worn by
women in the Nebraska Amish community. They do not wear bonnets.

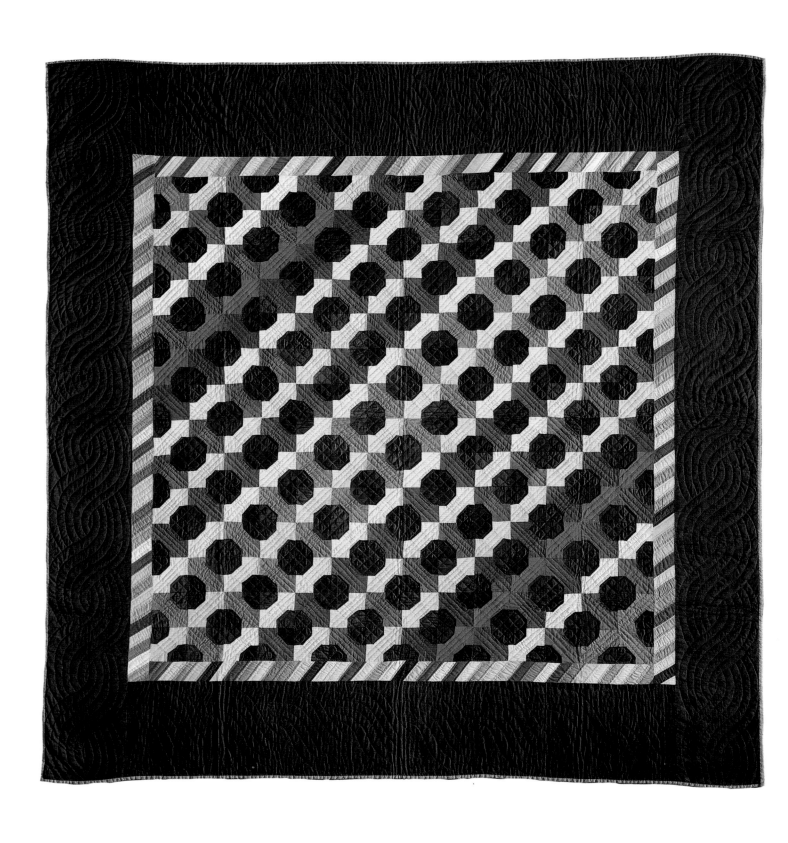

Bow Tie
Holmes County, Ohio, circa 1925–35 • Made for Mrs. Homer Miller by her mother.
Plain-weave cotton percale, chambray poplin, cotton sateen, twill-weave wool serge
80 × 85 • Eve Granick and David Wheatcroft

Amish Quilts: Their Beginnings

Early 19th Century Quilts

Though the written record attests to the existence of quilts among the Amish as early as the 1830s we have only a vague idea of what these first textiles might have looked like. The overwhelming majority of Amish quilts known today were made between the 1880s and the 1960s, and most of these quilts were produced in the 20th century. The number of quilts dating from the 1890s is relatively small and the number from the 1880s is even smaller. While estate inventories do indicate the ownership of quilts among the Amish in the years between the 1830s and the 1870s, it is important to remember that only a few quilts are listed in these documents, and existing quilts from this time period are extremely rare. At present we have only two known examples dated before 1870.

Both the survey of estate papers and the examination of the few known pre-1880s quilts suggest the strong possibility that the production of any type of quilt, plain or pieced, and their use in Amish homes was very unusual in the period from 1830 to 1870.

Between the late 1860s and the early 1880s the practice of quiltmaking, particularly of pieced quilts, seems to have developed rather suddenly in the Amish community. The number of quilts listed in estate papers during these years increases noticeably, and there are a handful of examples which are either dated or reliably traced to this period.

The 15 years from about 1870 until 1885 can be considered a transitional stage. It is during this time, in the course of one generation, that Amish women discarded more traditionally Germanic bedding styles, like blankets, featherbeds and coverlets, and embraced a new tradition of quiltmaking.

It is evident from both the public record and from the quality of craftsmanship exhibited in late 19th century Amish quilts that Amish women knew about and practiced some quilting before the 1880s. The question remains then, what did these earliest Amish quilts look like? While estate papers offer a great deal of information and are an important research tool, they are curiously silent on this subject. With only one exception, Amish inventory listings offer no detail beyond the words "quilt" or "bed quilt," which appear sporadically among the other bedding and textile items. The words, "one woolen brown quilt," in the 1849 inventory of Stephen Kurtz of Mifflin County are the only description found among the hundreds of inventories that were examined. This lack of description is not limited to Amish inventories. Among the estate paperwork of both Pennsylvania Germans and "English" families, details about quilts are limited and unusual.

Since the historical record offers so little information about the appearance of early Amish quilts, we are forced to rely solely on the few examples which have survived. There are

thousands of extant examples of quiltmaking by other American women from the 1850s, 1860s and 1870s. We have only a handful of quilts which are dated or accurately traced to this time that were made and used by Amish women.

The earliest, existing, dated Amish quilt currently known is illustrated on the left. Made in Mifflin County, Pennsylvania, the front of the quilt is constructed from two panels of fine, plain-weave, indigo blue cotton. The back is made from two large pieces of plain woven fabric as well, although the weave has a looser, coarser appearance. All of the seams, bindings and quilting are sewn by hand. The thread is a coarse, brownish, handspun cotton, and the initials, "B P," and the date, "1849," are embroidered in white cotton thread.

A similarly designed quilt is owned by the Indiana State Museum. This quilt was brought to Indiana by an Amish family who originated

in Lancaster County, where the quilt was likely made. The Lancaster example is also constructed from two large panels of fabric sewn together to create a one color quilt. The material on the front is a glazed, dark blue, plain-weave cotton and the back is made from a lightweight brown wool. This quilt has the date, "1869," and the initials, "G D," quilted in the center.

In both of these pieces the quilting designs fill the entire surface. In the Mifflin County example the quilting is patterned after pieced blockwork in its placement and design. The Lancaster County example is quilted in the style of a Center Square with a rope design along the outside borders, a grid of crossing lines through the center section, and stars double stitched in the corner areas.

The simple and carefully crafted one color quilt seems to be a logical first step in the

Plain Quilt
Mifflin County, Pennsylvania, dated "1840," initialed "B.P."
Plain-weave cotton • The People's Place Quilt Museum
The binding along two sides was made by turning the backing material over the front. A
yellow, plain-weave cotton binding is sewn by hand along the top and bottom ends of the quilt.

evolution of Amish quilts. Just as Lancaster women selected the outdated Medallion style quilt in the late 19th century, Amish women in the mid-19th century made an entirely plain quilt, reminiscent of earlier American linsey-woolsey and calamanco quilts. The inherently conservative nature of Amish culture permits change only in relationship to the larger outside society. What has been discarded by other American women as being out of fashion is then acceptable for possible adaptation in the Amish community. When Amish women did begin quiltmaking in the mid- and late 19th century, they appear to have deliberately chosen the most conservative and outdated styles.

Modern examples of the plain one color quilt can also be found today. In some of the most conservative Amish groups in Indiana and Canada, the making of pieced designs has been specifically forbidden by church rules, from the 19th century to the present day. This prohibition on piecework and multicolored patterns is practiced among some of the Old Order Mennonites as well. One woman, a member of an Old Order Mennonite group in Pennsylvania, stated quite emphatically in an interview that cutting up material and sewing it together again was "just for pride."[1]

The few extant examples, the written record and modern prohibitions on pieced designs, which still exist in a few communities, all suggest that simple, one color designs were the first type of Amish quilts. Before the 1870s there is no evidence to date of any pieced pattern quilt-making among the Amish. In the years between the earliest mention of quilts in Amish inventories — 1831 — and the mid-1870s, only 22 notations of quilts exist in the estate paperwork of Amish families out of the hundreds of inventories examined. The production and ownership of quilts before the 1870–1880 period was most likely the exception rather than the rule, and the few items that existed at one time have

(above) **Plain Quilt**
Purchased in Indiana, probably made in Lancaster County, Pennsylvania
Dated "1869," initialed "G.D." • Glazed plain-weave cotton and wool
Indiana State Museum collection

(below) **Bars**
Circa 1800 • Glazed calamanco
America Hurrah, New York

31

disappeared into rag bags or the burn pile.

While there is little supporting evidence of any widespread quiltmaking tradition until the 1880s, there are a few quilts which can be dated to the 1870–1880 period. These few quilts represent the tentative beginning of the Amish quiltmaking tradition, which developed so dramatically in the last decades of the 19th century and the first few decades of the 20th century.

The early pieces which have survived are an important link in the story of Amish textiles. There are fewer than two dozen known examples which can be traced to the 1870s and early 1880s, and fewer than half of these are actually dated on the quilt. A significantly greater number of quilts exist from the later 1880s and 1890s, although they are rare as well. The differences between the earliest examples and those which followed help to illustrate the changes taking place in both Amish and American culture during the mid-and late 19th century. These changes included a significant shift in patterns of textile consumption, and they suggest a transition in both decorative and social traditions among the Amish.

These earliest quilts share certain characteristics that can help to identify them as the products of these transitional years. Color is one of the most striking elements. Browns, tans, olive greens, pumpkin, indigo blues, rust colored reds and the occasional pieces of turkey red or citron yellow are quite distinctive. These colors were used in later quilts as well, but the earliest examples from the 1870s and early 1880s are notable for the lack of brighter and more varied colors which are found in quilts from the late 1880s and 1890s. The first experiments in synthetic dyeing did not take place until 1865. The discovery and distribution of new colors to consumers took place fairly rapidly, but it was not until the mid- and late 1880s that dye manufacturers and textile factories were able to offer the large diversity of bright

Nine Patch
Circa 1890–1900
Heavy napped wools • 62 × 80 • Joan Fenton and Albie Tabackman, Quilts Unlimited

Plain Quilt
Dated "Feb 8 1898," initialed "AD"
Plain-weave cotton percale • 68 × 87 • Jonathan Holstein and Gail Van der Hoof

and relatively colorfast materials which can be found in late 19th century Amish quilts. The earlier quilts depend on a more "natural" color scheme. A side-by-side comparison of quilts from the 1885–1910 era with those from the earlier years reveals some of these differences.

Fabric is another element to consider in examining early quilts. While a few small pieces of homespun materials can be found occasionally in the earliest Amish quilts, the goods are predominately factory produced cottons and wools. The cottons are usually quite fine, lightweight plain weaves. Wools may be either finer dress wools, both in twill and plain weaves, or heavier pieces of flannel and suiting wools.

Quilting thread is often brownish or black, and the quilting tends to cover the entire surface of the quilt, even if the design is only a simple grid of lines. Double stitched lines are another example of the careful attention to sewing which characterizes earlier quilts.

The earliest Amish quilts are generally simple in their pattern and design construction. Nine Patches, or a Nine Patch variation, a Center Square, large block arrangements and an occasional Irish Chain or simple triangles are the most usual choices. The Amish quilts of these earliest years are strikingly sparse when compared to contemporary American quilts of the period. A look at the quilts of the most conservative groups, the Swartzentrubers in Ohio, the Mifflin County Nebraska Amish and the Amish of Adams and Allen County Indiana, offer important insight. Each of these groups formed its quiltmaking tradition with restrictions based on a desire to maintain the "old way." Among the Swartzentrubers, Nine Patches and simple block designs in two or three colors were standard. In Mifflin County, only Nine Patches and simple Nine Patch variations were permitted. In Indiana, the one color plain quilt was the only choice. Both in pattern and color schemes, these communities have attempted to continue the oldest traditions well into the 20th century.

Many factors and influences moved Amish women from the home production of traditionally German styled linen and woolen textiles to the limited use of factory manufactured materials, and finally to the unrestricted consumption of purchased fabrics. A more detailed look at the larger American culture of the 19th century and its effect on the Amish, as well as a consideration of population statistics and the influence of rather traumatic changes in the Amish church during the 1860s and 1870s, may shed further light on the story of 19th century Amish quilts.

Nine-Patch Variation
Purchased in Clark, Missouri; probable place of origin is Ohio or Somerset County, Pennsylvania
Circa 1870–80 • Plain-weave cotton • 67 × 81 • Michael Oruch

Center Square
Lancaster County, Pennsylvania, dated "1875," initialed "G.D."
Plain-weave wool • 81 × 85 • Dr. and Mrs. Donald M. Herr
This is the earliest dated Center Square that has come to light.

Growth and Change in the Amish Church during the 19th Century

In the atmosphere of growth and expansion throughout North America during the 19th century, the Amish church faced growing dissension within its ranks. The division which created the Old Order Amish as a distinctive and formalized group did not occur overnight. Gradual changes in both the Amish community and the larger society began as early as the 1820s, growing in importance through the 1830s, '40s and '50s.

In 1862 the first in a series of meetings was called for ministers from all the Amish communities to discuss the direction and future of the church. Unable to reach an agreement on important congregational differences, the Old Order Amish withdrew from the main body of Amish Mennonites. In doing so, they established an identity as a group, separate and markedly different from the prevailing world around them. Standards governing dress, transportation, social and religious practices and even quiltmaking were defined to reflect the spiritual differences they felt. Just as the 17th century schism led by Jacob Amman was based on many issues, this important division was the result of several factors, but primarily the concern that the church was becoming too accommodating to the surrounding society and losing its purity and faithfulness.

Like other Americans in the late 18th and early 19th centuries, some Amish families were part of a westward migration movement to the farmlands which opened for settlement across the ever expanding frontier. The desire for land fueled the development of "mother-daughter" communities that originated in Pennsylvania, then spread westward to Ohio by the beginning of the 19th century and finally into Indiana, Illinois and Iowa by mid-century. As the older communities grew, the need for more farm land at an affordable price forced Amish families to seek new areas to settle where their children could own farms and raise the next generation.

This westward movement, while providing additional land, also exacted a toll on group unity. Families moving into the frontier areas of the Midwest were beset with problems and circumstances different from those in the more established communities in Pennsylvania. The quality, quantity and accessibility of basic goods available to a family in Indiana were much lower than to a family in Pennsylvania. The cost of starting a new farm on the frontier meant a less comfortable standard of living for the early midwestern family. Because they were consumed with establishing their farms, these pioneers had less time and energy to create and maintain home furnishings. What they had they used hard, and little has survived. Estate inventories through the first half of the 19th century indicate that Amish families in Ohio and Indiana generally owned fewer objects than their counterparts in Lancaster and Mifflin counties in Pennsylvania.

Living on the Indiana prairie was vastly different from living on an established farm in Lancaster. Removed from the mother communities, and in many cases from the oldest members who normally held the line against change, the more thinly populated communities in the Midwest held less firmly to certain rules. There they had more interaction with non-Amish neighbors, since settlers were forced to rely upon each other for assistance. This interaction seems to have fostered more rapid acceptance of quiltmaking among the Amish, particularly in Ohio. There, throughout the 1850s and 1860s, quilts appear with slightly greater frequency in the inventories of Amish families than is recorded in Pennsylvania communities. In the more affluent Amish settlements in the East, the typical Pennsylvania German bedding traditions — coverlets, feather beds and haps —

seem to have dominated longer. Although we have more surviving heirlooms from these communities, there is scant evidence of quilts in the inventories.

Not only was life more difficult in the Midwest, but there were also a greater number of "outside" influences. In the years between 1816 and 1860 nearly 3000 Amish Mennonites emigrated from Europe to America.[2] The influx of these European "sisters and brothers" created some turmoil in the church. Most of the new arrivals found the American Amish to be far more traditional than they were, and though they did make initial contacts with the existing group, they ultimately formed their own communities and congregations and eventually merged with the Mennonite Church.[3] Meanwhile, they left a somewhat liberal mark on the Amish community, especially on certain church leaders and members who were open to a less conservative point of view.

Some of the difficulties in the Amish church were simply a result of steady population growth. During the 18th and early 19th centuries the growth of the church was relatively slow. The fact that the Lancaster and Mifflin communities were only large enough to require one church district each until the 1840s indicates just how small the Amish population was. At mid-century, however (and again in the 20th century), the Amish population increased dramatically. As the number of church districts and ministers grew, there was increasing difficulty in reaching agreements on even comparatively minor issues. Differing practices and an ever widening interpretation of the rules created great tensions.

The size of the Amish population is critical when considering the issues of church unity, but it is also an important factor in estimating the number of quilts that might have been produced by Amish women in the late 19th and early 20th centuries. The U.S. Census of 1890

counted the American population at some 63,056,000 people.[4] A religious census made by the government that same year found only 2030 adult members of the Old Order Amish church. Adding children and unbaptized youths brings the estimated total Amish population in 1890 to 3700 people.[5] If every adult Amish woman had made one quilt in 1890, there would have been only 1000 quilts. From that inflated total, one would have to subtract a large percentage of quilts which would have been lost to heavy use, time and the general fragility of textiles. It is understandable, then, why so few 19th century Amish quilts remain. In contrast to the abundance of late 19th century American quilts, Amish quilts are comparatively rare. The following chart provides figures which may be useful in calculating the possible number of quilts made in the 20th century, based solely on population.[6]

If internal population expansion, the influence of new Amish immigrants and the general western fever that gripped America in the 19th century brought some destabilization to the Amish community, the world outside the Amish community created pressures and problems for the Amish as well. The accelerated pace of change in industry and the impact of

Grandmother's Dream
Lancaster County, Pennsylvania • circa 1890–1910
Twill-weave wool • 44 × 44 • Dr. and Mrs. Donald M. Herr

Year	Number of Church Districts	Population	Females	Number of Church Districts in the Three Largest Settlements:		
				Lancaster County, PA	Holmes County, Ohio	Elkhart and Lagrange, Indiana
1890	22	3,700	1,800	5	6	4
1900	32	5,300	2,650	6	7	6
1910	57	9,500	4,750	9	8	8
1920	83	14,000	7,000	11	13	16
1930	110	18,500	9,250	12	16	12
1940	154	25,800	12,900	18	24	18
1950	197	33,000	16,500	25	40	25
1960	258	43,000	21,650	38	49	29
1970	343	57,000	28,800	47	70	37
1979	526	85,780	42,890	60	103	47

technology on American life threatened the simplicity of rural life. The Amish were not exempt from the transformation of formerly isolated rural communities into part of a large national economic network. The last quarter of the 19th century was in particular an era of tremendous growth in transportation, communication and the production of consumer goods. Two additional social forces — a period of religious revivalism and the Civil War — added stress to the Amish community.

The first half of the 19th century was marked by a growing religious sentiment, sometimes called the "Second Great Awakening." This intense and emotional religious movement sparked a period of self-examination and renewal of religious commitment among many American Protestants. By the 1860s this "Awakening" had stirred many Mennonites as well. This more emotional approach to religious life was contrary to the life of disciplined faith, rooted in suffering and humility, that was practiced by the Amish. Yet the missionary zeal of the revivalists and the appeal of having the assurance of salvation drew some away to join other churches during these years.

The Civil War, which engulfed the nation in 1861, proved to be as disruptive to Amish life as the American Revolution had been in the 18th century. Although the Amish refused on religious grounds to participate in the war effort, their communities became embroiled in the turmoil which ravaged the entire country.

Faced with these internal and external threats, a group of Amish ministers and bishops met during the 1860s and 1870s to try to resolve the growing differences among congregations. No solution was achieved, and gradually over a number of years two separate groups, the Old Order Amish and the Amish Mennonites, emerged.

In the years in which these divisions occurred, about one-third of the total Amish population was identified as Old Order. These people were mostly the descendants of the colonial Amish.[7] Of the Amish population living in Lancaster, Mifflin and Somerset counties in Pennsylvania, Holmes County in Ohio, La-Grange and Elkhart counties in Indiana, the Arthur, Illinois, area and Johnson County, Iowa, the largest proportion became Old Order.

In contrast, the majority of the Alsatians who immigrated in the early part of the 19th century became Mennonites, and only a small number of this group went with the Old Order. Those who did formed distinctive and quite conservative communities in Indiana and Ontario.

Taking into account all the change and turmoil within the Amish community during these years, it seems understandable that we have no examples of pieced Amish quilts made before the 1870s. Other Pennsylvania Germans, including the Mennonites, began quiltmaking as early as the 1830s and 1840s. Estate records show that the Amish did not make many quilts of any type during the first six decades of the 19th century. In these years they held persistently to traditional German bedding forms: the chaff or feather bed, blankets and coverlets. In the 1860s and 1870s, when cultural practices and visual symbolism were important points of contention, pieced quiltmaking was not a typical Amish custom. It was only in the years following the separation of the Old Order Amish and the less traditional Amish Mennonites, after the Old Order had clearly identified themselves and stabilized their church, that pieced Amish quilts began to appear. Perhaps only then was it deemed safe by the group to experiment with a cultural form already in use by related groups and the larger society. In fact, it was not until the 1880s that quilts and quiltmaking seem to have reached any significant level of popularity among Amish women.

Plain Quilt Variation
Mifflin County, Pennsylvania • Byler church
Made in the winter of 1906 on the John Lee
Peachey farm. A hired boy who lived on
the farm that year helped with the quilting.
Plain-weave cottons • Esprit collection, San Francisco.

Miniature Variable Star
Holmes County, Ohio, dated "1895"
Plain-weave cotton percale, chambray • 71 × 87 • Darwin D. Bearley collection
This extremely fine quilting is done in a variety of colored threads. This quilt is the work
of Dena Miller.

40

Textiles: Their Changes from 1750–1950

Textile development is a revolutionary story that moves from the spinning wheel to the computerized power loom, from homespun to polyester.

In the 18th century, textiles constituted a major portion of the total value of a family's possessions. They required a larger percentage of a household's income than any other item, apart from land. The high value of textiles is evident in the inventories and vendue papers of families in the 18th century and well into the 19th century.

The colonial family's bedding and clothing materials were a combination of imported and domestic goods, as well as homemade textiles. Fabrics imported from Europe came primarily from England and were sold in the port cities of Boston, New York, Philadelphia and Baltimore.[1] Although these goods did reach the countryside, they were costly, and it appears that Amish families had little use for these fine imports. A European traveler through Pennsylvania in 1794 noted that "the German farmers also manufacture coarse material for coats, skirts and all their shirt items. On every farm they cultivate enough flax and hemp and also raise what sheep they need for linen and cloth."[2]

Lancaster was one of the most active areas in Pennsylvania. In 1786, with a population of some 700 families, 234 families were involved in manufacturing enterprises. Among these were 14 hatters, 36 shoemakers, 25 tailors, 25 weavers of wool, linen and cotton, and four dyers. There were also five hemp mills and one fulling mill within 10 miles of the town.[3]

The legal restrictions imposed on the colonies by England and the basic cost of establishing manufacturing facilities severely limited the domestic textile industry in America until after the Revolutionary War. In contrast to the primitive American textile factories of the period, European manufacturing was revolutionized by important new textile production techniques and machinery. It was not until the early 19th century that the spinning jenny, the flying shuttle, the power loom and the application of the steam engine to the spinning and carding process, reached America.

During the years following the American Revolution, heavy promotion of American enterprises and industry by political and social leaders fostered much development. The beginnings were tentative, and the movement of technologies from Europe to the United States involved the clandestine shipment of machinery from England and the illegal immigration of the man who would become the father of the American textile industry — Samuel Slater.[4] During the last decades of the 18th century and the first years of the 19th century, the basic groundwork for the industrialization of textile production in the United States was laid.

The textile industry grew steadily in the first years of the 19th century. New businesses connected with various aspects of carding, spinning and weaving sprang up in many places. Factories in New England turned out cloth in stripes and checks, bed ticking, and ginghams and fabrics for shirts, sheeting and counterpanes. Philadelphia factories made diaper cloth, jean, cotton jerseys, blankets, fustians, cord and velvets.[5]

Despite huge gains in the establishment of industry in the New World, England continued to maintain her supremacy in the field of factory textile production. During the first decades of the 18th century, American factory-produced textiles gained ground slowly. The majority of cotton, flax and woolen materials were still being made at home by families for their own use.[6] Amish inventories from this period support the premise that rural Pennsylvania German families used homegrown and homemade fabrics and supplemented these with small amounts of domestically manufactured materials. The inventory of Christian Beiler reveals a variety and quantity of textiles common to this era.[7]

Inventory of Christian Beiler
Lancaster County, Pennsylvania, 1804

His wearing apparell	7 yards of planket
a quantity of linen	bedcase and bedsheet
2 bed and bedstead	linen table cloth
2 bed and bedstead	7 towels
7 yards of linen	heckled flax
1½ yards of linen	woolen yarn
4 yards of linen	linen yarn
12 yards of tow	flaxen yarn
7½ yards flax linen	3½ yards of linen
11 yards of flax linen	woolen yarn and wool
5 yards of blane [plain] fustain	flax and hemp
5¾ yards of woolen cloth	flax and hemp
5¾ yards of worsted lincy	flax and some tow
311 yards lincy	coverlet and a blanket
worsted lincy	3½ yards of bed stuff
planket	11 yards of linen
8 yards of linen	6 pound of cotton yarn
spinning wheel	great wool wheel
quantity of linen cloth	bag of hemp seeds
quantity of tow	bag with flax seeds

From the 1820s until the middle of the century the growth of the American textile industry was dramatic. Each year new factories opened, new machinery designed from the latest English models was put to use, more spindles were added, the investment value of manufacturing concerns increased and the yardages and variety of fabrics produced grew steadily. In the ten years between 1830 and 1840 the number of spindles in production increased from 1,246,000 to 2,284,630 and the dollar value of manufactured textiles jumped from $26 million to $46 million. According to the census of 1850, textile manufacturing constituted a capital investment of $81,667,000, and some 1200 factories employed 103,600 people in the production of printed, plain and mixed cotton and woolen goods.[8]

During these years the shift from home-produced textiles to factory-made goods took place gradually and at varying rates across the country.[9] In the 1820s home manufacture was still an integral part of American farm life. A small variety of manufactured materials was available, but families depended heavily on the flax and wool they grew and processed at home.

Wool broadcloth and cassimere were two of the earliest textiles produced in American mills. Other factory products included nankeen, corduroy, jersey (a knitted wool), serge, linsey-woolsey, flannel and muslin.

Between the 1820s and the 1840s the predominance of home-produced materials diminished rapidly and the importance of factory-made textiles increased. Some households continued doing their own spinning and weaving, but most now purchased the majority of their clothing and household fabrics. Cassimere was still a staple woolen, and satinet and Kentucky jean were widely available. Finer goods, such as cashmere, merino and delaine, grew in popularity among American women for dress fabric.

During these years the Amish continued producing much of their own cloth, doing so into the 1850s and early 1860s. Despite their heavy cultural preference for linen and home-made textiles, the Amish and other Pennsylvania Germans did buy small amounts of raw cotton and some other factory-made textiles. Amish inventories from this period mention woolen cloth, cassinet, flannel, muslin, linsey and the ubiquitous linen and flax goods. These excerpts from Mifflin County inventories are typical of those found in Lancaster County as well, during the 1840s and 1850s.[10]

Inventory of Michael Yoder, 1843

3 yards of cotton flannel
8 yards of drillin
8 yards ticking
1½ yards muslin

2 remnants of flannel
7 yards of blue muslin

Inventory of David Hartzler, 1844

4 coverlets
3 haps
7 feather ticks
9 bolsters and 2 pillows
3 spinning wheels
1 large wool and reel
2 blankets and 11 sheets
1½ yards of cassinet
7½ yards of cassinet
2½ yards of flannel
4½ yards of home made cassinet

Inventory of Christian Zook, 1852

2½ yards of linsey
4½ yards of cloth
4½ yards of cassinet
36 yards of muslin

Farther west in Ohio, the importance of flax and the spinning wheel lingered longer. These items are evident in Amish inventories well into the 1860s. In fact, they were so vital to family and home life that the "widow's portion" was a legally defined and standardized section of every will in Ohio. The "widow's portion" included all spinning wheels and weaving looms, the family stove, all of the religious and school books of the family, one cow, 12 sheep and the wool shorn from them, all the wool yarn and cloth manufactured by the family from these animals, all of the flax, yarn and thread made by the family, and the clothing and wearing apparel of the family and the deceased. It also included cooking utensils, all bedsteads and $100 worth of personal property.

Inventories in Holmes and Wayne counties in Ohio indicate that homemade textiles were as important for the more western Amish families as they were for the Pennsylvania Amish of the early 19th century. These inventories from Ohio illustrate some of the typical materials found among the Amish in the 1840s and 1850s:[11]

Inventory of Issac Yoder, *1841*

one lot of muslin
15½ yards of muslin
a lot of yarn
16 yards of linen shirting
5 yards of woolen cloth
spinning wheel
2 flax hatchels

Inventory of Sarah Schrock, *1848*

2 quilts
bed curtains
flax hatchels
one piece of muslin
one piece of blue flannel
one piece of blue muslin
37½ yards of flannel
13 yards of flannel
6½ yards of brown flannel
2 pieces of brown cloth
12 yards of muslin
1 yard of linnen

Inventory of John Zook, *1854*

25 yards of flax linen
15 yards of bleached muslin
3 yards of linen
3½ yards of broadcloth
canton flannel

As the 19th century progressed, cotton gradually replaced flax as the primary domestic fabric throughout the country. By mid-century cotton had moved from last place to first in importance in household textiles. Home-manufactured fabrics were quite important through the 1820s and 1830s, particularly in rural areas. By the 1840s, while some home-spinning and weaving were still practiced, the majority of household fabrics were factory-produced materials that were purchased new.[12] That was true even for households in the West who were further removed from manufacturing centers. By 1850, most of the basic fabrics that had been produced or imported during the colonial period were still available, but their fiber content and even the per capita consumption of these goods had changed noticeably.[13]

Although the Amish did not rely exclusively on home-produced textiles after the 1840s, they seem to have maintained spinning and weaving traditions for at least a decade longer than their non-Amish neighbors. Slowly, however, even in Amish homes, homemade materials were eventually replaced by products of the New England textile mills.

One American textile tradition the Amish appear to have embraced as readily as their non-Amish neighbors was the woven coverlet. In the early part of the 19th century, thousands of handweavers emigrated from Europe to America. Among these immigrants were Mennonites who supplemented their farming income with weaving. The jacquard loom or loom attachment first arrived in America during the 1820s. The invention of a French weaver, this loom made possible the creation of complicated patterns, pictorial elements and elaborate borders. Jacquard-style coverlets became extremely popular with Americans during the 1830s and '40s. The Amish considered the Jacquard coverlet too fancy; they used only the traditional overshot harness looms to weave coverlets or *debbichs* in simple patterns of two or three basic colors. Even after coverlet weaving lost popularity and disappeared from rural

(opposite) These are examples of woven blankets and coverlets that were used in Amish households throughout the 19th and early 20th centuries. The coverlet on the far right is an example of Jacquard weaving which was popular with Pennsylvania German families. The Amish considered this style to be too fancy for use in their homes.

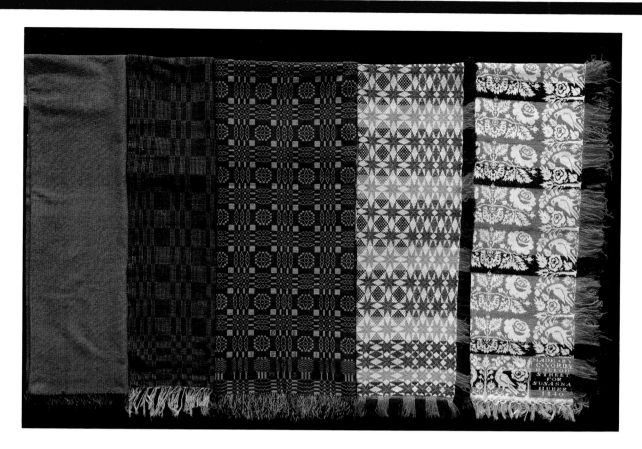

American homes, the Amish continued to make and use this type of bed covering.

From 1845 to 1900 astonishing changes came to all aspects of American life. Textile technology was no exception; each advance seemed to spark additional discoveries. The sewing machine was patented in 1846. Mass marketing of the invention began in 1856, and during the next three decades the sewing machine became a standard fixture in American homes. Singer and Howe sold more than 130,000 machines in the four years between 1856 and 1860 alone.[14] The Amish appear to have accepted this new technology as rapidly as their neighbors. Even the earliest Amish-pieced quilt tops from the 1870s and 1880s were sewn together entirely on the treadle sewing machine.

In the factories, major advances in spinning and weaving were paralleled by discoveries in chemistry and textile dyeing.[15]

By the late 1850s and 1860s a great variety of commercially produced fabrics were available to American women. These were still costly commodities, especially for families living outside the eastern urban centers. Woolen textiles in particular were expensive, and so were supplemented by hand-produced goods. Families who raised sheep could take their wool to the local fulling mill where the woolen yarns were woven into blankets and coarse textiles by local hand-weavers.

For those without financial restrictions or religious cautions, however, the purchase of factory-produced goods became commonplace. The most typical materials of this period included wool merino, broadcloth, cashmere, challis, alpaca, mohair, brilliantine, sicilian, serge and twill, cotton calico, osnaburg and nankeen. Cotton percale, which was introduced in 1865, gained immediate and widespread favor.[16]

From 1861 until 1865, the Civil War consumed the energies and resources of the American people. In these years the cotton market of the South was decimated and the old plantation system destroyed. When the War finally ended, a period of rebuilding brought dramatic changes in both American industry and culture.

Woven Blanket • Lancaster County, Pennsylvania • Dr. and Mrs. Donald M. Herr
Overshot Coverlet • Indiana • Michael Oruch
Overshot Coverlet • Ohio • The People's Place Quilt Museum
Overshot Coverlet • Lancaster County, Pennsylvania • Dr. and Mrs. Donald M. Herr
Jacquard Patterned Coverlet • Lancaster County, Pennsylvania • Dr. and Mrs. Donald M. Herr

During the post-Civil War period the westward migration movement regained new vigor. Thousands of Americans packed up their belongings to follow the trails to the frontier. Much money and energy were devoted to transplanting the American family westward. Despite romantic notions of a wild new land, most of the immigrants brought with them middle class values and the desire for a "civilized" lifestyle. They quickly settled the frontiers, and as economic links were formed with the East, factory-produced textiles rapidly replaced the production of homemade materials completely.

The inventories of Amish families from the last decade of the 19th century reveal the decline and disappearance of home-produced fabrics and the decreased value of textiles in general. As the older generation passed away, spinning wheels and flax hatchels were replaced by sewing machines and quilting frames. From the 1870s onward, Amish families from all communities listed quilts among their possessions with increasing frequency. The extensive listings of linen and flax materials were gone, as were the detailed descriptions of yardages of each type of fabric. Clothing and bedding materials no longer headed the inventories, nor were they assigned the high monetary value they held in the earlier years of the century.

The move from individual self-sufficiency to a reliance on produced goods took place gradually, and the Amish accepted the changes more slowly than other rural families. Their resistance was based on a strong, and probably accurate, conviction that interaction and interdependence with the outside world and its modern technologies would diminish and perhaps destroy the Amish community and its doctrine of separateness from the world. The formation of the strictly conservative group known as the Nebraska Amish, during these years, indicates that concern.

As the 19th century drew to a close, however,

Inventory Book • Mifflin County, Pennsylvania, inscribed, "written by Eli Peachey for Barbara E. Sharp February 13, 1874." This page lists 3 happs, 1 blanket and 2 coverlets, along with some dried fruit and linens.

changes were inevitable and unavoidable, even for the Amish. Improvements in transportation and communication led to an economy that was increasingly interconnected on a national scale, leaving little rationale for home production and self-sufficiency. The creation of sophisticated financial and industrial institutions touched all aspects of rural life. While the Amish struggled to maintain the older ways and resist the encroachment of modern society, the old textile traditions disappeared and new traditions evolved to take their place. It is especially noteworthy then, that during this period of increased industrialization in American life, the first examples of piecework quiltmaking appeared among the Amish. Although there are a number of 19th-century examples, the majority of Amish quilts were made in the 20th century. The story of 20th century textiles is therefore intrinsic to the study of these quilts.

In the first years of the new century, advances in technology and chemistry and the growth of the textile industry continued unabated. The inventions and discoveries of the late 19th century were improved upon and enlarged.

The creation of rayon in the last years of the 19th century grew out of efforts to make artificial silk. The impact on textile history of these experiments was profound. The ability to create yarns and fabrics from something other than the traditional fibers transformed the textile industry once more. The spinning of rayon yarn began in 1905 in England. In 1910 the American Viscose Corporation opened its first successful commercial rayon plant. Between 1915 and 1925 rayon was introduced and gradually developed as a marketable textile fabric. The word "rayon" was coined in 1925 to replace the label of "artificial silk." In 1926–27 delustered rayon and rayon crepe were developed, and during the 1930s all types of rayon goods appeared in the marketplace. Rayon's use alone, and in combination with natural fibers, increased year by year.

During the Depression the need for inexpensive materials made rayon a highly marketable fabric. Its popularity continued through the 1940s as the Depression gave way to World War II. The war created terrible shortages of natural materials; out of sheer necessity, synthetics and synthetic blends became the most widely used materials during the period. Even the Amish, who had continued to use cotton and wool, were forced to accept the new materials in a time when consumers had little or no choice of fabric selection.

The technological discovery of polyester took place in 1941, and in little more than a decade it was established as a textile staple. Acrylics followed in the 1950s and gained widespread use in the late 1950s into the early 1960s.

During these years of rapid change and discovery in the textile industry, the Amish, along with everyone else, could use only those fabrics which were available. Amish women tried to avoid the fads and fashions of new materials, but when the traditional natural fiber textiles such as henrietta, wool batiste and sateen disappeared from the marketplace, they had no choice but to accept newer fabrics. For example, wool henrietta was a standard offering in the Sears catalogue until 1920. In the Fall/Winter 1920–21 issue only cream-colored henrietta was mentioned, and by 1925 no type of henrietta was included at all. Batiste was another traditional woolen offered in the Sears catalogue during the early 1930s. By 1935 it too had gone the way of henrietta. Cotton sateens, available through most of the 1930s, disappeared after 1939.

Many of the new materials developed after 1940 were embraced quickly and happily by Amish women. The relaxation of rules in many church districts during these years allowed for greater diversity in the women's choices of color, weave and fabric type. Particularly in

Ohio and Indiana, a wide assortment of materials in lighter colors and fancier weave structures found their way into Amish clothing and quilts. These new fabrics made a strong and irreversible impact on Amish quiltmaking. Though the admirer and the collector of early Amish quilts may be dismayed by this growing diversity or by the introduction of polyester and acrylics, most pragmatic Amish housewives were satisfied with the price and quality of these fabrics.

The advent of synthetic materials hastened the decline of quilting skills as the 20th century progressed. It was simply easier to do fine stitching on wool batiste or plain weave cotton than on synthetic textiles. Good quilting requires soft and resilient fabrics that will accept and bend to the quilting needle.

Not only are synthetic materials more difficult to quilt well, synthetic batting requires less quilting to hold the batting in place. Consequently, the generation of women who learned quiltmaking on synthetic fabrics with synthetic batting abandoned the intricate needlework of their mothers and grandmothers. Just as Bishop Beiler bemoaned the passing of weaving and spinning skills in the 1860s, so, too, older Amish women comment about modern practices and young women who hurry through their quilting.[17]

It was more than just different or new materials, however, that caused Amish quilts to change. One cannot ignore the fact that the women who made quilts in the 1950s and 1960s were different from their grandmothers and mothers who created quilts from 1880 to 1930. The Amish change more slowly than the general American population, but they do change, and they must do so to insure their survival as a group. To progress from being flax cultivators to being consumers of manufactured textiles required steady but gradual changes in both thinking and practice.

In the late 19th century two factors coincided to foster an atmosphere which permitted quiltmaking to flourish. In the post-Civil War industrialization of the United States, commerce and industry had developed sufficiently to make a great deal of inexpensive, colorful and fine quality materials available to the public. At the same time, the religious and social life of the Amish community had stabilized enough to allow an artistic textile tradition to evolve. These conditions appeared together at a time when women still possessed excellent sewing skills. The era of homemade materials and hand-sewing was not a distant past.

By the 1950s, American life was radically different than it had been at the turn of the century. The Amish community changed as well during these years, albeit more slowly. Tremendous increases in population contributed to the growth of older Amish communities and the founding of many new settlements throughout the eastern and midwestern United States. The basic structures of Amish life remained unchanged, but the community was forcibly exposed to various aspects of American life. Schooling and taxation issues brought the Amish community into the courts and the public eye. Some of the vast array of consumer products created by industry in the 20th century gradually became intrinsic parts of Amish life.

As the discoveries and inventions of synthetic dyes and increased factory production affected 19th century Amish quiltmaking, so, too, the development of synthetic materials and the ever-increasing mechanization of American life affected 20th-century Amish women. The changes in Amish textiles and quiltmaking reflect the social, economic and industrial history of the country at large and the Amish in particular.

Fabric

To understand quilts requires some knowl-

48

edge of the materials from which they are constructed. Although the subject of fabric is an extensive one, it is helpful to be aware of a few basic facts about the types of materials commonly used by Amish women in their sewing work. Understanding the common terminology employed in the description of fabrics and weaving is also useful.

There are two types of materials: natural fibers and man-made or synthetic fibers. Each has its own variety of weaves and finishes.

Weaving is a mechanical process in which warp and weft threads are interlocked. The warp threads run across the length of the fabric. The weft or filling yarns cross the warp and run across the width of the material.

Finishing describes any number of chemical and physical techniques used on the finished woven material to enhance or change its appearance. Typical finishes include bleaching, napping, calendering, sizing with starch or gum, and mercerizing.

Weave describes the way a fabric is constructed. There are three basic weave patterns: plain, twill and satin weave. Plain weave is the simplest and least expensive method. In plain-weave fabrics, the filling is simply passed over one warp thread and under the next across the length of the fabric. Each row alternates this under-and-over pattern. The result is a cloth that looks like a simple grid.

There are some variations to the plain weave which may enhance a fabric, making it a little fancier in appearance. In general, Amish women have traditionally used the simple plain weave. In quilts and clothing however, it is possible to find fabrics that show a ribbed effect or employ the basket weave. Both of these plain-weave variations achieved some popularity among Amish women in the years after the 1940s. Rib plain weave is made by using fillings that are heavier than the warp thread, as in poplin, or by using warps heavier than the fill-

Detail shows contrasting weaves:
Black — sateen weave • Brown and brown/green — twill. The twill weave is enhanced in the one piece by use of green and brown threads. • Light brown — plain weave
Detail shows contrast of plain and sateen weaves:
Blue — Indianhead cotton, plain weave • Black — rayon sateen, sateen weave

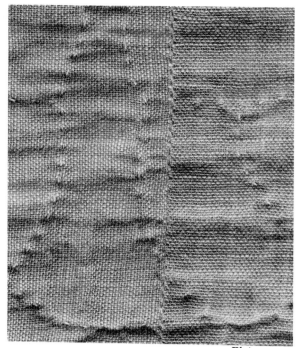

Plain weave

ings, as in Bedford cord.

Another method of enhancing the plain weave is to vary the size of the warp and weft yarns and to use uneven yarn at irregular intervals. Crash, shantung and pongee are examples of fabrics created with this weaving technique. Variation can also be created by using different degrees of twist in the warp or filling yarns and by spinning the yarn so hard that it twists and crinkles, as in crepe. Chambray is still another example of the enhancement of plain weave. By using a warp thread that differs in color from the white filling threads, a more attractive material is created. Chambray was and is a very popular fabric among the Amish, and it can be found in all types of clothing and quilts from the mid-19th century to the present day.

Some of the most typical plain-weave fabrics used by Amish women in both clothing and quilts are batiste, broadcloth, calico, cambric, challis, chambray, crepe, flannel, georgette, gingham, homespun, muslin, nainsook, organdy, percale, pongee and soisette.

The second major fabric weaving pattern is the twill weave. Considered to be the most durable of all the weaves, it, too, comes in many variations. In twill, the filling yarn is interlaced with the warps in such a way as to form diagonal ridges across the fabric. Like the plain weave, a number of variations of twill weave are created by the use of yarns of different sizes, qualities and colors, as well as through the application of different finishes. Twills used by the Amish include broadcloth, cashmere, covert cloth, denim, drill, gabardine, jean and serge. These fabrics are made in cottons, in synthetic materials, in mixtures of cotton or wool and synthetics, and in 100 percent wool.

Satin weave is the third major weaving technique. Based on the principles of twill, satin weave is identified as a separate technique because of the appearance of the finished material. In these fabrics, the front side exhibits

Detail shows contrasting weaves and materials:
Blue — plain weave, muslin quality • Red — plain weave, muslin quality • Green — plain weave, broadcloth • Dark pink — plain weave, Indianhead • Light pink — sateen weave, sateen
Detail shows contrasting plain and twill weaves: Red — plain weave, rayon • Green — twill weave, rayon/wool blend

more warp than filling threads. A variation of this method is the sateen weave (or filling-face satin weave), in which the front of the fabric shows more filling than warps, thus creating a sheen across the surface of the material.

Cotton sateen was an extremely popular fabric among the Amish for many years and is easily identified by both the weave and its overall appearance. The front reveals a smooth, soft lustrous surface; the back of sateen-woven fabric has no luster. Again, as in twill and plain weaves, variations in the warp yarn and in the finishing processes can give the fabric different appearances. The sateen weave was used in both cottons and rayons.

Weave and finish are two essential aspects in the appearance and identification of a fabric. Another important element is a fabric's fiber type. There are four major, natural fibers: wool, cotton, silk and linen. Among the most widely used synthetic fibers are rayon, nylon, polyester and acrylics. The fabrics most common to Amish sewing are wool, cotton and the synthetics.

Wool

There are two types of wool fabrics: those made with woolen yarns and those made with worsted yarns. Woolen yarns are generally softer and more loosely spun. They are used for the softer, bulkier and heavier woolen fabrics, such as tweeds and coating goods. Worsted yarns are used for the clear surfaced and hard textured dress and suiting fabrics, such as gabardine, serge and poplin. The worsted woolens, along with wool batiste, are the fabrics found most often in Amish clothing and quilts.

Wool is generally regarded for its softness, warmth and resiliency. Wool also absorbs light rather than reflects it, thus making colors appear deeper and richer. In Amish quilts made of wool, the color is enhanced. Wool is, however, more sensitive to soap and water and prone to

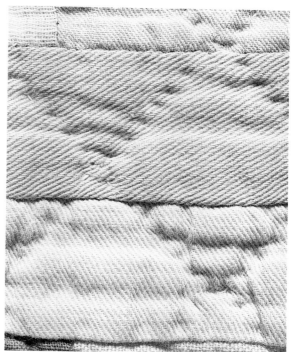
Twill weave

Sateen weave

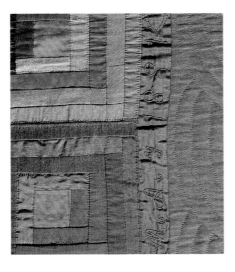

moth infestation, so that it requires more care in its maintenance and laundering. Wool goods for both dresses and quilts were standard among the Lancaster Amish into the 1940s. Most other Amish communities used more cotton than woolen materials.

Cotton

Cotton is perhaps the most widely used fabric in the world today. It is the cheapest and most available natural fiber. It is durable and easily cleaned, it dyes well, accepts a large number of different dye and finish treatments and can be woven into a diverse number of products.

Cotton goods have been used extensively by Amish women since the 19th century when cotton largely replaced flax linen for household goods. From the 1850s until the 1950s, cotton was the preferred material for all homemade clothing in all Amish communities other than Lancaster.

Synthetics

Synthetics have been with us much longer than one might guess initially. "Synthetic" describes any fabric made of fibers that are chemically produced. Rayon, the first synthetic, was followed by nylon, polyester and acrylics. All of these materials were the result of research and experimentation which began in the 1880s and has continued unabated to the present day. The value of synthetic fabrics lies in their flexibility and diversity. In addition, their cost is comparatively less than traditional fibers.

Although many Amish women did cling to the use of traditional cottons and woolens, since the 1930s and 1940s they have used synthetics extensively in both clothing and quiltmaking. When polyester appeared on the market in the 1950s, the Amish turned quickly and wholeheartedly to the fabrics of the 20th century.

Plain- and twill-weave wools, circa 1890–1900
Plain-weave cotton percale, circa 1880–90
A mixture of cotton and cotton/rayon materials in plain- and sateen-weaves, 1950

Identifying Fiber Types

Learning to identify fabrics by their visual and tactile clues is a skill requiring practice. Printed materials tend to be easier to date than the solid colors used by the Amish, since prints follow recognizable fashion trends. But printed materials are rare in Amish quilts and so we must rely on other information. Amish women made quilts for a limited number of years and used a narrower range of fabrics than the general American population. Although learning to identify the materials found in Amish quilts requires time, sensitivity and practice, it is not an insurmountable task.

It is helpful to handle and compare different fabrics and to examine materials whose fiber type and period of manufacture are known. Collections of materials from textile sample books can be found in libraries and archives of many museums.[18] Collections of Amish clothing and fabrics are also helpful guides. It was a tradition for an Amish bride to give swatches of the fabric used to make her wedding dress, and often that of the groom's suit, as "favors" to her guests and friends. These keepsakes are an invaluable index in determining both the age and types of materials found in quilts. Finally, a careful look at collections of quilts that are accompanied by accurate provenance is an excellent source of information on fabric.

To identify any fabric type, the first test is that of touch. More technical laboratory methods can be used, but since that is frequently not possible, it is often necessary to rely most heavily on a developed sense of touch. When examining materials in a quilt to determine the fabric type, feel the material with several different fingers. Run your hand across the cloth in all directions and, if possible, brush a section of the fabric against your cheek or on the skin above your lips. Think about the sensations of warmth, coolness, softness, roughness, pliability, strength or smoothness that the fab-

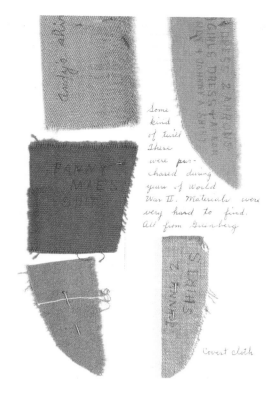

(below) **Amish Wedding Samples**
Two collections of wedding dress samples are pictured here — one from Lancaster and the other from Indiana. A popular custom in many Amish communities was to give guests swatches of material from the wedding dress and suit of the bride and groom. These leftovers from the sewing work were carefully labeled with names and dates, and treasured by women as mementos of their youth.

(above) **Pages from Fabric Book**
This book of scraps was made by an Amish woman living in Indiana. A great lover of material, this woman saved and labeled the many different fabrics she used over the years in her sewing. Many of the scraps were sent to her mother in Ohio in her letters, to show her mother what the family was wearing.

ric exhibits. Cotton tends to feel cooler, softer and smoother than wool or synthetics. Wool is usually soft, pliable, scratchy and warm. The synthetic fabrics tend to feel harder and more slippery, as well as less pliable than either wool or cotton material.

Woolen goods are most easily identified by rubbing the material on one's face. Wool has a distinctly soft, scratchy feel. Cotton and synthetic fabrics are often more difficult to distinguish and, in fact, many synthetic fabrics are actually a mix of natural and synthetic fibers. Fabrics made of 100 percent rayon have a particular soft, lustrous feel, which, with practice, can be readily identified by touch and appearance.

Touch and appearance are the main methods available for examining the materials in quilts. If a strand of fiber can be isolated without damaging the quilt, examining it under a microscope or using the burning test can help to accurately determine the fiber type.

Various fabrics react to flame differently, burning at different rates and leaving different residues and odors. The following list outlines the reactions of various materials to the burning test method of identification.[19]

Cotton	Cotton ignites and burns quickly. There is a slight odor of burning paper and a small amount of light ash residue.
Wool	Wool ignites and burns more slowly than cotton and it can be easily extinguished. Burnt wool fiber leaves a strong odor like burnt feathers or hair.
Rayon	Like cottons, rayon ignites quickly. It burns more rapidly than cotton and there is little residue or ash.
Nylon	When ignited, nylon will melt before it burns. As it burns, it shrinks from the flame and forms a hard, round bead. There is also a slight odor like celery.
Polyester	These fabrics also fuse and shrink from flame. Dacron, Kodel, Fortrel and Vycron melt and burn slowly. Kodel produces a slight soot; Dacron has a slightly sweet odor; Kodel smells like burning pine tar. All four fibers leave a hard, round, black bead of ash.
Acrylic	These behave as polyester does, leaving a brittle, black bead of ash.

A pick glass or linen counter is a small, portable and inexpensive tool which offers high magnification for examining the surfaces of fabrics. It is the most useful tool for looking at weave structures. Under a pick glass, wool may appear fuzzier than cotton. Rayon and polyester fibers appear smoother than cottons or wools. Magnification may help to verify visual and tactile impressions of a material.

Although a pick glass can provide a relatively precise look at a fabric surface, a microscope makes it possible to accurately examine and identify a fiber's structure, as each textile fiber has its own distinctive shape. There are, however, certain manufacturing and finishing processes such as mercerization and delustering that affect the appearance of fibers under the microscope. Also, a dark colored fabric cannot be identified because light does not pass through the fiber shaft in sufficient quantity to illuminate the fiber structure.[20]

From the microscopic examination of a single fiber to the overall visual impression of the whole quilt, all elements of a quilt need to be considered in order to determine its content and age. Focusing on a single factor can be misleading. The fiber type and fabric varieties, the colors, the design, the scale of piecework and the quilting all provide invaluable information about the origins and make-up of each quilt.

Textile Dyeing

Textile dyeing is the process of saturating yarns or woven fabric with color. "Home dyed" or "natural colors" are terms frequently applied to the fabrics found in early Amish quilts. These are often misleading descriptions because, like the arts of spinning and weaving, the practice of home-dyeing textiles with natural dyes was a craft virtually forgotten by Amish women by the time they began making pieced quilts in the 1870s.

As with other aspects of textile production, increased industrialization in the mid-19th century had turned fabric dyeing almost exclusively into a factory job. Although women continued to do some dyeing at home, this usually involved purchasing packaged dyestuff from the store and tinting or retinting small amounts of material. As cottons and wools became increasingly available in a wide variety of colors at reasonable prices, the practices of weaving and dyeing cloth in the home became unnecessary and obsolete. Amish women appear to have accepted this change as readily as other American women. Although many older Amish men and women can recount stories passed on to them by their parents and grandparents about various aspects of life in the mid-19th century, most of these elderly members of the community have nothing but the vaguest notions about the making of homemade dyes.

Although the *production* of home dyes is only a faint memory, the *process* of home dyeing is not unfamiliar to Amish women today. Everyone interviewed said that they did dye materials at home, and they mentioned a variety of commercial preparations: RIT, Putnam's, Perfection, Cushing and Diamond dyes. These were used by their mothers in the late 19th century and early 20th century. In the 1930s, 1940s and 1950s, they used these dyes themselves. Particularly during the Depression there seems to have been a great deal of home-dyeing of white muslin feedsacks. In hard times, this material was used for everything from dresses to shirts, underwear, diapers, sheets, toweling and quilts.

Commercially prepared dyestuffs first appeared on the market in the 1860s. In 1863 the Howe and Steven's Dye company began manufacturing and distributing a series of "Family Colors." These were "dye balls" and packets of natural dyestuff, ground into powder, then mixed with powdered mordants. The ease and accuracy of these premixed solutions made them very popular, and by the end of the 19th century commercial preparations for home dyeing could be purchased at drugstores and country stores in the most remote parts of the United States.[21]

There are two general classes of dyes: synthetics created by chemists, and natural dyes derived from plant, animal and mineral sources. Natural dyes were the only type available until the mid-1800s. They were employed by factories, by housewives and by professional dyers who ran small businesses. Textile dyeing was a craft, dependent upon limited natural substances and traditional recipes and formulas. The most commonly used dyestuffs in America were indigo for blues, madder and cochineal for red, fustic, quercitron and chrome for yellow, logwood and chrome for black, and sumac for neutral shades.[22] In Pennsylvania, black dyes were also derived from walnuts.[23] In the late 18th century, new inorganic mineral colors such as iron, buff, antimony orange, Prussian blue and manganese yellow were introduced.

Indigo, one of the oldest dyestuffs known, was one of the most basic and widely used textile dyes in America. Even after synthetic indigo was developed in 1870, the methods for producing it at marketable prices were not available until the turn of the 20th century. This is one of the "natural" colors that can be found with great frequency in Amish quilts from the 19th century.

Madder was another of the staple dyes for wool and cottons until the development of synthetics. Dyeing with madder was a difficult and complicated process which originated in India and spread to other eastern countries, including Turkey. One color produced by madder dyeing is called Turkey Red. Materials colored with Turkey Red were extremely popular and widely used in American quilts during the 19th century, and much time and effort was put into developing this dyeing process in America. In 1840 in Lowell, Massachusetts, one factory alone produced more than ¼ million yards of cotton fabric dyed in madder colors.[24]

Throughout the 19th century cochineal was also considered a staple dye. Cochineal produced crimson, pink and scarlet on wool and it continued to be used heavily even into the early part of the 20th century. The shades of red found in 19th century Amish quilts, from light pinks to the deepest scarlets, were colored either naturally or synthetically, since during those years both types of dyeing were used. Natural yellows were the product of fustic, quercitron and chrome, which were introduced in America in the 1830s. Chrome yellow was a successful cotton dyestuff and was considered the best of the yellow cotton dyes throughout the second half of the 19th century.[25] Chrome and manganese yellows can be found in early Amish quilts, including the earliest 1849 example from Mifflin County. Chrome yellow of all shades was a popular color for all types of American quilts during the 19th century.

By mid-century, the textile industry was becoming a sophisticated and booming business. Home-weaving was largely a thing of the past and factories produced millions of yards of fabrics each year. Yet despite the dramatic growth, materials produced on increasingly refined machinery continued to be dyed by methods which were practically medieval. The discovery of synthetic dyes altered all of this almost overnight. Several tentative laboratory experiments with dyes occurred during the early 19th century. In 1865, W.H. Perkin discovered the first analine dye. The race to develop new colors and methods for dyeing threw chemists into a frenzy of activity. From the beginning the Germans, and to some extent the English, dominated the synthetic dyestuff industry. Every year after 1865 witnessed the creation of one or more new colors as chemists systematically worked through the varieties of aniline, azo, sulphur and indigosol dyes, discovering many possible combinations. The products of this chemical research were enthusiastically received by the public who were eager for the variety of new bright colors. By the end of the 19th century a large number of brilliant and easy-to-use dyestuffs were available to the textile industry. Factories turned out millions of yards of bright and richly colored fabrics. The eye-dazzling, brilliant colors present in the most memorable Amish quilts were possible only with the advent of synthetic dyes created in the chemistry laboratories of Europe.

At the turn of the century, after the initial public enthusiasm for the new dyes subsided and the commercial success of synthetic colors was assured, development of new colors slowed while the search for increased fastness grew. One of the most serious drawbacks of the earliest synthetic dyes was their tendency to bleed, stain and fade when washed. During the late 19th and early 20th centuries, experimentation and research led to improvements in dye manufacturing, production machinery and increased colorfastness.

By the late 1880s, German manufacturers were producing a large diversity of attractive, clean, bright and relatively fast colors. In fact, in the early years of the 20th century, the term "German Dye" was considered a one-word description of the best product available. Consequently, during World War I the German monopoly of the industry caused shortages of dyestuffs in this country. The problem became so severe that it affected even stampmaking and bookkeeping. Advertising in the *Sugarcreek Budget* in October of 1915, Garver Brothers wrote:

> Dye stuffs are becoming very scarce and some goods will be very scarce after a while and hard to get if the war in Europe continues much longer. On account of the unfortunate conditions in Europe there is a real famine in materials, for coloring yarns and colored goods of all sorts have gone way up in price. The prices on some cotton goods have doubled.[26]

In the years following World War I, chemistry and organic chemistry became huge industries in the United States. American manufacturers threw themselves into the development of technology and production for domestic dyestuffs. In just three years, between 1917 and 1920, over 100 companies were founded to produce synthetic dyes.[27]

The discovery and development of new manmade fibers fostered new research in textile dyeing. Chemists continued to seek improvement for the process of coloring both traditional natural fibers and the new synthetics. During the 1920s, 1930s and 1940s researchers continued to work on enlarging the color palette and increasing colorfastness. In 1956, 109 years after Perkin's first synthetic creation, an entirely new chemical principle of reactive dyeing was discovered for dyeing cotton and other fibers. Reactive dyes actually react with fiber

molecules to form a new chemical compound. This process enabled manufacturers to create brilliant new colors with maximum fastness.

Although many of the earliest Amish quilts do contain material colored by natural dyes, by the 1880s and 1890s natural dyes were far less prevalent than synthetic dyes. By the 1870s and 1880s Amish women were purchasers rather than producers of fabric, and so they became dependent upon the dictates of the marketplace. The synthetic dye industry was well established by the time any significant number of Amish quilts were being produced.

Textile Sources for the Amish Community

The materials found in Amish quilts, almost without exception, are the product of factory manufacturing. During the past 100 years Amish women have purchased an ever-increasing quantity of dry goods from a variety of sources. In interviews, older Amish women spoke of several places from which they, their mothers and grandmothers obtained materials. Those most frequently cited were local stores, traveling salesmen who frequented the Amish community year after year, the mail-order departments of Montgomery Ward and Sears, and several businesses that operated locally and nationally, run by merchants who catered specifically to the Amish community.

A survey of the *Sugarcreek Budget* through the years provides a great deal of information about these businesses and the types of goods available during various periods, as well as their costs. Montgomery Wards' and Sears' mail-order catalogues give insight into both the evolution of textiles and the parallel social changes that have taken place in the United States during the past 100 years. Interviews with the granddaughter and son of one of the early traveling salesmen, and with some of the merchants who operated stores in Amish communities, provide much colorful and accurate information on the fabric-buying practices of Amish women.

The Traveling Salesmen

From colonial times onward, the traveling salesman was an important fixture in the lives of rural Americans. Until the emergence of general stores in the mid-19th century, peddlers brought almost everything, from pins and needles to commissioned portraits, to families living in the countryside. The traveling peddler is a stock figure in American folklore. Selling door to door was hard work at best, but men who perhaps felt too constrained by the regularity of farming or factory work, or who simply had an itch to travel, could earn their living by supplying a variety of products and services to rural communities. Before the days of nationally run chains and standardized goods, Amish women purchased many things, including dry goods, from these traveling businessmen. The tradition of country peddlers was an integral part of rural life, and throughout the Amish communities some of these men became almost legendary.

In the later 19th and early 20th centuries, the eastern cities were filled with immigrants looking for work. Peddling provided economic opportunities for those newly arrived Americans. Many of the traveling salesmen who brought fabrics to the Amish were Jewish merchants with access to the textile wholesalers and jobbers in New York and Philadelphia. Carrying heavy celluloid suitcases filled with materials, they traveled in caravans, working through the coal regions and farmlands of Pennsylvania during the spring, summer and early fall. As winter approached they headed south to ply their trade among the cotton farmers who had collected on their crops, enjoying the more moderate climate which eased the arduous work of walking and carrying large cases of fabric.[28]

Jack Barsky was an early peddler who happened upon the Amish communities around Lancaster and realized quickly the value of the Amish as steady customers. Here were women who purchased large quantities of goods because they required materials for nearly every piece of their families' clothing. They bought every year, but their needs were limited to specific types of fabrics. With a network of friends and relatives, Amish women could help spread the name of a salesman who had treated customers right, and such men found themselves welcomed into households throughout the communities. Although many American women had begun to embrace the ready-made clothing industry, the Amish continued as consumers of vast amounts of yard goods. Several peddlers realized that they could build their entire business by carrying goods from the cities to these communities. They were able to offer fabrics at prices below those asked by the local merchants because they sold materials known as remainders and closeouts — fabrics available from textile jobbers in the cities at a fraction of the cost paid by standard wholesale purchasers.[29]

Barsky's fame grew out of his ability to remember everyone's name (not always an easy task in an Amish community, where there may be numerous Lydia Beilers or Rachel Stoltzfuses) and to calculate prices accurately in his head even while conversing on a variety of subjects. Others followed Barsky's lead, and two particular families became heavily involved in selling to the Amish communities in Pennsylvania, Ohio and Indiana. Nathan and Sam Greenburg and their cousin Isaac Korsch all began as peddlers in the 1920s and 1930s, as did M.A. Spector. In later years their children and grandchildren enlarged and changed their businesses. Between the 1920s and the 1960s these peddlers and their families supplied a great deal of the materials that went into Amish quilts.

Spectors operates today as both a mail-order business and a retail store with four locations in Ohio and two in Indiana. They offer household items along with their dry goods selection.

Sam Greenburg worked as a traveling salesman for many years and brought his son William "Sam" Greenburg into the business in the 1940s. His granddaughter Joyce Brown took over from her father in the 1960s and today runs a mail-order service and still travels to various communities. She operates the business under the name of her grandfather and is even called "Sam Greenburg" by many of the Amish who remember her father and grandfather.

Peddling is work that requires good bargaining skills, stamina and a sense of humor. These men genuinely enjoyed dealing with the Amish and made good friends among them. They would return year after year to the same farms, witnessing the birth, childhood and coming of age of thousands of children. Many Amish women commented that the materials for their wedding dresses were gifts of the traveling salesmen. One woman in Indiana noted that she had eight daughters and Sam Greenburg seemed to know when it was about time for a wedding, because he would always show up with just the right goods and present them to the girl as a gift.[30]

In their wheeling and dealing, peddlers offered various inducements to buy. There were discounts for large purchases and "free pieces" to sweeten the deal. (The free pieces were usually fabrics that were not selling well, but they were tokens of goodwill and a successful business tactic.) Particularly in the 1940s, when materials of any kind were difficult to find, peddlers carried a variety of fabrics unfamiliar to Amish women. If the salesman didn't know the correct name of a fabric he was selling, he would simply invent a name. Peddlers had to be familiar with fabrics, their structures and brand names, but they also enjoyed adding new words to the Amish vocabulary. One particular cloth was named by William "Sam" Greenburg, "Pettijohn cloth," a label derived from the names of two boys in his family, Peter and John.[31]

Peddlers found good customers in the Amish community for more than their dry goods. They also brought with them amusing stories, pleasant conversation and messages from other communities and relatives. In that way they played a small but important role in the Amish community. Even men and women who had never purchased goods from the Greenburgs or Spectors, knew their names because they were frequent and regular visitors in Amish homes throughout the United States.

The Sugarcreek Budget

The Sugarcreek Budget is a national weekly newspaper which has served the Amish and Amish Mennonites since the 1890s. Begun as a newspaper for the area around Sugarcreek, Ohio, it grew over the years to provide information and news of the groups' communities throughout the United States, Canada and Latin America. Early advertisers in The Budget included land and railroad companies anxious to solicit business from the Amish. Agents for health and farming products were also steady advertisers, and textile distributors and dry goods retailers realized the advertising potential of The Budget from the outset of the paper's existence.

Early advertisers included Garver Brothers, Weaver and Mast (later Weaver Brothers), the Sugarcreek Woolen Mills and H.E. Putts, all from Ohio, and the Clinton Woolen Mills, Dembusky, and Gohn's from Indiana. Some of these early companies are still in business today.

In the 20th century, Sam Greenburg, Spectors, W.L. Zimmerman, Yoder's and Rubinson's advertised their retail operations and provided mail-order service as well.

One of the first advertisers in The Budget, The Sugarcreek Woolen Mills, offered "all wool and cotton warp blankets of all colors . . . satinets, cassimeres, flannels and stocking yarns of all colors" in the 1890s.[32] From Indiana, the Clinton Woolen Mills near Goshen advertised "all wool coverlets, bed and horse blankets, heavy cloth, hand knit socks and mittens, woolen batting and custom work."[33]

A full-page advertisement by Weaver Brothers in April 1895 offers a glimpse of the variety and prices of the materials most commonly used at the end of the 19th century by Amish women.[34]

Our Buyer Has Just Returned From N.Y.C. Where He Has Been Searching For Bargains
We sell best plain Berlin calicoes at 5 cents a yard.
Also good plain calicoes at 4 cents a yard.
Plain brown and white, blue and white and black and white ginghams at 5 cents a yard.
Very fine plain gingham in all colors.
Best Manchester chambrays at 10 cents a yard.
A big line of cottonades and jeans.
Plain sateen from 6 cents a yard and up.
Half wool Alpaca at 9 cents a yard.
In lace and embroideries we can beat the Jews.
Good machine thread in black and white is 2 cents a spool.
Best 6 cord thread by Clarks O.N.T.

Dry Goods at Wholesale Prices
plain calico — 4 and 5 cents
plain gingham — 6½ cents
best chambray — 10½ cents
heavy gingham — 7½ cents

black sateen — 8 cents and up
Lancaster ginghams — 4½ cents
plain indigo blue muslin — 8½ cents
34-inch cashmere, half wool — 14 cents
36-inch cashmere, half wool — 17 cents
20-inch cashmere, half wool — 9 cents
extra heavy blue and brown denim —
11 cents

Always on the lookout for the best prices and the variety of materials necessary for their family clothing, Amish seamstresses purchased materials from a variety of sources. Many women bought extensive yardages, often by the bolt. All of the family clothing was made at home with the exception of shoes, men's hats, socks and underwear. In certain communities these last two items continued to be homemade well into the early 20th century, and in some cases, still are today.

Generally Amish women do a concentrated amount of sewing at particular times of the year. The middle and late summer and the middle of winter are the most common periods for large purchases of goods. William Greenburg recalled that he always sold a lot in the summer when women were preparing for school clothing and for weddings, which traditionally occur in October and November. Several advertisers in *The Budget* capitalized on these seasonal ups and downs by stocking large quantities prior to the period of Amish women's heavy sewing work. In the summer of 1900 Garver Brothers carried this advice to the reader:[35]

Buy All Your Fall Goods at Garver Brothers
Heavy denim
9 oz. denim in black or brown
Kentucky jean
heavy drilled wool cassimere
best plain black calico
Omega black sateen
Fine black sateen
fine bleached muslin

large sheets of cotton wadding white or dark
best grey chambray ginghams
Cocheco oil colors
plain dyed fine muslin cloth

Garver Brothers

Garver Brothers in Strasburg, Ohio, was a very large and prosperous operation. Begun in the late 19th century, this business continued into the 1950s. Almost every Amish woman interviewed mentioned that her family had patronized this store, either directly or through mail order.

Their advertisements in *The Budget* are full of information. When Garver Brothers began soliciting business from the Amish community in 1894, they asked *Budget* readers to "help us by sending or bringing samples of such goods as you wear."[36] The advertising copy for the store featured a chatty, personal style and offered political and economic information as background for the prices. Readers were frequently encouraged to stock up because they never knew what conditions might prevail in the cotton or wool markets and "buying now will surely pay in the long run."[37]

Advertisements from different periods indicate the changes in textiles that were available from the late 19th century through the 1950s. The cashmeres, batistes, percales, sateens and henriettas that were the stock in trade until the 1920s were replaced by synthetics in the 1930s and 1940s. By 1949 Garver Brothers' "most popular dress fabric — rayon spun challis" was available in a bright array of new colors, such as bottle green, African brown, aqua and peacock blue.[38] Plain-colored Quadrigal percale, the finest and best of all the 80-square percales, had guaranteed fast colors and a special "needlized" finish to make it ideal for quilts. A full spectrum of light green, copen blue, royal blue, orchid, lavender, wine, rose, coral, yellow, navy, aqua, tan, dark brown and black were typically used in quilts and clothing of this period.

Dembusky and Gohn's

C. Dembusky in Goshen and George Gohn in Middlebury were two businesses that served the Amish community in Indiana. Both advertised weekly in *The Budget* from the early years of the 20th century until the 1940s and 1950s. Both were small, family-run operations that catered specifically to the Amish trade. Gohn's, which specialized in producing finished Amish men's suits, employed a number of Amish women in the Middlebury area as seamstresses and tailors to produce those suits. Mail-order service was a large part of the business of both these companies, as it was for Garver Brothers and Spectors in Ohio. One such advertisement is shown on this page.[39]

Yoder's Department Store

When Dembusky and Garver Brothers closed their businesses in the 1940s and 1950s, others arrived to take their place. Yoder's opened in Topeka, Indiana, in 1942 as a small operation run by one man and his family. The business expanded quickly and soon the Yoders were operating three stores at once in both Topeka and Shipshewana. From the first years, dry goods were sold along with a variety of other household products. Mr. Yoder estimated that in the 1940s and early 1950s almost half of his fabric sales were to the Amish. As his business grew, that percentage decreased over the years. Cotton and rayons were the mainstay of his stock; the only wools he sold were for men's suits. Generally he shopped for materials at three different wholesale houses in St. Louis, obtaining goods from a number of companies, including Cloth of Gold, Springmaid, Eli and Walker, Indianhead Mills and Pepperell Mills. In later years, salesmen representing different mills and textile houses in Chicago and St. Louis began bringing samples and seeking orders.

Yoder's did some advertising in *The Budget,* particularly in the early years, and also always did quite a bit of mail-order business at the request of customers.

Mr. Yoder observed that in all his years in business, the Amish women in the area around Shipshewana were very quality conscious and anxious to obtain materials they had found satisfactory year after year.[40] His best-selling dress fabric through the 1950s was a spun rayon, plain-weave fabric with a soft feel like challis. Made from 100 percent rayon, this fabric sold in black, brown, navy, dark green, dark grey and lighter colors for children's clothing. Yoder said that when polyester came on the market in the late 1950s, Amish women purchased it by the bolt for family clothing.

Yoder's Department Store in Shipshewana, Indiana, operates today as a large department store and grocery.

W.L. Zimmerman and Rubinson's

Dembusky, Gohn's, Yoder's, Spectors and Garver Brothers were the largest and most successful operations in Ohio and Indiana for many years. In Lancaster, W.L. Zimmerman and Sam Rubinson's stores were the most frequently mentioned local sources for fabric.

W.L. Zimmerman was founded in 1909 by a man who "left off farming cause he didn't have the feet for it."[41] His three sons, all of whom were born in the apartments above the store where the family lived, continued the family business when their father retired. Recently the third generation has taken over management of the grocery, hardware and oil-delivery service which grew out of the original general store.

A few years ago when a local Amish woman started a fabric store down the street, Zimmer-man left the dry goods business entirely. For almost 70 years, however, W.L. Zimmerman sold piece goods obtained through wholesalers in New York, Baltimore and Philadelphia. Zimmerman carried the whole line of standard goods popular with Lancaster Amish women.

Mr. Zimmerman's observations on the fabric buying practices of the Amish are similar to other merchants. He confirmed that the most important changes in fabrics came during World War II and in the post-war period. Even though the Amish complained about it, they were forced to accept new types of materials in the mid-and late 1940s. In subsequent years, the variety of colors and types of fabrics that were acceptable to Zimmerman's customers increased steadily.

Sam Rubinson's was another popular source of materials for women in the Lancaster area. Rubinson operated a department store in New Holland which he opened in 1914. Early success led to the enlargement of his business and a new store was opened in September 1921. At his Grand Opening Sale, poplins in all colors sold for 35 cents a yard, unbleached muslin went for 10 cents a yard and extra high quality cretonne cost 25 cents a yard. By the 1930s Rubinson was offering mail-order service to Amish women all over the country. Rubinson's never achieved the national following of Spectors or Garver Brothers, but they did sell a lot of material by mail-order.

Rubinson's advertisement on a 1937 wall calendar, which he distributed to his customers, announced, "What ever you need in Amish Dress Goods — Amish clothing — Amish hats and shoes. Write to the biggest Amish store — Get samples and our low prices." The listing of dress and household fabrics Rubinson offered was extensive and indicative of fabrics typical to the Lancaster area in the late 1930s.[42]

Dress Goods of Every Kind
Write For Samples Of
All Wool Batiste, Men's Suiting, Cottande Pantings, Moleskins, Corduroys, Blue And Black Denim, Blue Bell Shirting, All Wool Flannels, All Wool Crepes, Apron Gingham, Cotton Flannels, Mohairs, Pebble Crepes, Ticking, Shawl Goods, Cap Goods, Rayon Flat Crepes, Silk Flat Crepes, Indianhead Linens, Muslins, Sheetings, Half Wool Crepes, Poplins, Charmeuse, Broadcloth, Linings, Veilings, Hemstitched Sheets, Pillow Cases, Bolster Cases And Dust Cloth.

Mail-Order Catalogues

The founding of two business ventures in the late 19th century — Sears & Roebuck and Montgomery Ward — was to have far-reaching effects on the lives of rural Americans. These mail-order businesses were only possible after a national railroad system was in place. Both national and local companies capitalized on the rail system and its ability to move goods quickly and efficiently from producer to seller to consumer.

The catalogues, or "wish books," of these two companies became a major source of entertainment, as well as consumer products, for people living outside urban centers of commerce. Like other rural families, the Amish found products and prices in these catalogues that were often unavailable in the local marketplace. The success of Sears and Ward was unprecedented; in interviews Amish men and women consistently mentioned these mail-order companies as sources they and their families used for materials. Examining the dry goods offered by these two companies from the late 19th century into the 1960s gives both a linear and nearly complete picture of the changes in American and Amish textile patterns.

In the early 1870s, Aaron Montgomery Ward was a traveling salesman in the Midwest. He had worked for several different firms in St. Louis and Chicago, selling dry goods. When he decided to start his own business he chose the farmer as his target customer. His familiarity with midwestern rural communities and their needs paid off quickly and handsomely. His first catalogue in 1872 was a single printed sheet listing about 50 dry goods items all priced at one dollar or less.[43] He sold out immediately. When Sears first entered the mail-order market in 1886, Montgomery Ward was a well-established concern. In 1886, Ward's catalogue was already 280 pages long and offered over 10,000 items.[44] Although Ward came first, Sears' growth was rapid and by the turn of the century had surpassed Ward in sales and profits.

Sears and Roebuck was founded in 1886 by a railroad clerk named Richard Sears. Wanting to supplement his income, he began selling watches and later jewelry by mail-order. Alvah Roebuck joined the business as a watch repairman and each year these men expanded their offerings. The catalogue grew from 32 pages in 1891 to almost 200 pages by 1894. In 1897 some 318,000 copies were mailed to families in the Midwest.

In 1895 dry goods first appeared in the Sears catalogue, including a few printed dress goods. By the next year the dry goods offering was vastly enlarged. Sears advertised sample swatches, about one inch square, that were free to the customer, but admonished the client to "make your request as specific as possible . . . so we can serve you prompt." The catalogue also notes that "it pays to get up club orders."[45]

The listing of fabrics in the 1896 – 97 catalogue was extensive and included many materials popular among the Amish during this period for both clothing and quilts. Colored henriettas, domestic and imported serges, alpacas and cashmeres were offered in a variety of widths, colors and prices. Twenty-two-inch

BLACK GOODS SPECIALTIES

57044   43¢

57057 $1.25

57051 69¢

57059 49¢

57059 A BLACK GERMAN HEN-RIETTA, strictly all pure wool, silk finished. Will hold its color to the last. This goods is well worth 65c. per yard, but we bought the output of the mills, and will give our customers the benefit. Width, 45 inches. Our special price, per yard....$0.49
A full dress pattern of 7 yards for....................$3.39

No. 57061 BLACK FRENCH SERGE, strictly all pure wool. It has a neat, small twill. This goods will not show the dust. This particular number is a decided bargain, and when our present stock is exhausted we cannot duplicate them again. Width of goods, 45 inches. Our special price, per yard....$0.49
A full dress pattern of 7 yards for....................$3.40

57061 49¢

57041 25¢

57042 38¢

57047 50¢

57054 75c

57049 55¢

FOR SAMPLES OF DRESS GOODS WRITE FOR BOOKLET 15H.

● **BLACK DRESS GOODS.** ●

SAMPLES OF DRESS GOODS SENT FREE ON REQUEST. ASK FOR 15H.

Union cashmere was available in medium, light and dark slate, olive, medium blue, medium brown, seal, tan, golden brown, cardinal, garnet, myrtle, navy and black for just nine cents a yard.

Henriettas and serges made from "positively all wool" came in all the standard shades, such as myrtle, wine, dark and light brown, navy and slate, for 25 cents a yard. Thirty-six-inch black cashmere also cost 25 cents a yard and solid-colored oil print dress cottons in cardinal, orange, grey, medium blue, scarlet, tan, black,

medium brown and turkey red sold for five cents a yard. Black sateens, covert cloth and cambrics, domestics such as denim, and bleached cottons and cotton batting were all offered.

Cotton batting was sold in 16-ounce rolls, and the catalogue noted proudly that "our batts are patent folded and not simply a wad of cotton to be repicked and put into the quilt in bunches. Each batt is nicely papered, folded and will open to the same thickness 36 inches wide and 7 feet long."[46]

Sears must have satisfied his customers, be-

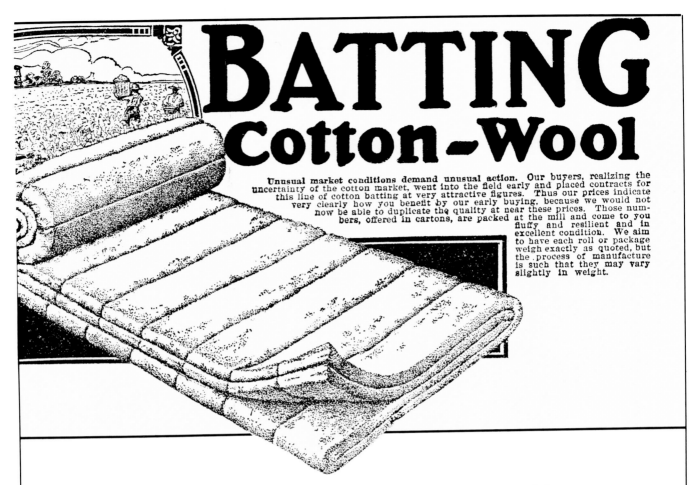

BATTING
Cotton-Wool

Unusual market conditions demand unusual action. Our buyers, realizing the uncertainty of the cotton market, went into the field early and placed contracts for this line of cotton batting at very attractive figures. Thus our prices indicate very clearly how you benefit by our early buying, because we would not now be able to duplicate the quality at near these prices. Those numbers, offered in cartons, are packed at the mill and come to you fluffy and resilient and in excellent condition. We aim to have each roll or package weigh exactly as quoted, but the process of manufacture is such that they may vary slightly in weight.

cause by 1902 the volume of samples that was being sent to customers had become so great that the company began requesting one cent per sample to help defray the expense of sample mailing. Furthermore, they begged the readers to send only for "such samples as you need."[47]

Woolen fabrics in the 1902 issue included a variety of black and colored serges, henriettas, cashmeres and broadcloths. Cotton scotch chambray in solid colored pink, blue, navy, tan, gray or brown was available for 10 cents a yard and fine colored dress sateens with "absolutely fast colors" were offered for 12 and 17 cents a yard in "all the fashionable staple colors as well as 'opera' shades."[48]

By 1905 the pages devoted to ready-made clothing had grown quite numerous. The dry goods listing had also expanded and the fabrics available included cashmere, henriettas, mohair brilliantine, heavy serges and cheviots, plain and fancy dress fabrics, lightweight dress goods, black dress goods, colored wash dress fabrics, sea island batiste cottons, mercerized sateens

and a large assortment of domestics, cotton battings, thread and notions.

The wool batiste so common to Lancaster quilts of this period was sold by Sears in solid colors, such as royal blue, green, cardinal, brown, gray, pink and black. A new fine-weave colored wool melrose was introduced, and the catalogue explained that wool melrose was a fancy weave with so little of the fancy effect that it might be termed a plain cloth. It was about the same weight of henrietta and came in all standard colors.

The fabrics offered in the 1910 catalogue were, for the most part, similar to the previous years; woolens and cottons in a wide assortment of colors and qualities were fully described. Prices for all-wool and part-wool fabrics had increased by 1910 and the colored batistes, cashmeres and henriettas, which had been priced in the 20- to 30-cent range in 1897, were now close to 50 cents a yard or more. Terms such as "cashmere and henrietta effect" and "wool faced" appeared frequently on the more

economically priced goods. In the cotton dress goods department, solid colored percales, plain colored chambrays, lustrola and improved poplins ran from six to 20 cents a yard.[49]

Mail-order catalogues touted their high standards as an important selling point and emphasized their commitment to customer satisfaction. In the second decade of the 20th century, Sears mounted extensive efforts to guarantee the standards of their goods by paying for the education of in-house experts and developing their own private laboratories for testing the products they sold. This effort was necessary because in the early part of this century, before standards were established and enforced by the federal government, textile manufacturers often mixed wool with cotton and lesser quality woolens and simply told their distributors that the fabrics were 100 percent virgin wool.

In the 1915 Sears catalogue, fabric names and prices reflected a new effort at honest labeling. All-wool henrietta cost only 27 cents a yard. Fine all-wool batiste sold for 42 cents, and the catalogue noted that "this grade of all wool batiste is a width and quality which is known in nearly every home in the country."[50] It was available in a large selection of colors. Cottons were sold in batiste weight, chambray, sateens and solid colored calico. The catalogue did mention that the colors of the fabric on the page were "as fast as it is possible to dye them" and cautioned customers to "wash them only in warm water with pure soap and then rinse in cold water."[51]

Although the war in Europe affected the United States in many ways before the country's actual involvement in the conflict, Sears & Roebuck managed to maintain its supplies and prices until 1917 when the United States entered World War I. In the 1918–1919 catalogue the dry goods listings began with an advisory: "Our great Dry Goods Department is prepared to give you the same service as always. Extraordinary conditions have made it difficult to secure the necessary supplies, but not withstanding these conditions our stocks are large and variety is great."[52] Prices jumped sharply, however, so that the plain colored chambray used by Amish women for quilts and clothing climbed from the 1915 price of nine cents a yard to 29 cents a yard, or $2.44 for a 10-yard bolt in 1918–19. Plain-colored sateens, another Amish staple, which cost anywhere from 10 to

20 cents in 1915, now cost 35 to 52 cents a yard. All-wool batiste, available in such a wide selection of colors for 42 cents in 1915, was now 98 cents a yard and only came in pink, lavender, light blue or navy. Even half-wool batiste was expensive at 73 cents a yard.

When the war ended, the American economy restabilized and started to develop rapidly in the post-war period. The changes taking place in American culture were also reflected in the Sears catalogue. In the spring 1919 issue, a full-page letter addressed directly to American women indicated the increased financial and social power that women had gained during the war years. The fabrics offered in the dry goods department were largely the same as previously, but the higher prices and shortages created by the war were still evident. Within two years of the war's end, however, the prices of cotton and wool dropped and the 1921 catalogue pointed out that "dress cottons are now reasonably priced."

One of the most noteworthy changes in the post-World War I period was the disappearance

from the market of the once-standard henrietta woolens. In 1921 Sears offered only cream-colored henrietta and some other cotton fabrics which were described as "henrietta finished." In the fall and winter catalogue of 1921, the woolens that were available included part-wool tricotine for 75 cents, mohair brilliantine for 69

COLORED SATEENS

Luster Finish Charmeuse Finish Satin Finish

Width, About 30 Inches.	Width, About 36 Inches.	Width, About 36 Inches.
20c A YARD 36K4827 A good quality medium weight bloom or silk finish cotton fabric. Universally in use for waists, dresses, petticoats, bloomers and various trimming purposes, including lining. One of our most popular grades. Guaranteed fast color with exception of the dark shades which will set after one washing. State color wanted.	**29c** A YARD No. 36K4830 This is a softly finished imitation silk fabric, made of fine cotton yarns, which have been woven so as to give a smooth silk-like texture to the cloth. Beautifully mercerized, and all colors are fast. There is probably nothing which would cut to better advantage, give more service and better satisfaction than this moderate priced, well made quality. We offer this cloth in competition with popular brands which are ordinarily offered for considerably more money. State color wanted.	**39c** A YARD 36K4832 This cloth represents the best that we could find in a domestic cotton yarn fabric. Highly mercerized, imitation silk finish. It is ideal for waists, petticoats, bloomers, trimming and linings. A beautiful fabric, and its fineness of weave makes it feel and look like satin silk. State color wanted.
COLORS	COLORS	COLORS
Light Blue Navy Blue Pink Garnet Light Black Brown Royal White Blue Cream	White Garnet Light Blue Slate Gray Cream Navy Blue Copenhagen Black Blue Chestnut Old Rose Brown Olive Green Pink	White Chestnut Light Blue Brown Cream Slate Gray Copenhagen Navy Blue Blue Black Old Rose Pink Myrtle Green Garnet
Shipping weight, per yard, about 4 ounces.	Shpg. wt., per yd., abt. 4½ oz.	Shipping wt., per yard, about 4½ ounces.

For sateen linings see page 807.

to 79 cents a yard, part-wool batiste for 69 cents and all-wool batiste for the extravagant price of $1.10 and $1.57 a yard. French and storm serge, which became very popular with Amish women for dress fabric, were more reasonable at 69 cents for the all-wool quality.

In the early 1920s Sears introduced several fabric trademark brands which became popular with Amish families. Indianhead was described by Sears as "the national all around everyday thrift fabric." Soisette, another registered trademark, was a soft dress fabric which many Amish women mentioned in interviews. Satellite sateen, which was Sears' exclusive brand, sold for 25 cents a yard. This became a staple fabric among Amish women for dresses and quilts, particularly in the Midwest.

By 1923, "Artificial Silk — Fashion's New Favorite Material" appeared in the catalogues. Although it was not picked up by Amish women when it was first introduced on the market, their use of rayon in a variety of fabric types became more and more prevalent after the mid-1920s. The traditional cotton and woolens which Amish women used were abundant and less expensive by 1925. In addition, all-wool batiste had dropped to 98 cents a yard and came in an increasing number of colors. Indianhead, Soisette, broadcloths, plain colored ginghams, chambrays and calicoes were also cheaper and more varied. Plain colored percale for 16 cents a yard came in such exotic shades as heliotrope, tangerine and cadet blue, and Indianhead and Soisette were sold in "fast" colors such as dark copenhagen, jade green, leather brown, rose and tan. Sateen appears to have been a very popular product in the mid-1920s, as Sears offered several brands in a variety of qualities and prices.

In the early 1930s there were important changes in the fabrics produced in the United States, and the catalogues reflect this shift. The Fall/Winter 1929–30 issue of the Sears cata-logue advertised dress woolens such as wool covert, washable half-wool cashora and non-shrinkable half-wool crepe, wool covert georgette, all-wool crepe romaine, wool twill, wool flat crepe and wool rep. The best all-wool batiste was still available in "all fashion colors" from 1930 through 1933, but by 1935 it too had gone the way of mohair, brilliantine, alpaca and henrietta. Rayon became increasingly important in mixed woolen fabrics, but the traditional cottons (Indianhead, sateen, Soisette, poplin, chambray and percale) were still more prevalent than cotton/rayon mixtures in the early 1930s. As the Depression began to take hold of the nation, Sears addressed the economic problems of rural farmers by lowering the prices of all its cottons and woolens and introducing inexpensive rayons with increasing frequency.

The Fall/Winter issue of 1930 noted that "prices in this catalogue are lower, much lower than any time in the past 10 years. This is the thrift book of a nation."[53] Indeed, Indianhead dropped from 39 to 35 cents, Soisette from 35 to 29 cents, satellite sateen from 24 to 19 cents

and best wool batiste to 89 cents a yard. In 1936 Sears celebrated 50 years in business with such Golden Jubilee Bargains as cotton percales and chambray for nine cents a yard and satellite sateen for 15 cents a yard. In the mid-1930s, the increasing use of rayon with wools and the predominance of pebble crepes, rayon flat crepes and various wool/rayon mixtures signaled the imminent demise of the woolens that Amish women had traditionally used in both quilts and clothing since the 1880s. Cottons were still widely available at relatively inexpensive prices, and percale, sateen and chambray were among the most commonly described cotton and dress goods advertised.

It was not until the 1940s that rayon began to make important inroads into the cotton textile manufacturing process. In the first years of the 1940s, "economy" cottons and "washfast" cottons were inexpensive and quite popular with Amish women. "Carefree cottons" offered the consumer a material which when laundered looked like new and needed no starch. It had a permanent "sealed in finish."[54] One fabric is noticeably absent from the catalogues by the end of the 1930s — the ever popular sateen.

From the early 1940s until 1946, after World War II ended, the availability of almost every item sold by Sears became an increasingly difficult problem for the company. Amish women everywhere verified this with their own memories of wartime shortage. Everyone interviewed mentioned that in those years you "made do with whatever fabrics you could get."[55] In 1945 fabrics were completely omitted from the Sears catalogue. Between 1941 and the spring of 1942 Sears dropped 31,000 items from its book, and the poor selection of dry goods in 1941 and 1942 became no selection at all by 1945.

World War II ended in 1945, and by the time the Spring 1947 issue of Sears catalogue was printed, the nation's economy was starting to produce for consumers once more. In 1947

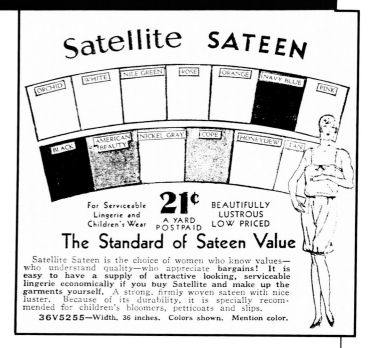

Sears was happy to announce that "good quality percales are back again — the biggest cotton value in years." Despite the optimism, however, these percales were only available in medium blue or rose, and little else besides rayons and cotton chambrays were advertised. A few wools and part-wool fabrics came in a very limited range of colors, and most fabrics were relatively expensive.

By the early 1950s the United States' economy was in full swing. Technologies developed during the war years were now applied to the production of consumer goods. Textiles were once again plentiful and inexpensive. Rayons, nylon, cottons and wools were all offered in the pages of the Sears catalogue. Alpaca-type rayon, rayon romaine, rayon crepes and rayon gabardine were advertised along with cotton broadcloths, washfast percales, Indianhead, covert and chambray fabrics. "Deep-dyed," extra-strength cottons now came in such colors as gray, bright rose, aqua, orchid, medium blue and pink. Throughout the 1950s the textile offerings emphasized synthetic and synthetic blend fabrics. Although there were no traditional all-wool offerings, 100 percent cottons such as organdy, nainsook, broadcloth, and a revived Amish favorite — sateen — were available.

Polyester came onto the market in the late 1950s and was first used primarily in combination with other fibers. In the Sears catalogue, wash-and-wear broadcloths of 65 percent dacron polyester and 35 percent combed cotton were a standard offering by 1961. For the quilters, 100 percent dacron polyester batting weighing 1½ pounds and measuring 72 × 92 inches could be purchased for $3.93. Glazed white quilting cotton in a one-pound weight was a better buy in 1961 at $1.27. In the early years of the 1960s, however, the cost and quality of polyester fibers improved rapidly, and by 1965 polyester was more efficient, because it required less ironing and no starch, and was more economical than the traditional cotton fabrics.

From the 1880s to the 1960s, textiles and textile production methods changed as radically as they had in the early and mid-19th century when fabric production moved from the home to the factory. The changes that occurred in products offered during these years by mail-order catalogues, merchants and peddlers are reflected in the changes of type and quality of goods used by Amish quiltmakers during those same years.

The fabrics offered in each era are the same ones to be found in the clothing and quilts made by Amish women. It should be noted that the fabrics used for a quilt's large borders and its back or "lining" are often the most accurate indication of the age of a quilt because they were usually purchased around the time that the quilt was put together. On the contrary, materials found in smaller patchwork were most often from the scrapbag, which usually contained both older and newer goods.

The information gathered from catalogues, advertising and interviews can be quite useful in dating quilts. It is information that helps to explain how and why Amish quilts have changed during the past 100 years. The social, scientific and economic history of this period have all had as large an influence on the look of Amish quilts as the sect's principles of religious faith and its guidelines affecting community aesthetics.

Broken Star
Holmes County, Ohio, circa 1925–35
Plain-weave cotton percale, cotton sateen • 78 × 79 • Darwin D. Bearley collection

Amish Communities: Their Distinctive Quilts

Community and Symbolism

Every Amish community shares certain symbolic practices which identify the members as part of a distinctive group. The conformity in clothing, the use of horses and buggies and the prohibition against high-wire electricity and telephones are all readily visible to the outsider. These are symbols that help to create a physical and emotional boundary between the Amish world and the outside world or the "English," as the Amish customarily refer to those who are not part of their church.

What may be less apparent to the casual viewer are the particular standards that each community adopts for itself. These preferences and rules are a sort of code that is understood within the group, and they are expressed in the choices of colors and designs used in clothing, quilts and other aspects of the domestic interior. The choices are themselves relatively unimportant; their greater significance lies rather in their power as a symbol of one's individual conformity to the group's decision and will. Frequently these are matters of small detail (the color of window shades or the width of a hat brim), yet the differences from one community to another are immediately recognized by an Amish person. If one talks with them about these variations, they will often express an almost surprisingly strong opinion of taste in these matters. They are sometimes lightly critical and often amused by the practices of different communities. One Amish woman, com-

menting on the buggy style of another community, said, "I wouldn't want to ride in one of those ugly orange-topped buggies."[1]

The link between clothing, particularly that worn by women, and quilts is obvious. Most of the patches for quilts were made from scraps left from dressmaking and family clothing. In fact, many women justified quiltmaking as a good way to use up those leftovers so they wouldn't go to waste. Usually fabric was purchased for the larger sections of a quilt, such as the borders or backs, which is why these parts of a quilt are often the most accurate indications of its age.

Just as certain dress colors and types of materials are predominant in various communities, so, too, the types of materials, the colors and patterns chosen for a quilt vary from Pennsylvania to Ohio to Indiana. When a family moves from one settlement to another, they adopt the clothing style of the new community. They are expected to conform to all the details of hem length, buttonholes, cap and bonnet styles, color and design of clothing.

By the same token, a quilt made in one community might not be acceptable to a new community's standards. For example, the families in the community of Cashton, Wisconsin, came from several different districts in Iowa, Indiana and Ohio. Part of their impetus in establishing the new settlement in Cashton was a desire to renew some of the church's stricter guidelines. They decided as a group that the use

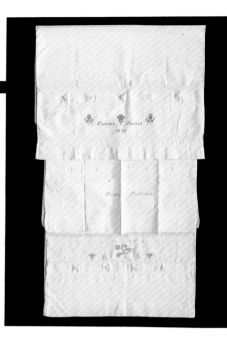

of white in quilts was unacceptable, and those with such quilts either put them away or sold them and made new ones. Conversely, a family moving into a "higher," more liberal church group might not use quilts that are considered too plain or dark. They would probably want new quilts that reflected the less stringent guidelines of the "higher" church.

Sometimes these details of conformity and symbolism can be minute. During one interview, a woman in Geauga County, Ohio, was asked to identify some old material that happened to be part of a child's dress. In looking at the goods she remarked immediately, "This isn't from here; we don't make our buttonholes this way."[2] These details and preferences can also be the source of much amusement and joking among the Amish. A traveling merchant who sells materials in Amish communities throughout Pennsylvania and the Midwest tells the following story:

Joyce "Sam Greenburg" Brown stopped to sell fabric in New Wilmington, Pennsylvania, one day after doing business in Mifflin County. Among her materials was a bolt of brown cotton. An Amish woman with two teenage daughters picked up the brown fabric and turned to her two girls saying, "Oh, I think I'll buy these nice goods to make you girls dresses." They all began to giggle and groan and even the merchant began to laugh. In Mifflin County, brown is a popular and widely used color among the Nebraska Amish. In New Wilmington, though its use is certainly permitted, most women consider it too ugly for a dress. Joyce Brown, who sells fabric in many communities throughout the country, explained that each settlement has its own ideas, and "they can't stand to see people wearing the 'wrong' colors or fabrics."

The members of each community practice nearly complete conformity in terms of clothing style and color. They purchase the same fabrics and sew their clothir in the manner agreed upon by the group. When certain types of goods become impossible to obtain because of changes in\the textile industry, the Amish must find a way to make the transition as a group.

In some cases the acceptance of new materials comes about in unusual ways. Joyce Brown recounted an experience in one Indiana community involving the white organdy which is used for aprons and caps. Organdy comes in various weights, whitenesses and weaves; it is available in both imported and domestic varieties. Different communities use different brands of organdy, but all of the women of each community must use the same type of organdy for their prayer caps, an article of clothing with high symbolic importance to the Amish. One day Joyce Brown brought a new type of organdy to a community in Indiana. The organdy traditionally used there was becoming increasingly difficult and expensive to obtain, and the merchant felt she might be able to supply a new brand more steadily and at a better cost. She began with the bishop's wife and was able to convince her of its quality and acceptability. When the merchant returned to the community several weeks later, everyone wanted the new brand of organdy.

Decisions about brown dresses or white organdy may seem at first glance to be rather small variations between communities, but these details represent deeper issues. Those differences and preferences also apply to quilts. In the next section we will examine the Amish of various communities and the similarities and differences in their quilts.

Embroidered Pillow Case Covers • Lancaster County Pennsylvania • Plain-weave cotton; Red embroidery thread
Dr. and Mrs. Donald M. Herr, The People's Place

Lancaster County, Pennsylvania

Lancaster County, Pennsylvania, is the site of the oldest, continuously occupied Amish community in the United States. The families who live here today are the direct descendants of the 18th-century immigrants who came to Pennsylvania; many of the Lancaster Amish occupy farms which have been in their families for two centuries.

Lancaster is a prosperous community and sometimes considered "fancy" when compared to other settlements (although Lancaster is comparatively conservative in practices related to technology). In this community more than in any other Amish settlement, the traditions of Pennsylvania Dutch culture and art are heavily intertwined with the Amish way of life. In addition to making quilts, the Lancaster Amish built furniture, painted fraktur, stitched samplers and hand towels, hooked rugs and knitted colorful socks and mittens. All of these objects reflect both the strong cultural link to the Pennsylvania German arts and the inherent conservatism of the Amish community.

Scholars generally consider the years between 1750 and 1840 as the period in which the Pennsylvania Dutch arts developed and flourished. The years after the 1840s were not the end of the culture itself, but by the mid-19th century, English and American influences on the Germanic community had asserted themselves so thoroughly that, it is generally agreed, the heyday of Pennsylvania German arts had passed.

The Amish involvement in the artistic renaissance created by the Pennsylvania Germans is difficult to gauge. Prior to 1840 the Amish population in Lancaster and in the United States was exceedingly small. In Lancaster there were only enough families to warrant one church district until the mid-1840s. We have only a few items of verifiable Amish origin, such as hand towels, samplers and an occasional example of fraktur, that date to the years before the 1840s. Most of the Amish-created arts and crafts were produced after the middle of the century. One of the most significant contributions the Amish made to Pennsylvania Dutch culture appears to be the persistence with which they preserved traditional forms long after other Pennsylvania Germans had abandoned them, rather than the production of an abundance or variety of early works.

The Amish in Lancaster were latecomers to quiltmaking, when compared to other Pennsylvania German women in the area, or even to their Mennonite cousins. Once the practice of pieced quiltmaking was established, however, it became a vitally strong tradition. Consequently, a Lancaster Amish quilt is probably the most easily identified and the most distinctive in its differences from Amish quilts made elsewhere in North America. From the earliest 19th century examples until those of the present day,

Door Towels • Lancaster and Mifflin counties, Pennsylvania. Four examples ranging from 1857 to 1902. The People's Place
The practice of embroidery on linen was a popular Pennsylvania German tradition. Largely forgotten after the 1850–1860 period, this practice was continued by Amish women into the 20th century.

the patterns of Lancaster quilts have remained basically unchanged. Other elements such as color, fabric, and the quality and quantity of needlework have altered considerably, but the choice of quilt patterns has been limited to a relatively few designs and their variations.

Patterns

The first thing we usually see when we look at any quilt is its pattern. In Lancaster quilts the most popular and frequently used patterns include the Diamond in the Square, Bars, Sunshine and Shadow, Grandmother's Dream, Double Nine Patch and Nine-Patch variations, Center Square and Baskets. Also popular, but less frequently made, were Lone Stars, Irish Chains, Crazy Patterns and Log Cabins. It is noteworthy that the earliest and the most traditional Lancaster patterns, the Center Square, the Diamond and the Bars, are all based on the Medallion-square format of quiltmaking.[3] Medallion-style quilts were popular with American women during the first half of the 19th century. By the 1880s, however, the fashion of blockwork quilts (patterns assembled out of small squares of piecework) had long since replaced the Medallion-style format. The choice of Amish women in the late 19th century of this highly outdated fashion seems to have been a deliberate attempt to make their quilts in accordance with Amish standards of nonconformity to "English" fashion.

The Diamond in the Square or Cape pattern is a design virtually unique to Lancaster County. Any use of this pattern outside Lancaster usually indicates a close family link to the Lancaster community.

Proportions and Design

Even if its pattern is common to other communities, a quilt can usually be readily identified as a Lancaster County production because

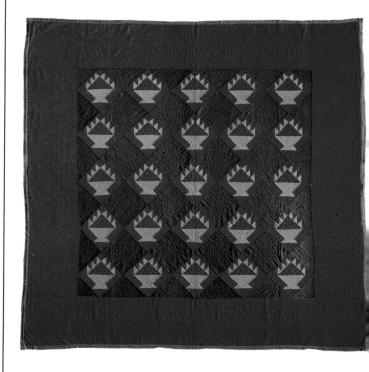

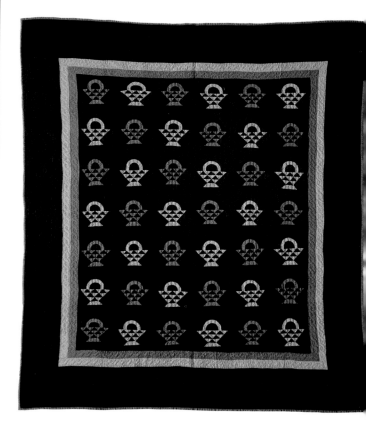

(above) **Baskets** • Lancaster County, Pennsylvania • circa 1920–30
Plain-weave wool batiste • 77 × 78 • Gail Van der Hoof and Jonathan Holstein
(below) **Baskets** • Holmes County, Ohio • circa 1930–40 Plain-weave cotton percale,
cotton sateen, white muslin back • 71 × 86 • Eve Granick and David Wheatcroft

Diamond in the Square
Lancaster County, Pennsylvania • circa 1920–30
Plain-weave wool batiste • 75 × 76 • Eve Granick and David Wheatcroft

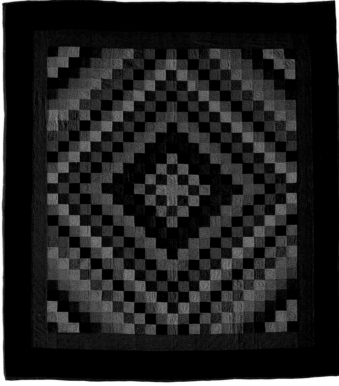

of its proportions, binding, quilting and fabrics.

Quilts made in Lancaster are usually almost square in measurement. The dimensions of full-sized quilts fall generally in the range of 70 × 75 inches to 80 × 80 inches. Bar quilts are frequently more rectangular than square, but that generality is not a hard and fast rule. Even block patterns, such as a Nine Patch or Baskets which are usually arranged in a rectangular configuration outside of Lancaster, are generally made into square proportions by the Lancaster quiltmaker, through the use of an equal number of blocks along the sides and across the width.

Another typical design proportion, which is helpful in identifying Lancaster quilts, is the use of particularly wide outside borders and large corner blocks. In quilts made in other communities, the outer border is usually between four and eight inches wide. If there are corner blocks, which is much less common, they too are proportionately smaller. In Lancaster County quilts the outside border measurement is almost double the width of others, measuring anywhere from 10 to 15 inches. The corner blocks, which are quite common, are proportionately larger.

Fabrics

Almost without exception, the fabric chosen for quilts in Lancaster, until the 1940s, was a fine, plain-weave wool batiste or wool twill cashmere. Other lightweight woolens were also used, particularly in patterns such as the Log Cabin or Sunshine and Shadow, which require a great deal of piecing, but wool batiste and wool cashmere were the mainstay of Lancaster Amish quilts. In the 1940s, when the Amish began to have great difficulty obtaining these traditional materials, they were forced to accept synthetics, cottons and wool substitutes. From the 1940s on, flat rayon, rayon crepes and a variety of mixed cotton/synthetic and wool/synthetic materials in various weaves and

(above) **Sunshine and Shadow**
Lancaster County, Pennsylvania • circa 1920–30
Plain- and twill-weave wools • 66 × 67½ • Amy Finkel
(below) **Sunshine and Shadow**
Holmes County, Ohio • circa 1940–50
Cotton, cotton rayon blend • 74 × 86½ • Michael Oruch

finishes were widely used in both quilts and clothing.

The persistent choice of fine wool and the subsequent use of synthetics contrast sharply with the traditions that developed in Amish communities outside of Lancaster County. In Ohio and in Indiana, fine wools were used for quilts, but with notably decreasing frequency after the early 20th century. There are some early and interesting heavy wool quilts from the late 19th century that were made in these areas, and also many examples of quilts made in fine woolens though the first decades of the 20th century. The difference lies in the fact that Amish women outside of Lancaster also used cottons such as percale, sateen and plain calico from the earliest quilts to the present day. The midwestern tradition of cottons in quiltmaking may help to explain why the difference between a pre-1940 and a post-1940 quilt from Ohio or Indiana is less dramatic than it is in a Lancaster-made quilt.

The selection of certain materials in post-1940 quilts made in Lancaster had unfortunate consequences for both their quality and value. Many of the materials and the dyestuffs used to color fabrics that were developed during World War II and the early postwar period were not particularly suitable for quilts. The fabrics did not hold up well and the colors faded or washed out with exposure to sun or water. The choice of these easily damaged materials was unfortunate as well, because many of the quilts made in this period displayed excellent craftsmanship and needlework. Many fabrics simply did not merit the handwork that went into them. Prices for these post-1940s quilts in the antique quilt marketplace reflect the instability and poor quality of their fabrics. These quilts generally realize only a fraction of the value that wool examples attain.

Patterns with many small patches, such as Sunshine and Shadow or Grandmother's Dream, often have a considerable amount of wool in them, even in examples as late as the 1960s. Lancaster women placed great value on fine wool and used these pre-1940 fabrics as long as they could. It is the fabrics in the large border areas and the lining that tend to reveal the age of a quilt. In those expanses the quiltmaker was usually forced to use the fabrics that were most available and most economically priced.

Quilt Back or Lining

The materials used for the backings of Lancaster quilts are another distinctive and identifying element. The use of figured or patterned goods for any part of a quilt is rare outside of Lancaster County. In Lancaster, however, although no patterned material was used on the quilt front, it was permitted for the backing or "lining," as it is often called by Amish women.

Printed goods can be helpful in determining when a quilt was made. Patterned fabrics are more easily dated than solid colors because print designs changed with the fashions of the time. (Whether the material is solid or printed, however, it cannot be used conclusively to determine either the age or authenticity of a quilt.) Lancaster County quilts from the late 19th and early 20th centuries show great variety in the type of materials used for quilt backings. Some have backs of solid colored cotton; others have a solid or printed cotton flannel. Linings made from printed cottons show great variety in designs: dots, diamonds, dashes, circles, plaids, flowers, chevrons, lines and squiggles of every sort. Cotton chambray in brown and white, black and white or blue and white was also popular backing material.

The presence of both solid colored and printed goods seems to indicate that the individual quiltmaker simply chose what she liked from what was readily available at the time. In any decade some Amish women chose printed

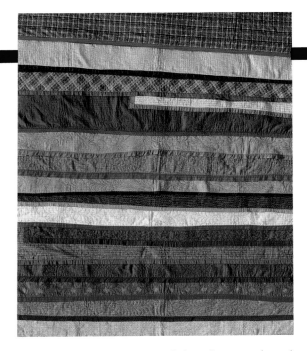

goods for the quilt lining, while others preferred a solid colored backing. Whatever the quilt backing, it should be examined and its age considered in conjunction with all of the other elements of the quilt.

Bindings

Even small details can help to identify when and where a quilt originated. The use of a particularly wide binding is another distinctive element of Lancaster quilts that sets them apart from quilts made elsewhere. In the Midwest and in other areas of Pennsylvania, the average quilt binding is generally between ¼ inch and one inch in width. In Lancaster quilts, the bindings are almost always wider, generally measuring between one and two inches. Some bindings are up to 2½ inches wide.

The front side of the binding was usually applied by machine and the back was either sewn on the machine or done by hand. Very often the corners were finished with hand-sewing.

Quilting

The large open field of colors that forms the design of a Diamond in the Square or Bars pattern, as well as the distinctively wide outside borders on Lancaster quilts, call for extensive quilting. The quilting done on Lancaster County quilts is often considered the finest done by Amish women anywhere. Though ex-

cellent quilting can be found in the Midwest also, particularly on early quilts, Lancaster women seemed to have given extra care to the needlework that held front, filling and back together.

Many of the quilting patterns are based on simple geometry: diamonds, concentric circles and lines. Other designs approach realism with bow ties, winding grapevines with fruit and leaves, intricately stitched fruit compotes and botanically correct renderings of flowers, such as roses, fiddlehead ferns and impatiens. There are a number of stylized designs that spring directly from the artistic traditions of Pennsylvania Dutch culture: hearts, stars, calla lilies, tulips and whirligig hexes. Feathered wreaths and feathered vines appear regularly on outside borders and corner blocks.

Quilting patterns can also help to determine the age of a quilt. The earliest quilts have fine but plainer quilting designs. The center field and corner triangles of the Diamond pattern are more likely to exhibit cross-hatching or diamond quilting than the stars or roses which appear in early 20th-century examples. Quilts from the years between 1910 and 1940 generally have the most elaborate quilting designs.

(above) These quilts display some of the great variety of fabrics which can be found on the backs or linings of Lancaster County quilts. From top to bottom they are arranged from the earliest examples of the 1870–1900 period, through the early 20th century, to the 1940–50 era.
(below) The pink binding is applied by machine-stitching to both front and back.
The blue binding is sewn by machine to the front of the quilt and then turned over to the back and hand-stitched.

The motifs are often double-stitched, a practice which fell out of use after the 1940s. As a general guideline, if the quilting is extensive and elaborate, the quilt was probably made in the 1920s or 1930s. Less quilting, less elaborate designs and certain motifs, such as the bow tie or the impatiens flower, are signs of a later quilt.

Color

One of the most striking elements of Amish quilts is their use of color. Although particular colors and color combinations have changed over the years, in some cases quite radically, there are also certain sensibilities that have persisted over time. Like other aspects of a quilt, color can help to distinguish a Lancaster quilt from those made in other settlements. The choice of colors for a quilt made in any period depended on two factors: both the variety of dyes and fabric colors available in the general marketplace, and the informal guidelines or group consensus about what was acceptable and desirable.

In early Lancaster quilts made before 1900, the color palette tended to be more muted or "natural," with softer, saturated shades of brown, medium and darker red, gray, medium and deep blues, greens and purples. In almost all cases these were not home-dyed fabrics. Instead they were dyed by the fabric manufacturer, although with natural dyestuffs derived from plant and mineral sources. The later, brighter colors and the contrasts they created were the result of the technological revolution which led to a vast variety of lively new colors, all created from synthetic sources. Some of the most striking and eye-catching Lancaster quilts used these brilliant and vibrant synthetic shades.

Over the first four or five decades of the 20th century, Lancaster quilts were dominated by a fairly bright and saturated color palette. Royal and medium blues, purples, red, wine, warm browns and tans, pink, teal, aqua, olive and parrot green are among the favorite colors used throughout much of the 20th century. In striking contrast to quilts made in Ohio or Indiana, where black was used extensively, black was used only rarely by Lancaster women. In pat-

Sixteen Patch
Lancaster County, Pennsylvania • circa 1870–80
Plain-weave cotton • 74 × 77
Dan and Kathryn McCauley

Sunshine and Shadow
Lancaster County, Pennsylvania • circa 1920–30
Wool • 82 × 82 • America Hurrah, New York City

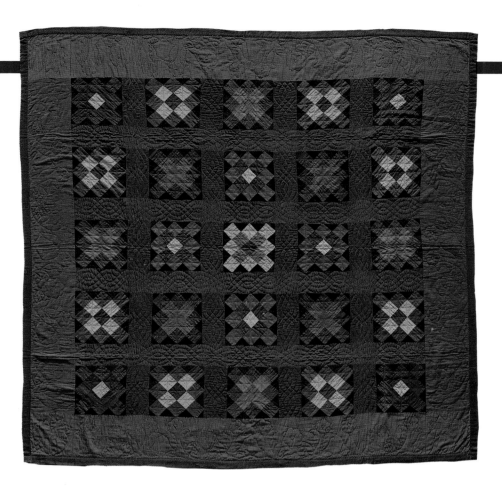

terns such as the Diamond or Center Square the use of black is virtually unknown. Although many Lancaster Amish recall no real color restrictions, they also note that white and yellow were not good choices, and these colors are found only infrequently.

After the 1940s, color choices for quiltmaking and clothing in the Lancaster settlement expanded notably, as it did in other communities. Pastel shades and intensely bright, almost harsh colors came into wide use. The traditional blues, greens, purples and reds remained popular, however, and they can be found quite commonly in quilts made through the 1960s.

Overview

Certain characteristics mark the three basic periods in Lancaster quiltmaking. Those periods are roughly defined as the late 19th century, the time between 1900 and the 1940s, and the years after 1940. These are only *general guidelines,* not hard and fast rules, but they may be helpful in recognizing the changes which have taken place over the last hundred years.

Quilts made before the turn of the century are distinctive for several reasons. The choices of color, patterns and fabrics were quite limited, especially when compared to quilts made in the same period in Ohio and Indiana. Colors used in Lancaster tended toward either more muted or deeper shades; brown, rust, wine, olive and forest greens are typical. If bright colors were used, they were frequently arranged in sharp contrast to the more "natural" shades.

Patterns made during this period included the repertoire of Lancaster designs — from the simplest Center Square to the Diamond, Bars, Double Nine Patch, Irish Chain, Log Cabin, Sunshine and Shadow and Grandmother's Dream. Center Square quilts are notable because they were rarely made after the 19th century ended. Sunshine and Shadows are more common in the 1920s and the years following than they are to the 19th century.

Wools, either batistes or twills, were the first choice of Lancaster women. There are infrequent examples of cotton quilts but these are rare.

Another exception in Lancaster was the

Album Patch
Lancaster County, Pennsylvania • circa 1920–30
Plain-weave wool batiste • 71½ × 72 • Eve Granick and David Wheatcroft

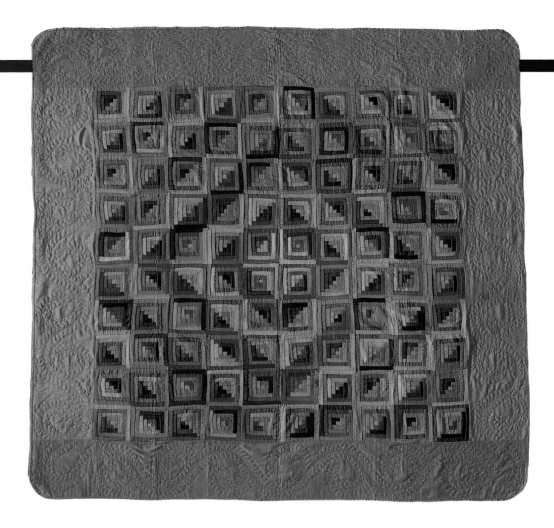

making of crib quilts. Unlike the women in Ohio, Indiana, or even in Mifflin or Lawrence counties in Pennsylvania, Lancaster Amish women did not produce crib quilts in any significant numbers. A 19th century Lancaster crib quilt is extremely unusual and valuable.

Quilts made in the years between 1900 and 1940 continued the traditions established during the 19th century. In this 40-year period, however, certain changes did occur. A great number of new colors were used and a marked preference for bright colors evolved. Certain color favorites remained — the ubiquitous blues, purples, greens and reds — but new shades and color combinations achieved popularity while the more muted browns, rusts and deep greens lost favor.

Fabric choices remained fairly constant during these years, but in the mid-1930s materials such as wool crepe and rayon/wool blends began to appear in quilts. The backing goods used in these years also reflect some of the gradual change in fabric technology and fashion

that were taking place. Solid colored cottons, various printed cottons and flannels, and colored chambrays were used throughout this period.

Although design proportions — the measured relationship between piecework and inner and outer borders — and the overall square shape of Lancaster quilts remained much the same between 1900 and 1940, the overall size of quilts increased gradually. Established quilting motifs also persisted during these years, though the amount of quilting and the intricacy of design generally decreased as time passed.

The changes in quiltmaking between the 19th century and the 1930s came about slowly and almost imperceptibly. On the other hand, the changes in quiltmaking that occurred during the 1940s and 1950s took place with dramatic speed. The developments in technology and the shortages and substitutions of traditional materials for new synthetics seemed to be the greatest causes of differences in the quilts made after 1940. Pattern proportions, quilting

Log Cabin
New Holland area, Lancaster County, Pennsylvania • circa 1890–1900
Made for Mrs. John Lapp by her mother. • Mixed wools, plain-, twill- and patterned weaves
84 × 84 • Dr. and Mrs. Donald M. Herr

Bars
Lancaster County, Pennsylvania • circa 1900–1915
Plain-weave wool batiste • 77½ × 77½ • Jonathan Holstein and Gail Van der Hoof

85

motifs and even colors, to a large degree, remained the same in these later years. The changes from batiste wool to crepe wool to rayon were rapid, and the shift was not particularly popular with Amish women. In one interview a woman mentioned rather wistfully that, whereas her two older sisters had purple batiste wool for their wedding dresses, purple crepe was her only choice when she married in 1944.

As one tradition disappeared, other changes crept in gradually. Pastel colors achieved a new popularity, especially in the 1950s. Even more importantly, the choice of color combinations changed noticeably in these years. The practice of arranging colors in sharp contrasts, lights next to darks or deep vibrant colors next to equally vivid tones, gave way to using more closely matched shades and more gradual contrasts.

Embroidered quilts, polyester fabrics and battings, and new patterns spelled the final demise of the traditional Lancaster Amish quilt. One woman, born in 1898, who wore a purple batiste wedding dress and owned quilts made only in batiste wool (including a "best Sunday quilt" in the Diamond in the Square pattern) made Ocean Wave crib quilts in white and mixed pastel colors for each of her childrens' first babies in the late 1950s and early 1960s.

Changes usually occur rather slowly in the Amish community, unless outside events combine to influence the practices of the group. In the early 1970s, when the Amish quilt was discovered by quilt collectors and antique dealers, changes occured rapidly and irreversibly. Amish quilts had evolved considerably over the years, but many of the old quilts were either still in use or owned by Amish families as treasured keepsakes. When these quilts suddenly began to bring such astonishing prices, however, many families sold them quickly.

Double Nine Patch
Lancaster County, Pennsylvania • circa 1935–45
Twill-weave wool, plain-weave cotton, cotton crepe
86 × 88 • Dr. and Mrs. Donald M. Herr

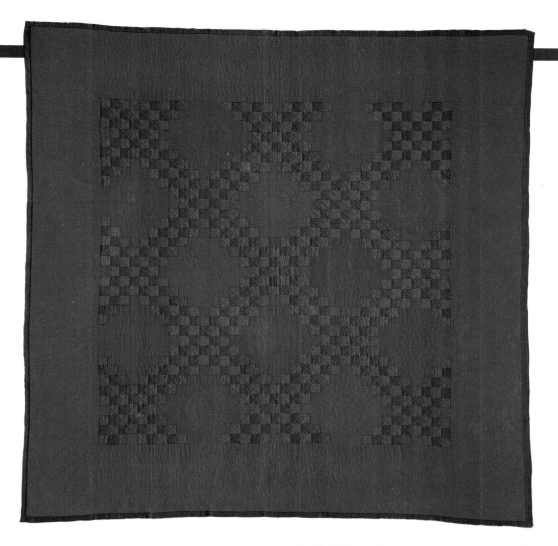

For many the decision to sell appears to have been a pragmatic choice. In many cases families needed money for farms or medical bills. When a rash of thefts began to occur, with quilts disappearing off clotheslines or out of blanket chests, families sold because of well-placed concern about owning such valuable property. Those who held out longer received increasingly larger sums of money; prices escalated rapidly during the 1970s and early 1980s.

The creation of a full-scale tourist industry and quilt market in the Lancaster area completely altered Amish quiltmaking. The quilts created by Amish women in the years between the 1880s and even into the 1960s were the result of closely defined group aesthetics. Innovation or originality were not the hallmarks of these quilts. Rather, craftsmanship, a love of color and strong tradition appear to have guided the hands of Amish women in Lancaster.

Mifflin County, Pennsylvania

The Amish have resided in Mifflin County, Pennsylvania, since the early 1790s, when several families from Lancaster and Chester counties followed the Juniata River upstream to arrive in the Kishacoquillas Valley. Mifflin County was formally organized in 1789 with Lewistown as its county seat. The area had been settled already for many years by the Scots-Irish. In the period preceding the arrival of the Amish, these pioneers began to leave the area in large numbers for the new frontiers farther west, and they sold their lands to the Pennsylvania Germans, who in turn were leaving the southeastern part of the state.

The Kish Valley, or Big Valley, as it is called by its residents, is a relatively small and geographically isolated strip of land bounded by two mountain ridges. The area is only about 30 miles long and four miles wide. Within this

Triple Irish Chain
Lancaster County, Pennsylvania • circa 1915–25
Plain-weave wool batiste • 81 × 82 • ESPRIT collection, San Francisco

narrow area resides a wide variety of Amish and Mennonite divisions, ranging from the "low" and most traditional Nebraska group to the "higher," considerably more liberal, Mennonite groups. There are five different and completely separate Old Order Amish groups in the Valley and seven different Mennonite affiliates. Each of these groups maintains a separate church with different rules and bishops. Each has a different set of visual symbols that help to distinguish it and maintain its social boundaries. Buggy style, clothing colors and style, house architecture and decoration, and the making and using of quilts are all determined by group rules. This high degree of diversity is particularly noteworthy because all of these factions grew out of the original single Amish church that existed as a unified group until the beginning of the 1850s.

The quilts made in Mifflin County during the past 100 years can be described as belonging to three general periods, in much the same manner as those made in Lancaster. There are

also some further descriptive divisions that are necessary, since each of the four Old Order groups in the valley had different quilting practices.

The Nebraska Amish

The Nebraska Amish are the most distinctive in the Big Valley, as they are the most traditional and conservative group in both the Big Valley and among all Amish groups in North America. The Swartzentrubers of Ohio and some of the strictest groups in Indiana are the only others who share a similar set of church rules or philosophy.

The Nebraska division was formally created in 1881, but the beginning of the group goes back to a separation which occurred in 1849. The seceding faction, headed by Samuel B. King, extolled more conservative attitudes and practices than the other Amish in the Valley. By the 1880s the most conservative members in King's group were disturbed by what they perceived as a growing liberalization within their

Nine Patch
Mifflin County, Pennsylvania, circa 1935–45
Plain- and twill-weave cotton, plain- and twill-weave cotton/rayon • 72½ × 81
Barbara A. Streibert

own group. Heated arguments erupted and a bishop from Nebraska, Yost H. Yoder, was brought in to attempt a reconciliation in the Samuel King church (see chart). When this reconciliation failed, those following Yoder's opinions separated to maintain a stricter church, and they became known as the Nebraska Amish.[4]

In embracing the most conservative interpretation of the *Ordnung,* the Nebraska Amish have retained the most traditional forms of dress, transportation and general lifestyle. Men wear brown, gray, and, sometimes, blue broadfall pants without suspenders, white shirts made in a traditional Pennsylvania German style, wide hat brims and long hair. Women's dresses, aprons, capes and prayer caps are cut and sewn from the most traditional patterns. The bonnet, which was adopted by all other Amish women in the 19th century, is not worn by Nebraska Amish women.[5] Their houses and barns are often unpainted, and families ride in white-topped buggies. Inside the Nebraska Amish home there are few concessions to 20th-century life. Humility, modesty and obedience are expressed in a very rigorous dress code and strict limitations against innovation or the use of modern technology. These regulations regarding worldliness extend into quiltmaking as well.

The quilts of the Nebraska Amish are limited in both color and design by church rules, and quiltmaking among this group never reached the proportions that it did in other Amish communities. That the quilt was an innovation in bed covering, not adopted by Pennsylvania Germans and the Amish until the mid- and late 19th century, may also have some influence on the restrained attention paid to quiltmaking among the Nebraska Amish.

Other groups in the Big Valley used a variety of quilt designs, but the quilts of the Nebraska Amish were governed by even stricter guidelines than the women in Lancaster followed. Four- and Nine-Patch variations were and continue to be the only patterns permitted. Further restrictions directed the choice of colors used to create these patterns. The brighter "synthetic" colors, so popular among other Amish women in the Big Valley and in other communities, were never permitted by the Nebraska church. Quilts and clothing were fashioned from a limited palette of traditional "natural" colors: browns, blues, darker purples, black, darker greens, yellow, ochre, tan and some darker reds.

Purchasing goods specifically for making quilts, particularly the fill blocks (between those that were pieced) and border sections, was a common practice among Amish women throughout the United States. In the Nebraska Amish community, however, this was generally less acceptable and women relied heavily on the leftovers from their sewing work. This frugal and strictly utilitarian attitude had several design consequences. Color and materials were restricted to those fabrics used in the production of family clothing. The quality of these materials and the range of colors were very limited when compared to those available to the quiltmaker in Lancaster or Ohio or even several miles away in the same valley.

If a Nebraska Amish woman ran out of scraps in one color while making a quilt for everyday use, she would simply substitute a second color to finish the pattern or borders. The concern for usefulness in a bedcovering was the guiding principle in most examples of Nebraska quiltmaking. Consequently, everyday quilts have a tendency to be very simple, at times even crude, and were made predominantly in the blues, browns and purples of dress scraps.

Special quilts, made either for Sunday use or marriage gifts, offered the only suitable occasions for utilizing finer materials or unusual colors. In these quilts there was also unspoken permission to lavish attention on both the design and quality of quilting. Yet in all aspects of quiltmaking, even in these finer examples, the Nebraska Amish women chose the simplest and most straightforward colors, designs and quilting motifs. In contrast to the elegance of a Lancaster Diamond or the touches of originality in Ohio quilts, the Nebraska quilt is a simple and modest expression of the community's interpretation of the proper way to live.

The Byler Church

The Byler church is an offshoot of the Samuel King division in 1849. When the Nebraska group was formed in 1881, those who differed with the strictly conservative decision of Yost H. Yoder formed their own church and pursued their own vision of a faithful Christian life. Although the Bylers are more liberal than the three Nebraska groups in the Valley, church members have maintained "lower" church styles than their cousins in the Peachey group. This is reflected in the styles of their homes, clothing and quilts.

This group is also directly related to the settlements in Lawrence County in western Pennsylvania and to some small settlements in western New York state. In each of these communities several visual and symbolic elements mark obedience to the church rules. Families drive yellow-topped buggies. Men wear blue chambray shirts and women wear a dark brown bonnet instead of the black that is used in all other communities. In the Byler community, the house exteriors are painted and the interiors are very simple and uncluttered. Small rag carpets, a wall calendar or family tree chart and hanging pincushions beneath the clock shelf are the only permissible decorative elements in the house. The simple painted or oak furniture, the green roller shades and white half curtains at the windows are identical from one house to the next.

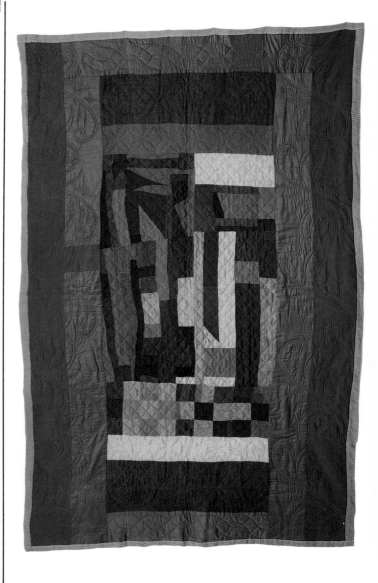

Nine Patch and Crazy Pattern
Mifflin County, Pennsylvania, circa 1910–20
Plain-weave cotton • America Hurrah, New York City

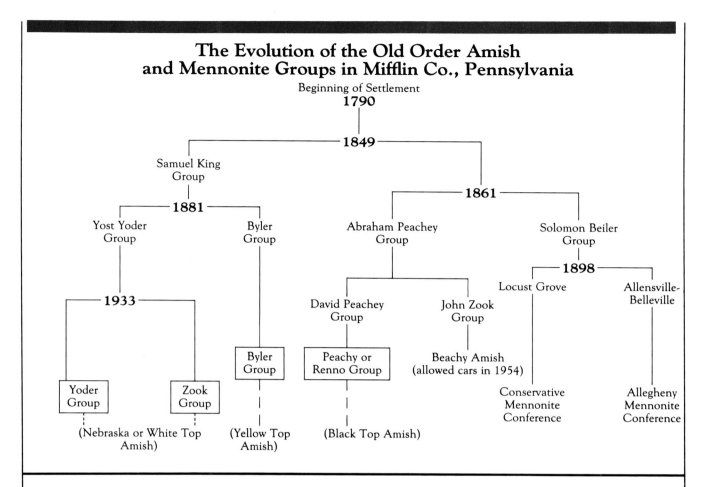

The Evolution of the Old Order Amish and Mennonite Groups in Mifflin Co., Pennsylvania

Beginning of Settlement
1790

1849

Samuel King Group

1881

Yost Yoder Group — Byler Group

1861

Abraham Peachey Group — Solomon Beiler Group

1898

Locust Grove — Allensville-Belleville

1933

Yoder Group — Zook Group

Byler Group

David Peachey Group — John Zook Group

Peachy or Renno Group

Beachy Amish (allowed cars in 1954)

Conservative Mennonite Conference

Allegheny Mennonite Conference

(Nebraska or White Top Amish) — (Yellow Top Amish) — (Black Top Amish)

The Peachey Church

The Peachey group (also known as the Renno Amish) evolved out of factions in the community that were more liberal than either the Nebraskas or the Bylers. Of all the groups that developed in the middle and upper Big Valley, only the Peachey church maintained its link with the larger Old Order Amish church. The Peachey and Byler groups do have some limited interaction, but the Peacheys are considered a "higher" church with a different standard of dress and decorative symbolism. Women wear dark, plain colors, black bonnets and white caps. The Peachey group are also called One Strappers locally, because the men use only one suspender. Their buggies are black-topped and their houses are painted and well maintained. They lavish a fair amount of care on their yards, gardens and flowers, and decorate the interiors of their homes with small and useful but decorative objects. Plaques with Bible verses, advertising calendars, family tree charts and houseplants are standard. Most homes display a corner cupboard with glass doors that is filled with colored glass and a collection of knickknacks.

The quilts made by women in the Byler and Peachey churches are not as distinctive in their overall design, pattern or color as the Nebraska quilts. Instead, quilts made by women in these groups tend to be more like Amish quilts made in other areas, but they also exhibit characteristics that can be considered unique or distinctive to the Big Valley.

Patterns and Design

Some of the early examples found in Mifflin County among both the Byler and Peachey groups reveal the links that existed between the Lancaster and Mifflin communities. In most cases, however, quiltmaking traditions in the Big Valley were more similar to those practices

that developed in Ohio and the Midwest. Early examples of Bars and Sunshine and Shadow designs are reminiscent of Lancaster patterns, but the overall rectangular proportions of the quilts distinguish them as the work of Mifflin County women. The full dimensions of quilts made in Mifflin County fall generally between 75 × 80 inches wide and 75 × 85 inches long. There is a great deal of variation from one decade to another, and even from one quilt to another in the same period, but the general rule seems to have been to make a quilt about nine or 10 inches longer than wide.

A variety of Four- and Nine-Patch arrangements were among the most popular and common designs pieced by women in the Big Valley. These blockwork designs were used exclusively in the Nebraska church and also widely among the Byler church members. Other patterns such as Jacob's Ladder, Tumbling Blocks, Irish Chain, Shoofly, Crazy Patches, Baskets and Log Cabins appear as well among both Byler

and Peachey families. In fact, Log Cabin quilts made between the 1890s and the 1920s in the Pennsylvania and Ohio communities are often strikingly similar. Without a family history or provenance, this example (see photo) by a woman who was a member of the Peachey church could easily be mistaken for a quilt made in Holmes County, Ohio, or in Lancaster, Pennsylvania.

One design scheme that appears with great frequency in Mifflin County uses a gridlike series of inside borders and blocks. This distinctive use of small borders to isolate the piecework can be found occasionally in quilts made in other communities, but it was a design arrangement that was especially popular in the Big Valley.

Fabrics

Unlike the women in Lancaster County who expressed such a strong preference for wool, Byler, Peachey and Nebraska Amish quilt-

Log Cabin
Mifflin County, Pennsylvania, circa 1900–1910
Plain- and twill-weave wool, brocaded fabric • Kelter-Malcé Antiques, New York City

(above) **Checkerboard**
Mifflin County, Pennsylvania, circa 1930–40
Rayon/cotton • 74 × 81• Michael Oruch
(below) **Sunshine and Shadow Variation**
Lebanon County, Pennsylvania • circa 1925–35
Made by Rachel Zook for her daughter Annie. • Twill-weave wool • 80 × 82
Dr. and Mrs. Donald M. Herr

93

makers adopted the midwestern tradition of using a wide variety of fabrics. Early quilts can be found in either cottons or wools; in fact, the use of both types of fabric in one quilt was also acceptable. As the 20th century progressed, cotton, cotton sateen and a cotton rayon fabric which was locally produced became the predominant choice of materials for quiltmaking in the Big Valley. Certain patterns such as the Log Cabin quilt were most frequently done in dress wools like mohair, cashmere and brilliantine. Although there was some use of batiste wool in Mifflin County, this fabric is found with much less frequency.

One of the most distinctive elements of a Big Valley quilt is the use of a particular fabric produced by the American Viscose Corporation. A manufacturer of rayon goods, American Viscose established a factory in Lewistown in 1921. This factory supplied dry goods to many area residents at an outlet store, and the Amish from all of the church groups in the valley were quick to adopt this new material for both clothing and quilts. A rather soft fabric with a dull, smooth finish, these cotton/rayon materials were used in quilts much earlier than rayon was used in Amish quilts from communities elsewhere. This fairly distinctive fabric can help a collector or dealer with some experience in recognizing fabric types to identify a Mifflin County quilt. There are a number of examples from this area, made during the 1920s and early 1930s, with this fabric. A Big Valley quilt can, therefore, easily be incorrectly dated because this material was used later in other communities, usually from the 1940s and on.

Quilt Backs or Linings

The backing material for quilts made in Mifflin County is very similar to linings found in most other Amish communities. A solid colored piece of fabric, usually of cotton or cotton/rayon, was the standard choice. Printed material of any type was not acceptable in the Big Valley churches.

Bindings

The quilt binding practices in Mifflin County are more closely related to those in Ohio and other midwestern Amish communities than to those in Lancaster. There are examples, particularly in early quilts, that show the wider bindings preferred in Lancaster, but, for the most part, women in all of the Old Order groups in the Big Valley used narrow bindings, anywhere from 1/4 inch to one inch in width.

Bindings were applied by one of three different methods: (1) A separate piece of fabric was chosen, with the color often matching the small inside border of the quilt. It was applied by machine to the front side of the quilt, then turned over to cover the quilt edges and either hand-sewn or machine-sewn to the backing; (2) in another common technique, the lining or backing fabric was simply turned over from the back to the front and hand-sewn or machine-stitched to form the binding; (3) less commonly, the material of the large outside borders was turned over from the front and sewn to the backing material to create the binding. The use of the quilt back turned front or the quilt borders turned back to make the binding was more widespread among Nebraska and Byler women than in the Peachey group. The overall

Box and Diamond
Mifflin County, Pennsylvania, circa 1890–1910
The name "Katie" is embroidered in the center.
Plain-weave cotton percale, chambray, cotton sateen • 31 X 42 • Eve Granick and
David Wheatcroft

appearance of these simpler bindings is less tailored or elegant and seems to be the result of a deliberate choice by the quiltmaker to produce a plain appearance.

Another rather common practice found in many communities, including the Big Valley, was the use of different colored materials in one binding. The top and bottom ends of the quilt were sometimes bound in a different color than the sides, or one side or part of one side was different from all the rest of the binding. Often this was the direct result of using the backing material to create the binding. Backs were necessarily pieced out of at least two sections of material. Sometimes several different pieces of fabric of different colors were used. Bindings made in this fashion seem less the result of design decisions than matters of expediency, where whatever fabrics were on hand were employed with little regard for the overall appearance of the quilt.

At the opposite end of the spectrum are some of the bindings applied to quilts made in the Peachey church district from the 1920s through the 1960s. Pieces of fabric, folded and sewn into the edge between the front and back of a quilt, formed a row of triangles, creating an extremely decorative and showy binding. Scalloped edges are another example of a conscious attempt at "English" style quiltmaking.

These various methods of binding quilts were not necessarily unique to the Big Valley. Rather, they describe the variety of choices available to Mifflin County women, a range of practices much greater than that found in Lancaster. Fancy binding techniques can be found in examples from Ohio or Indiana, and very simple bindings were made in these communities as well, particularly among families belonging to stricter or "lower" church districts. In Mifflin County, the choice of a quilt binding did reflect, in part, one's membership in a particular faction within the Big Valley. Those belonging to the Nebraska groups generally selected the simplest methods, and those in the "higher" Peachey group experimented with more "worldly" touches.

Quilting

Like bindings and piecework patterns, quilting motifs also point to the shared traditions of the Big Valley and other Amish communities. Mifflin County was an early settlement, and families from the Big Valley were often part of the movements westward to Ohio, Indiana and other midwestern states to begin new communities. Many of the most common quilting patterns used in the Big Valley can also be found in other areas. Popular patterns were used repeatedly and handed down from one generation to the next. Designs found in the earliest 1849 example were still being applied to quilts in the 1940s.

There are also a few motifs, particularly popular in the Byler and Nebraska groups, that were generally limited to the Big Valley or to quilts from Lawrence and Mercer counties in western Pennsylvania, where the Byler church established a "daughter" settlement in the 1840s.

In contrast to the intricate feathers, fruit baskets and rose branches of Lancaster are the flat, stylized designs found in Mifflin County.

Detail-Back and Bindings A. Binding is applied by machine. Top and side are bound with two different materials. B. Binding is applied by machine and made from a separate piece of material. C. Flag binding D. Chambray backing material is turned over the front and machine-stitched for the binding.

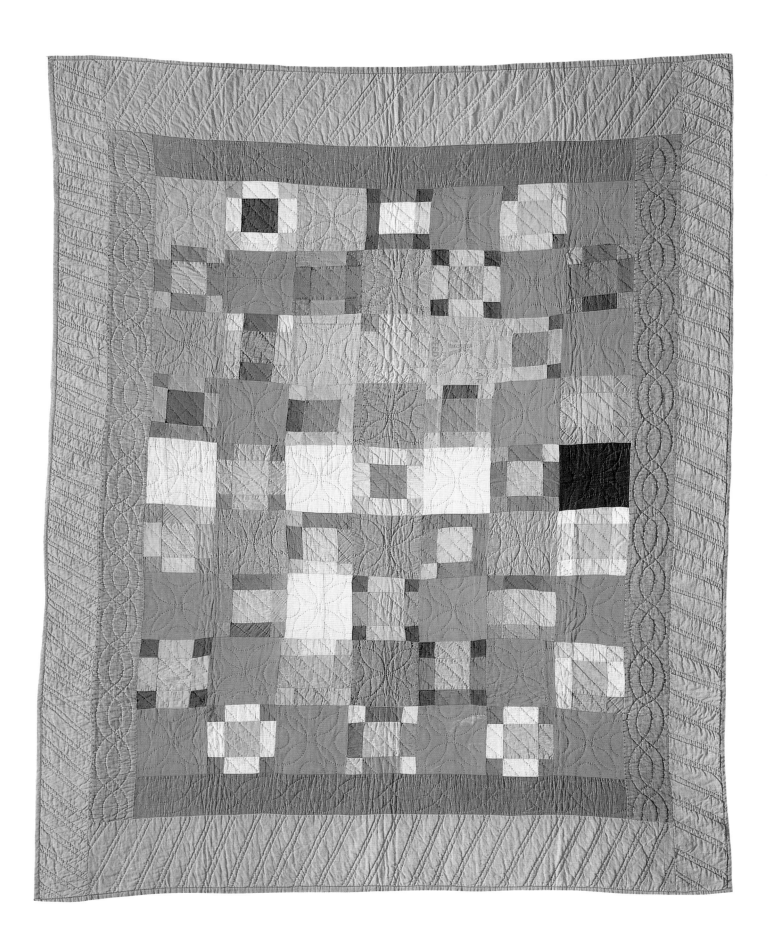

Nine-Patch Variation
Mifflin County, Pennsylvania, circa 1925–35, made by Elizabeth Zook Yoder
Rayon/cotton, chambray, muslin, feedsacking, twill- and plain-weave cotton • 56 × 70
Bill and Connie Hayes

Common outside border designs on Nebraska quilts include the chain, twist or fan. Long, simple, diagonal lines in one direction or two sets of diagonals crossing to form a diamond were also used frequently in all of the Old Order church groups. Variations on pinwheel and leaf geometrics can be found on inside borders and in the fill blocks.

The blackberry leaf vine was popular in both the Nebraska and Byler groups, particularly in earlier quilts. This pattern also migrated westward with families who left Mifflin County to begin new settlements.

The Sprucie Heart is another example of a local design. Flat, stylized tulips, leaves, hearts, baskets and geometric variations can be found on the earliest quilts where the design was often double-stitched. In the later 20th century the use of double-stitching eventually disappeared.

The quilting motifs and the general quilting skills of women in Mifflin County changed just as they did in Lancaster and other settlements. By the 1940s, the number of stitches per inch and the amount of thread used for quilting had dropped noticeably. Although the more conservative groups continued to make the same type of quilts in much the same color schemes and designs as their parents, as they do even today, the overall quality of sewing work deteriorated rapidly after the 1940s and 1950s.

Embroidery

The use of embroidered or cross-stitched initials on a quilt was a practice largely limited to Lancaster and Mifflin counties, where it was common. In Mifflin County it is found most frequently on Nebraska style quilts. Embroidered initials appear both in late and early examples; among the Nebraska Amish this practice has persisted as a tradition for many years.

Nebraska Amish women limited their embroidery work to two or three initials, but women in the Peachey church occasionally used colored thread work in the body of the quilt design. Turkey track or fence row stitching on crazy patterns was acceptable decoration in the Big Valley, as it was in Lancaster and other communities. The most "wordly" examples of embroidery work can be found in quilts produced in the 1920s and 1930s by the Peachey church group on their white and one-color quilts.

Color

There are Mifflin County quilts which are indistinguishable from those made elsewhere, but there are others whose colors are distinctive enough to help identify them as products of one of the Old Order groups in the Big Valley.

The color scheme of Nebraska quiltmaking (along with their pattern and quilting traditions) can usually be readily identified by even the casual viewer. In sharp contrast to the subdued "natural" tones of these quilts are the exceedingly bright colors which were popular, particularly among the Peachey Amish. In their quilts made as early as the 1920s, bright pinks, greens, oranges, blues, yellows and purples can be found. These brilliant shades were sometimes combined with deeper blues, browns or even blacks, but they were also used distinctively in combination with one another: pink next to orange, or pink and green, vivid fuchsias and turquoise pieced together with orange or

Detail Quilting
Chain • Mulberry leaf and vine
Flat tulip • Parallel lines
97

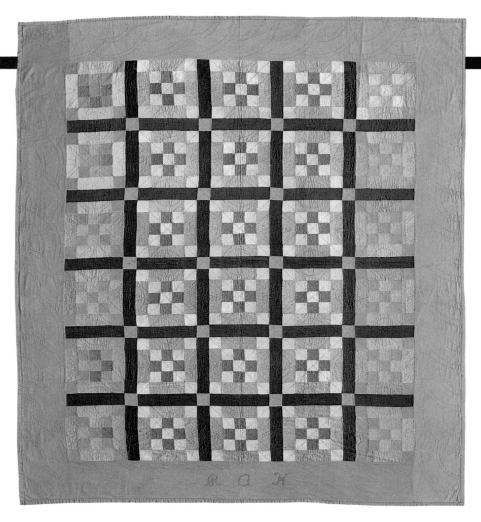

green. The visual impact of these strong colors can be either disconcerting or strangely beautiful. The palette of strong colors used in the Big Valley is somewhat different than that found in Ohio or Indiana. In those communities, showy, vibrant colors were also well liked, but they were frequently pieced on black backgrounds, which framed the effect of the brighter, hotter shades.

Those Big Valley quilts that were pieced from a more subdued palette of colors are difficult to identify specifically. Color choices do follow the same trends that prevailed in other Amish communities. In the early 20th century, deeper, brighter tones dominated. New colors and pastel colors made their appearance in the 1940s, 1950s and 1960s. Two particular colors, orange and a golden yellow, did appear frequently in Mifflin County throughout the 20th century, in contrast to many other Amish communities where there were spoken and unspoken rules against their use.

Quilts made even today in Mifflin County remain fairly unchanged in their color schemes.

Nebraska Amish women have maintained the same traditions for 100 years. Their material may be polyester and the quality of dyestuff may be different today, but their basic color choices are largely the same as they were in the 19th century: tans, blues, purples, wines and browns. In the Byler and Peachey districts the selection of colors has been more affected by fashion, but strong blues, purples, greens, pinks and even orange have remained perennial favorites.

Overview

The three general periods described for Lancaster quiltmaking also apply to Mifflin County (see pages 83–87). These are broad divisions, and the distinction between quilts made before and after the 1940s is less clear in the Big Valley than it is in Lancaster. Some significant differences do exist, however, between late 19th- and early 20th-century quilts, and quilts made in the 1920s, 1930s and 1940s. In the early years wool was used, but plain- and twill-weave cotton fabrics were equally important. By

Nine Patch
Mifflin County, Pennsylvania, circa 1930–40
Cotton/rayon, cotton sateen, plain-weave cotton • 66 × 74 • Private collection

the 1920s and 1930s, wools were barely used at all in Big Valley quiltmaking.

The introduction of rayon in quiltmaking took place quite early in Mifflin County, and the preference in some church groups for bright colors also appeared as early as the 1920s. "English" practices, such as choosing blue and white goods or using purely decorative embroidery work, came long before the 1940s, and, in fact, appear to have diminished in importance by the later period.

As is also the case in Ohio and Indiana, new patterns and pastel colors signal quilts made after the 1940s.

By the 1950s and 1960s, quilting skills had noticeably diminished among women in the Big Valley. Many continued to use traditional patterns and colors, but the appearance of polyester materials and fewer quilting stitches are important visual cues in identifying a later quilt.

In contrast to their great-grandmothers in the mid-19th century or even their grandmothers in the late 19th century, 20th-century Amish women in the Big Valley seem to have been more interested in pieced patterns and color arrangement than in the art of fine quilting stitches as practiced in Lancaster. There are examples of beautiful quilting in the Big Valley, but, in general, the quilts from this Amish settlement are more related to those made in Ohio or Indiana, where piecework patterns and the arrangement of colors dominated the quiltmaker's attention.

The quilts made in the different church districts of Mifflin County from the 1880s to the present day mirror the development of traditions in a small and closed community. The Nebraska Amish were among those least affected by the whims of fashion, and their quilts reflect a persistent vision of absolute simplicity. Women in the Byler church also maintained strong traditions for many years. It was among the Peacheys, the most liberal of the Big Valley

(above) **Diamond in the Square**
Mifflin County, Pennsylvania, circa 1935–45
Plain-weave cotton muslin, embroidery thread • 76 × 78 • Private collection

Mifflin County use of orange.

Double Nine-Patch Chain
Mifflin County, Pennsylvania, circa 1920–30
Plain-weave cotton percale, cotton/rayon,
cotton sateen • Rosalie Gallagher

Old Order groups, that the greatest variety of quilts were made.

Just as Lancaster County was a "mother" community to Mifflin County in the 18th and early 19th centuries, Mifflin County in turn became the "mother" community for new settlements in western Pennsylvania, Ohio and further west. Those who moved from the Big Valley carried with them their quilts and their quiltmaking customs.

Somerset County, Pennsylvania

The frontier area of Somerset County was officially opened for settlement in 1769, and the Amish were among some of its very earliest pioneers. They came to Somerset from communities in Lancaster and Berks counties, in search of cheap land and isolation from proselytizing religious groups.

Throughout its long history, the Amish settlement in Somerset has experienced many difficulties, and the community has remained small. Two factors played an important role in its lack of growth: the geographical position of Somerset County as the "jumping off" place for the westward migration movement, and the church divisions that occurred in the mid- and late 19th century, when the Amish Mennonites and the Old Order established more formalized rules governing church life.

This community was often the first stopping place for the second wave of Amish Mennonite immigrants who came to the United States in the years following the War of 1812. Somerset was something of a way station, and families arrived and left constantly, contributing to a certain lack of stability within the community. Most did not stay long in Pennsylvania, pushing on as soon as they had raised funds to pioneer in Ohio or Indiana or Illinois.

(above) **Trip Around the World**
Mifflin County, Pennsylvania, circa 1930–40
Chambray, cotton sateen, plain-weave cotton, cotton/rayon • 74 × 84 • Private collection
(below) **Delectable Mountains**
Mifflin County, Pennsylvania, circa 1920–30
Plain-weave cotton, cotton sateen • 78 × 79 • Private collection

101

In the mid-19th century there were three different Amish settlements firmly established in Somerset: the Glades, the Connemaugh and the River congregations. Of these three groups, only a portion of the River congregation remained Old Order. The other groups either disbanded and moved westward or changed to various degrees of Amish Mennonite and Mennonite affiliations. It is notable that even the portion of the River congregation that maintained its Old Order ties made a unique change by building a meetinghouse in the early 1880s.[6]

One of the most important aspects of the Somerset community is its link to the midwestern Amish settlements. Somerset was the first "daughter" community of the old Berks County, Pennsylvania, settlement, and in turn it became the starting point or "mother" community for the Amish districts in Holmes County, Ohio, Elkhart and LaGrange counties in Indiana, Johnson County in Iowa and Moultrie and Douglas counties in Illinois. The vast majority of midwestern Amish families can trace their family lines to relatives who resided

in Somerset County at one time in the 19th century.

Because the Somerset community stayed so small, only a few quilts from there remain to be examined. As families moved westward they took with them their household goods, including quilts and coverlets. Most likely some of the earliest quilts made in Somerset were carried from Pennsylvania to other states. Inventories in the Somerset County courthouse show that Amish families, and Mennonites as well, adhered to typical German textile traditions. Listings of flax, linen, coverlets and blankets predate any mention of quilts or purchased materials. A number of Amish Mennonites were listed in the tax records as weavers through the early 1830s, and coverlets are mentioned with great frequency in Amish and Mennonite inventories well into the 1880s.

In quiltmaking, the Amish of Somerset reflect their historical, social and emotional ties to both the older ways of the East and the newer practices of the Midwest. In late 19th and early 20th-century quilts from Somerset, the block

Log Cabin
Mifflin County, Pennsylvania, circa 1900–1910
Plain-weave cotton • ESPRIT collection, San Francisco

design was the most commonly used; the designs chosen were most often the simplest patterns — One and Nine Patches and their variations. Color choices also tended to be fairly conservative compared to midwestern examples, and the quilting, while sufficient, was neither abundant, fancy, nor particularly unique to Somerset. As among the Nebraska Amish in Mifflin County, the Amish in Somerset leaned toward utility and modesty.

Perhaps the social and religious strife that affected this community throughout much of the 19th and early 20th centuries is subtly reflected in its quiltmaking. Those who chose to keep themselves humble and remained Old Order Amish did not participate in the making of showy and unnecessarily fancy quilts. In Ohio and Lancaster, where community solidarity was never as much of an issue as it was in smaller communities, there seems to have been a much greater tendency toward some self-expression, experimentation in color and design, and a greater freedom to indulge in elegant quilting.

(left) **Flying Geese in Bars**
Somerset County, Pennsylvania, circa 1890–1910
Heavy wools • 64 × 77½ • Norma J. Wangel

(above) **One Patch**
Somerset County, Pennsylvania, circa 1890–1910
Plain- and twill-weave wools • 32 × 68½ • Norma J. Wangel

Bars
Somerset County, Pennsylvania, dated "MAR 1949"
Plain-weave cotton, cotton/rayon • 67 × 76 • Norma J. Wangel

Ohio

Of the three major Amish settlement areas in the United States — Lancaster County, Pennsylvania, Elkhart and LaGrange counties in Indiana, and the Ohio counties of Holmes, Wayne, Stark and Tuscarawas — those in east central Ohio constitute the largest concentration of Amish living in North America and, indeed, in the world. The Amish came to Holmes and Tuscarawas counties early in the 19th century. There they founded settlements which have grown and spread into several contiguous counties in Ohio, and have provided population for almost every Amish community in other midwestern states.

The first families who settled in Tuscarawas, Wayne and Holmes counties came from Somerset and Mifflin counties in Pennsylvania. Though there were a few families who staked land claims before the War of 1812, the real establishment of these areas came in the two decades following the end of that war. In the subsequent years of the 19th century the Ohio frontier was settled by massive numbers of immigrants of all religious and ethnic backgrounds.

The history of the Amish and Amish Mennonites in Ohio is a complicated and often confusing story.[7] Throughout the 19th century, the flow of immigrants from established communities in Pennsylvania, as well as the arrival of the European Amish Mennonites, meant a steady increase in both the population and the diversity of congregations. For the most part, however, the Old Order Amish were remarkably successful in developing stable and prosperous communities in the rolling hills of eastern Ohio.

Aside from the difficulties of beginning and maintaining communities, one thing is evident from both the public records and private family histories of Amish families in the early years of

Log Cabin Lone Star
Holmes County, Ohio, circa 1930–40
Plain-weave cotton percale, cotton/rayon blend, plain- and twill-weave wools, white muslin back • 70 × 71
Darwin D. Bearley collection

105

the 19th century. In moving to Ohio these people chose a harder lot in life than their relatives who remained in Pennsylvania. The first settlers put up small log houses with puncheon floors and oiled paper windows. Some of these structures still remain on Amish farms today, though most were eventually either enlarged and incorporated into the newer frame houses or taken down. All of the furniture, cloth for clothing and bedding, and many of the small household objects were produced at home throughout much of the first half of the 19th century. The widow's portion was a standard section of all estate papers and points up the importance of the home production of textiles in the Ohio communities, even after its significance had already diminished among Pennsylvania families.

As the 19th century progressed, estate inventories reveal changes in textile production among the Ohio Amish that mirror events in other communities. These excerpts from the estate papers of two different Amish women, one who died in 1861 and one who died in 1892, illustrate the changes that occurred within just one generation of 30 years.[8]

Catherine Hershberger Holmes County 1861	Barbara Hershberger Holmes County 1892
lot of towels	toweling
cushen (cushion)	new flax cloth
shawl	shirts
quilt	bed sheets
planket (blanket)	1 tick case and slip
coverlet	2 lounge sheets
planket	stockings and socks
planket	apron
flax heckel	thread
cotton	handkerchiefs
spinning wheel	table cloths
4½ yards linen	5 yards sheeting

12 yard linen	4½ yards bleached
14½ yards linen	muslin
paches of linen	7 white caps
6 yards cloth	2 wool shirts
wool wheel	dresses
thread	4 yards carpet
stocking yarn	frock coats
balls thread	pants
3 piller (pillow) slips	woolen shawl
8 towels	roll of oilcloth
bed slips	4 bed and bedsteads
6 tablecloths	1 blanket
4 sheets	1 comphort (comfort)
3 pieces shemery	1 wool blanket
piece blue muslin	1 small quilt
	1 quilt
	1 loungequilt
	8 yards cloth

A survey of estate papers from the 1830s through the end of the 19th century reveals that the spinning wheel and home produced fibers and handwoven textiles had lost their importance by the 1870s.

By the 1880s a substantial number of quilts are included in many Amish estate records. One of the most noteworthy aspects of these listings is the early dates at which quilts do appear in the Ohio communities and the relatively large number that are listed in inventory and estate vendue papers. The earliest notation of quilts in Pennsylvania Amish inventories is in Mifflin County in 1836, and there are only a few references to quilts or quiltmaking tools such as quilt frames throughout the 1840s, 1850s, 1860s and even 1870s in Pennsylvania. In Ohio, the first listing of quilts appeared in 1831 in Wayne County. Though quilts do not appear in Amish estate papers with the same frequency as they appear in the inventories of non-German families in Ohio, they do appear more frequently than in Pennsylvania Amish documents. The inventory of Catherine Miller, for example, who

died in Holmes County in 1875, lists six quilts, four coverlets, quilt patches and an assortment of other bed textiles such as sheets, cases, pillow slips and blankets.[9]

We can only speculate about the appearance of the earliest quilts cited in inventories prior to the 1870s. It seems likely they were plain productions and, although more citations do appear in Ohio than elsewhere, the numbers are still small. Only a handful of surviving examples date from the 1870s and 1880s. Quilts made during these years and in the last decade of the 19th century are extremely rare. Descriptions of the characteristics of the few extant quilts can only be guidelines, but with these in mind we can begin to differentiate 19th-century Ohio quilts from early 20th-century examples. Further differences in style, color, quilting and fabrics appeared as the 20th century progressed. By examining the particular fabrics, patterns, colors, quilting, backings and bindings we can begin to place Ohio quilts in particular time periods.

Patterns

It is the patterns of Ohio quilts — with their variety, complexity and originality — that make them so striking. Ohio Amish women developed a large repertoire of pattern designs, from the simplest plain or inside border quilts and two-color block designs, to the most intricate piecework of Railroad Crossings, Spiderweb Stars and Ocean Waves.

Patterns were not limited to a central, single or even traditional design. Every part of the quilt top and back was considered in the arrangement. Inside and outside borders were sometimes enhanced by diamonds, sawtooths, zigzags and keyboard piecework. Sawtooth bindings and bindings pieced out of several different colors also appear. Patterns were sometimes combined to enhance their visual effect, and some rare quiltmakers simply invented their own patterns and geometric variations.

Design was not restricted to the front of the

Original Pattern
Holmes County, Ohio, dated "1883," initialed "JJY, LLY, EB, JB"
Plain-weave cotton • 74 × 91 • Darwin D. Bearley collection

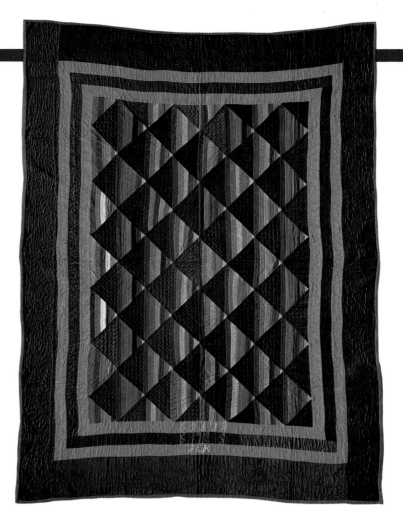

quilt. It is not uncommon to find a quilt with a piecework pattern on the front side and a plain border design on the reverse or lining side — two quilts in one.

Almost every conceivable piecework pattern can be found in Ohio quilts and, on rare occasions, examples of applique work as well. Certain patterns were particularly popular in various periods or within certain church districts or families. For example, the Swartzentruber group, the most conservative of the Ohio Amish, has always maintained a strict *Ordnung.* Plain quilts, Monkey Wrenches and Shooflys, usually pieced from blues, wine reds and blacks, are the most common patterns found in the homes of these conservative Amish families. Women in other church districts in Ohio have been guided by more liberal standards. They made both simple plain quilts and highly pieced and highly prized examples such as Railroad Crossings and Log Cabins.

Many patterns chosen for Amish quilts were

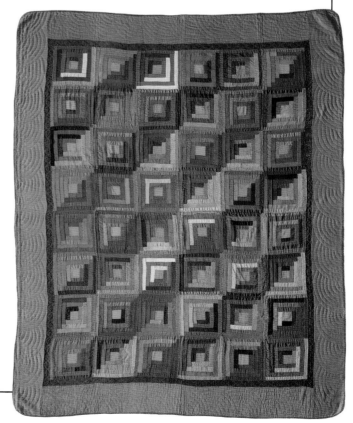

Roman Stripe
Holmes County, Ohio, dated 1912," initialed "IJY JEK"
Plain-weave cotton, cotton sateen, plain- and twill-weave wools;
reverse side is a plain inner border quilt done in black and red cottons.
59 × 82
Eve Granick and David Wheatcroft

traditional designs which were repeated over and over from one generation to the next. Some patterns were specifically related to "English" quiltmaking discoveries or fashions that were subsequently adopted by Amish women. The Double Wedding Ring pattern, for example, was developed and popularized among American women in the 1920s. Although there are a few examples of this pattern among Amish quilts in the 1920s, the vast majority of Amish Double Wedding Rings date from the 1930s onward. Broken Star is another example of a design which did not appear before the 1920s. On the other hand, patterns such as Log Cabin, Spiderweb or String Stars, and Roman Stripes, all of which are based on a strip method of piecing, are more common to the last decade of the 19th century and the first 20 years of the 20th century.

Fabric

Until the late 1940s, Amish women in Lan-caster, Pennsylvania, used fine wool for their quilts almost exclusively. In contrast, women in Ohio preferred very different materials. Wools can be found in early quilts, particularly Log Cabin patterns, but fine, plain-weave cottons also appeared quite early and seem to have been more popular than wool for quiltmaking even in the 19th century. Lancaster quilts were made predominantly of a soft, plain-weave batiste wool; when wools were used in Ohio quilts they were more often the hard-surfaced wools such as brilliantine and mohair. But although wool fabrics such as brilliantine, mohair, serge and even batiste were widely used in Ohio for dresses in the late 19th and early 20th centuries, cotton was still the predominant choice of fabric for quiltmaking. The number of cotton quilts far outweighs the number made of wool.

The high cost of finely woven dress wools probably contributed in part to the Ohio preference for cotton, but other factors were perhaps more important. The weight and texture of cot-

(left) **Log Cabin** • Berlin-Winesburg area, Holmes County, Ohio • Dated "1891," initialed "M.A.Y." • Plain-weave cotton percale, plain- and twill-weave wools, batiste, broadcloth, brilliantine, serge, black taffeta • 67½ × 87 • Darwin D. Bearley collection
Log Cabin •Berlin-Winesburg area, Holmes County, Ohio, dated "1914" • Plain-weave cotton percale, plain- and twill-weave wools, batiste, broadcloth, serge • 65 × 82½ • Darwin D. Bearley collection

These two quilts were made by a mother and daughter. The first, made in 1891, has many typical 19th century characteristics. The choice of colors, materials and the rounded corners all reflect 19th century Ohio quiltmaking traditions. The second quilt, made by the daughter 23 years later, illustrates the power of tradition and the influence of change. The daughter chose to make her quilt in the same pattern and in many of the same fabrics. The selection of colors with more use of black and the fancier strip border are an indication of the changes which occurred in Ohio quilts from one generation to the next.

ton lent it more readily to the detailed type of piecework favored in Ohio. Cotton is a less "fluid" fabric than wool and more adaptable to the process of cutting, arranging and seaming small pieces on the sewing machine.

Because cotton was used in Ohio quilts from such an early date, the changes that occurred in Lancaster quilts in the early 1940s, when wool became difficult to obtain, were not so apparent in Ohio quilts. The fine cotton sateens that were highly favored by Ohio quiltmakers did disappear from the marketplace and were replaced by a glossy rayon substitute, but other traditional cottons continued in steady use throughout the 1940s, 1950s and even into the 1960s. Cotton muslin, both good quality and the feed bag variety, was an important fabric for Ohio Amish women. During the 1930s and 1940s in particular, feedsacking and inexpensive muslins were used for almost every conceivable purpose, including quiltmaking.

The introduction of synthetic fabrics, such as rayon and rayon blends in the 1940s and polyester in the late 1950s, was less noticeable in Ohio quilts because the overall appearance of these new fabrics was similar to cotton. Many quilts from the 1940s and 1950s incorporate a variety of cottons, rayons and rayon blend materials. A careful examination of all of the fabrics in a Ohio quilt is necessary when one is attempting to determine its age. There may be many pieces of old cottons or sateens interspersed with materials from a later date. Often the borders and backing material reflect most accurately the time period in which the quilt was made.

Linings

A solid colored piece of fabric was the most popular choice for a quilt backing among Ohio Amish quiltmakers. Linings can be found in all colors, including black and white. In many Ohio communities the use of white muslin for a

(above) **Baskets**
Holmes County, Ohio, dated "1950"
Plain-weave cotton percale, cotton/rayon sateen, cotton/rayon blends • 36 × 46
Michael Oruch
(below) **Railroad Crossing**
Holmes County, Ohio, circa 1920–30
Plain-weave cottons, percale, chambray, cotton sateen • 46 × 47 • Eve Granick and David Wheatcroft

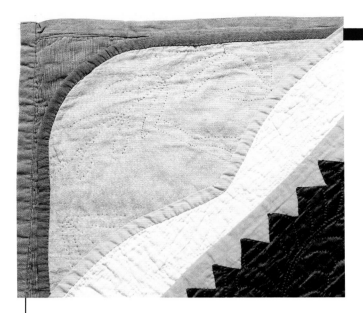

backing material was fairly common from the 1930s onward. Thus, although the majority of quilts do have a colored lining, white muslin is not necessarily indicative of either a late or reproduction quilt.

Sateen, chambray and plain-weave colored cottons were the favorite fabric types of the Ohio quiltmakers. Linings were either pieced out of leftovers from family sewing or purchased specifically for the quilt. Most quilt backs were put together from two or three panels of fabric seamed on the machine to give a solid appearance. If leftovers were used, several different colors were often put together in a random fashion.

There are many examples of quilts from Ohio in which special attention was given to the quilt backing. These are double or reversible quilts with piecework patterns on the front of the quilt and an inside border, plain quilt pattern pieced for the backing. This type of quilt does appear in all periods, but it is more frequently found in quilts made before the 1940s.

Bindings

Although most quilt bindings are indistinguishable from one community to the next, there are a few defining elements that can be described. In Ohio the width of quilt bindings generally falls between ¼ inch and one inch. Most often quilt bindings were made from a separate piece of material prepared specifically for the binding. The color was often chosen to match the small inner border or one of the

many colors in the quilt pattern. Bindings were applied by machine to the front of the quilt and then turned over the edges and either handsewn or machine-sewn to the backing.

In early examples from the 19th century, quilt corners and the bindings were frequently rounded rather than square. This design, although not limited exclusively to early quilts, can be considered in conjunction with other supporting elements as a reliable signal of a quilt made before or around the 1900s.

Another variation found with some frequency in Ohio was the applied sawtooth binding. These bindings required extra work and must surely be considered a fancy touch. In later quilts, from the 1940s through the early 1960s, scalloped edges became quite popular. This type of scalloping can be found in earlier American quilts, but it was not a practice among Amish women until the mid-20th century; even then it appears only in church districts which expressed more liberal attitudes toward quiltmaking.

Quilting

Quilting not only holds the layers of fabric together, it is an important element in the design and appearance of a quilt. In Lancaster, fine quilting was a major part of the quilt's overall design. In Ohio, quilting usually took a back seat to the pattern and piecing. Very fine quilting was, however, an essential element of the plain inside border quilt, and it is vital to the appearance of two- and three-colored block patterns. Several motifs were popular among Ohio quiltmakers for these two types of quilts.

In quilts with more complex design and piecework, however, quilting diminishes in importance. The viewer is more struck by color and design, and it seems that the quiltmaker expended most of her energies in the piecing. The outside border is often the only area where any extensive quilting appears. In the piecework

Bindings can be applied in several different styles. These are examples of binding methods found commonly on Ohio quilts:
1. The most common binding is straight with squared corners.
2. While rounded corners appear frequently on early quilts, they were also popular throughout the 20th century.
3. Scalloping of the edge and binding is more common to the post-1930 period.
4. Sawtooth bindings took a great deal of time and careful needlework to apply. They became popular in the 1920s and 1930s.

Inside Border, Plain Quilt Variation
Geauga County, Ohio, circa 1925–35
Plain-weave cotton percale • 67 × 90½ • Darwin D. Bearley

112

pattern area, quilting is usually limited to a series of lines that follow the seams of the piecework.

Fine stitching and particularly elaborate quilting patterns often signal an earlier quilt. Although different colored thread can be found in both early and later examples, most often black or brown thread was used in earlier quilts. White thread is more common in examples made after the 1930s and 1940s when pastel colors became popular. However, it is possible to find white quilting thread in early 20th-century quilts. Usually the choice of quilting thread was based solely on the colors of a quilt, white thread being used for lighter colored materials and black for darker fabrics.

Color

Ohio Amish quilts come in every imaginable color. The simplest arrangements are found in the plain quilts made of one background color and one, or perhaps two, contrasting colors for the inside borders and binding. Two-color block quilts are also quite common in all periods, again with one color as a background and a second contrasting color chosen for the pattern. In earlier quilts from the 19th century and very early 20th century, the background was usually blue, brown or red. The color schemes of these quilts were usually quite saturated and rich. Black backgrounds, which became so dominant in Ohio quiltmaking, were not popularized until the 20th century. It was during the years between the 1920s and 1940s that black became a dominating border and background color choice. Browns, blues and reds continued in some use, but black became far and away the favorite of Ohio Amish women for the backgrounds of their quilts.

The range of colors in Ohio quilts expanded rapidly in the early 20th century. As technology made more and more shades available to the consumer, the quilts of the 1920s and 1930s were created in rich, bright and eye-dazzling arrangements. By the late 1930s and early 1940s a palette of pastel colors gradually gained favor in many of the more liberal church districts, although the most conservative groups continued to make quilts in darker and deeper tones. In the 1940s some Amish women combined pastel colors with bright or dark shades, but stopped short of making the entirely pastel quilts that became so popular with American women after the 1920s.

Certain colors were not available until the 1940s and 1950s, and these can act as accurate markers of a later quilt. Particular shades of turquoise, green and purple, as well as specific color combinations, can be helpful in accurately dating quilts made in the 1940s and later.

When you look at any antique quilt, remember it may have been heavily washed or used on a bed which sat in direct sunlight. The colors you see today are not the colors chosen by the quiltmaker. Time, light, soap and water have diminished many of the original color schemes.

Overview

Quilts made in Ohio fall roughly into the three time periods described in other communities: the late 19th century, 1900–1950, and the years between 1950 and 1970. The differences between these eras, however, are much less distinct in Ohio than in some other communities.

The Amish communities in Ohio were a more diversified group than those in Lancaster. Although Holmes County had only a few more church districts during the 1920s and 1930s than Lancaster had, Ohio's variety of "high" and "low" church groups was much greater. This diversity is well represented in Ohio quilts, as some women adopted new ideas, colors and materials quickly, and others continued the older traditions into the 1960s and 1970s. By the 1950s the population of the Ohio commu-

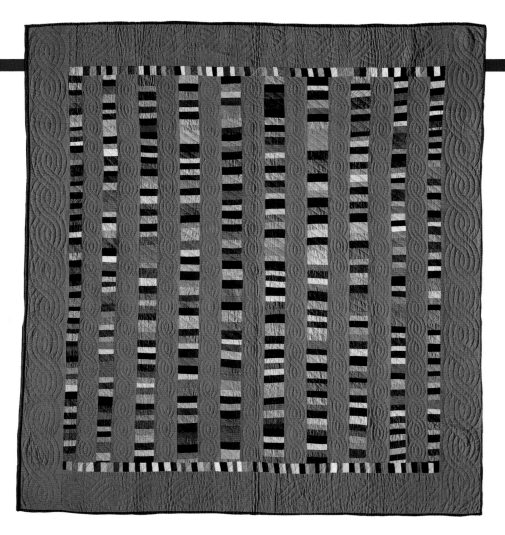

nities was almost twice that of Lancaster, and the variety of groups and the effect of intermarriage from one district to another makes any detailed descriptions or distinctives of Ohio quilts difficult.

In general, Ohio quilts made in the late 19th century were pieced from either cotton or, less frequently, dress wools. There are also a few examples of quilts from Ohio and other midwestern communities that were made from heavier flannel and suiting wools. These almost always date from before the turn of the 20th century. Among 19th-century Ohio quilts, simple block designs in two and three colors predominate, but there are also the rare and striking examples that exhibit complex piecework and a great variety of color and quilting designs.

The practice of making crib quilts was quite strong in Ohio, compared to Lancaster County traditions. Women in Ohio made many more crib quilts than their counterparts in Lancaster.

In the years following World War I, quilt-

(above) **Chinese Coins**
Plain City, Ohio, circa 1930–40
Plain-weave cotton percale, chambray, Indianhead cloth, cotton sateen, plain- and twill-weave wools • 76 × 84½ • Michael Oruch
(below) **Double Irish Chain**
Barr's Mills, Holmes County, Ohio, dated "1884," initialed "DY"
Plain-weave cotton percale, plain-weave polished cotton • 78 × 92 • Darwin D. Bearley collection

making underwent some important changes in the Ohio communities. The use of black backgrounds became increasingly popular. Brown, blue and red backgrounds, rounded quilt corners and the more muted "natural" colors of the late 19th and early 20th centuries were replaced. Bright deep colors of every imaginable hue and combination appeared. Added to that were squared corners and larger overall proportions, giving the quilts of the period from 1920 to 1940 a different appearance. Color contrasts were sharper and designs became bolder and often more complex, creating striking visual effects. Many consider the quilts made during this period to be the finest and most distinctive examples of Ohio Amish quiltmaking.

By the 1940s the most liberal groups in Ohio began adopting "English" styles and influences. Pastel colors and new patterns such as the Flower Garden or Lover's Knot appeared. The heavy use of black lost favor with young Amish women who considered black and dark colors "too old-fashioned."

Between the 1930s and the 1960s changes slowly filtered through all of the Ohio districts, with only the strictest groups maintaining the traditional styles. Remember that change takes place slowly in the Amish community. For many years women continued to make traditional blue and black or red and black blockwork quilts, along with the less distinctly Amish patterns and colors that began to appear after the 1930s. By the mid-20th century older patterns were often noticeably altered or modified by new color choices and piecing proportions. Even when a quilt's pattern, colors or quilting motifs were largely "traditional," the quilting stitches were usually not as fine and the size of the blocks and the pieces making up the blocks were frequently larger. As the Amish adopted the use of larger sized beds, the overall dimension of their quilts increased as well. More and more synthetic materials appeared in the period after 1940. The use of polyester battings and

Broken Star
Holmes County, Ohio, circa 1930–40
Plain-weave cottons • 81 × 81 • Judi Boisson

115

materials in the 1960s, and the development of a quilt market and tourist industry surrounding the Amish in the 1970s and 1980s finally altered forever the quilts of the Ohio Amish.

From the earliest 19th-century examples, quilts made in the Ohio Amish districts reflect a distinctly different type of community from those in Lancaster or the smaller 18th- and 19th-century Pennsylvania settlements. In Ohio the Amish found enough land and a particular type of geography to permit various church districts and factions to develop their own way of life without the stress of enforced geographical proximity. The hills and valleys of Holmes County provided certain physical boundaries which made the emphasis on rigid conformity and strict visual symbolism seem less necessary and less possible.[10] Symbolism and the *Ordnung* were still vitally important in the Ohio communities, and the principle of plain dressing certainly helped to stabilize Amish communities to a greater extent than the Mennonites were able to achieve. But many Ohio Amish districts do appear to have developed more liberal attitudes than their Pennsylvania brothers and sisters about the smaller details of daily life.

It is unclear how much interaction with "English" neighbors influenced quiltmaking in Ohio, since the Amish did have strong, well defined communities. Certainly the quilts of the Ohio Amish fulfilled the requirement to be "different from those of the world." Women in Ohio did not, however, appear to have felt compelled to restrict that difference to particular quilt patterns, as they did in Lancaster, or to particular quilt colors, as in the Nebraska Amish communities of Mifflin County.

Why were the Amish women in Ohio such great experimenters when compared to their Lancaster or other Pennsylvania cousins? Was this a matter of permission or choice? What social and economic factors influenced the Ohio communities in the late 19th and early 20th centuries to foster the creative efforts of these women?

By the time the Ohio Amish began pieced quiltmaking in the 1870s and 1880s, the settlements there were well established and prosperous. Ohio was no longer a frontier and those who had resisted the urge to move farther west had established thriving farms and businesses. The Amish communities in Holmes County in particular were examples of stable congregations. It is this community stability and economic security which seems to have played such important roles in sustaining the outburst of quiltmaking creativity.

These 19th-century and early 20th-century examples (see Figures 00 and 00) are the work of women who had enough leisure time, church permission and a personal inclination or talent to create quilts of extraordinary beauty and complexity. These are bedcoverings which far surpass simple utility. Both the quilting and piecework of a great number of early Ohio quilts suggest that aesthetic sensibilities were very strong among women in these communities. The solidarity of their church groups, the economic security of their home lives and the trends in fabrics and fashions of the time all

Flower Garden
Holmes County, Ohio, circa 1935–45
Plain-weave cotton percale and muslin, creped cotton • 35 × 38 • Joan Fenton and Albie Tabackman, Quilts Unlimited

coincided happily. By combining their traditional sewing skills with strong color and design aesthetics, these women produced a group of truly unique quilts. The balance between complex design and simple, ordered geometry, and the combination of convention and creativity achieved new dimensions in the quilts of Ohio Amish women.

Lawrence County, Pennsylvania

Located only a few miles from the Pennsylvania-Ohio border, the history of the Lawrence County settlement is closely linked to both the Byler church group in Mifflin County, Pennsylvania, and to the Holmes and Geauga county settlements in Ohio. In the late 1840s, population growth of the Mifflin County Amish settle-

(above) **Grandmother's Dream Variation** • Holmes County, Ohio, circa 1930–40
Plain-weave cotton, chambray, rayon/cotton, cotton/sateen • 73 × 76½ • Judi Boisson
(below) **Railroad Crossing** • Walnut Creek, Holmes County, Ohio, dated "1888" • Made by Melinda Miller
Plain-weave cotton percale • 69 × 89 • Eve Granick and David Wheatcroft

ment required the division of church groups into three different districts. Conflicts and a growing difference of opinions were being experienced, and clear-cut factions had begun to develop among the Mifflin County group. In 1847 several men from the Big Valley travelled 175 miles on foot to survey Lawrence County for a possible settlement. Finding suitable land, a small group of families moved in during the next few years, and in 1849 the Amish church in Lawrence County was formally organized, the same year that the first formal division of the Mifflin County Amish occured. Over the next decade these transplanted Mifflin County families were joined by others from Ohio. The first minister, Dan Byler, was the grandson of Hans Beiler, the first bishop of Mifflin County. He was ordained with help from the church elders in Holmes County. From the beginning then, this community has shared religious, social, familial and cultural ties with the Byler church of Mifflin County and with the Old Order groups from Holmes County and later from Geauga County, Ohio.

The Lawrence County community has enjoyed great stability and steady growth since its founding. Only one split occurred, when a small group of families withdrew in 1856 to form the Maple Grove Mennonite Church. The Old Order group has grown from the few founding settlers to include over 350 families and 12 districts in and around New Wilmington. Families have also moved into neighboring Mercer and Crawford counties and there are a number of small isolated settlements in nearby northwestern Pennsylvania and southwestern New York as well.

Predictably, the quilts made in the New Wilmington area combined aspects of Mifflin County quiltmaking practices with traditions found among Ohio Amish families. There has been a great deal of intermarriage and migration among families from Mifflin, Holmes, Geauga

and Lawrence counties over the years, and the quilts found in Lawrence County reflect this.

The majority of quilts made in this community appear to be block patterns; Nine Patches, Shoofly, Jacob's Ladder, Baskets and Stars were all popular. Overall patterns like Ocean Wave or Railroad Crossing, which are found in Holmes County, are rare among Lawrence County quilts. Piecework tended to be nicely done but not overly elaborate. The pieced piano key borders or sawtooth bindings used in Ohio are absent among Lawrence County quilts. Blue, purples, greens, grays, browns and burgundy are among the most popular colors. Yellow, white and bright red, while not explicitly forbidden, appear only rarely. The use of black as a background color is not unheard of, but it appears to have been less popular in Lawrence County than in Ohio, and more in keeping with Mifflin County traditions.

Like Amish quiltmakers in other communities, the women of Lawrence County have created quilts over the last century which reflect the standards of their settlement in various periods. Fabrics, colors, quilting and, to some extent, patterns have evolved and changed with

Double Nine Patch
Lawrence County, Pennsylvania, circa 1925–35
Plain-weave cotton, cotton sateen • America Hurrah, New York

118

time. New Wilmington has been a prosperous and stable settlement. Unlike the communities of Holmes County, however, the basic standards for the decorative arts have remained "plainer" and strongly tied to the Mifflin County Byler church.

Indiana

Indiana contains the third largest community of Old Order Amish in the United States. These settlements were begun in the 1840s by families from Somerset, Pennsylvania, from various communities in Ohio and by the newly arrived European Amish and Mennonites of Switzerland, the Alsace and South Germany. The communities were all founded during the years when the pressures and conflicts of the impending Old Order/Amish Mennonite schism were building. Accordingly, the history of the Amish church in Indiana is a story of numerous divisions and great variations among church districts and *Ordnungs.*

Amish life in Indiana in the 1840s and 1850s was largely ruled by the demands of developing new farmlands out of the midwestern prairie. The inventories of the early families in La-Grange and Elkhart counties indicate that life was difficult with much hard work and few fancy possessions. In the first years, the Amish, along with all pioneers, were consumed by the tasks of cutting timber to clear the land for plows, building log houses and crude furniture, tilling and draining the insect-infested wetlands, hunting and storing food supplies and making clothing, shoes and candles.

This personal memoir, written by Rosina Gerber in 1914, provides some details of the early days in Indiana.[11]

We left Wayne County, Ohio on April 3, 1854 to move to Adams County where father had bought 160 acres for $3400.00. [The author was at that time 12 years old.] Father and mother and two small sisters went on the train. My brothers, Peter and Solomon, and sisters Mary, Fanny, Anna and myself went in wagon. We were on the road eight days. Our new place had a two room log home, a log barn, a small orchard and a well. We soon built an addition to the house and cleared all the land but 20 acres.

We had a strong church in our community. They held meeting every two weeks. The meeting was held at the homes of the members and often times in the barns if the houses were not large enough. Church service would last until 1 p.m. and the people stayed for lunch. They took the plank benches which were used for seats, put them together and covered them with table-cloths. Then they set out bread and butter, apple butter, pickles, stewed dried apples and coffee. Two weeks later they would meet at the home of another member. It took about a year to get around once.

We raised sheep in those days. Mother and the girls would spin the wool and father wove it into cloth. The bolts were too large to wash by hand so they had "kickings." They would put the goods in the middle of the floor inside a circle of chairs tied together. The men and boys rolled up their trousers and when the warm soap suds were poured on the cloth they would kick and kick until they thought it was clean . . . In those days we cut our wheat and oats with a cradle, raked it with a hand rake and tied it in sheaves by hand . . . Things have changed so much in my life.

The account of frontier life that Rosina

Gerber offers is interesting not only for its details, but also because she describes her family as Mennonites. The domestic and church life among Amish and Mennonite families did not differ so greatly in those early years. For both, life entailed a lot of hard work and community fellowship.

As the rifts developed between the Old Order and those families that eventually chose the Amish Mennonite church, the similarities between the two groups gradually disappeared. Some of those who left the established communities in Ohio and Pennsylvania and moved on to the Indiana frontier also eventually chose to follow the leadership of men who were willing to drop many of the traditional symbols and practices of Amish life. Over several generations the traditional garb was exchanged for more worldly clothing, beards were shaved or trimmed back radically, church houses were built, Sunday schools and the use of English in the church service were introduced.

On the other hand, the Old Order Amish in Indiana today are the descendants of those who resisted these innovations in the 19th and early 20th centuries. They rejected religious evangelism and avoided the intrusions of such modern conveniences as electricity, cars and motorized farm machinery.

Amish families were highly divided as these changes occurred. Some joined the strictest groups; others, more liberal factions. In Allen County the few newly immigrated Amish Mennonites, who aligned themselves with the Old Order, developed highly conservative church districts. There were also many who left the Amish church altogether for Mennonite or Protestant church affiliations. The variety of these groups is reflected in the variety of quilts found in both Amish and Mennonite homes in Indiana.

Amish women in Ohio seem to have embraced quiltmaking fairly early. There is at least some mention of quilts found in the inventories of Ohio Amish families prior to the 1870s, although we have no extant examples. In Indiana many inventories of Amish and Mennonite households reveal virtually no listing of quilts before the late 1870s and early 1880s. In fact, Indiana Amish and Mennonite families seem to have owned few objects in the 1860s and 1870s, in sharp contrast to their counterparts during the same time period in Ohio and Pennsylvania, whose household inventories were extensive and valuable.

In 1863, the property of Joseph C. Yoder of LaGrange County was sold at public sale. The estate listing is more extensive than many from this era, but these excerpts from the textiles and bedding items are typical of the period.[12]

1 lot of bed clothes	taken by his widow
1 lot of bedding	taken by his widow
1 lot of flax	taken by his widow
1 wool wheel	sold for $4.00 to Fanny Yoder
Bed tick	taken by his widow
1 comfort	sold for $1.50 to Fanny Yoder
1 coverlet	sold for $1.00 to Catherine Yoder
sheeting	sold for $1.00 to Fanny Yoder
loom and furniture	sold for $9.25 to Joseph Weirick
1 lot of bed clothes	sold for $2.35 to Benjamin Keim
trunnel bed	sold for $4.25 to Henry Yoder
Bedstead and bedding	sold for $17.25 to Henry Yoder
Bedstead and bedding	sold for $10.00 to Catherine Yoder
Bedstead and bedding	sold for $10.00 to Fanny Yoder

Bedstead and bedding   sold for $10.00 to Christian Yoder

Coverlets, or *debbichs,* as they are often called by the Amish, along with various types of traditional Germanic bedding forms such as comforts, blankets, bedticks, pillows, bolsters and cases, were predominant in inventories in Indiana well into the 1870s. Typical inventories of various Amish families from that period also included bedsteads, bed and bedding, spinning wheels and reels, wool wheels, cotton and linen thread and a variety of fabrics such as "pant's stuff," jean, muslin, ticking, denim, calico, cassimere, coat lining, flannel and linen.

The monetary value of spinning wheels and looms remained high through the 1860s, bringing between one and five dollars at Amish estate sales in these years. By the late 1870s, however, this previously important piece of household furniture had been largely replaced by purchased textiles and sewing machines, and spin-

ning wheels were listed in estate inventories and vendue papers at only a fraction of their former value.

The change from a dependence on home-produced textiles to the newer practice of purchasing materials is inextricably linked to the rise of interest in quiltmaking. It is uncertain exactly when women in Indiana began to make pieced quilts, but the earliest known examples date from the mid-1870s. Throughout the 1880s and 1890s, quilts appear with increasing frequency in the inventories and vendue papers of Indiana Amish families.

The quilts made in Indiana in the late 19th and early 20th centuries were very strongly related in design, color and materials to those being made by Ohio Amish women during the same time period. There are also, however, some aspects of Indiana quiltmaking that are distinctive and noteworthy. By examining a large number of quilts made in Indiana and comparing them to those made in Ohio, we can

Bow Tie
LaGrange County, Indiana, circa 1920–30 • Mrs. Levi E. Miller
Plain- and twill-weave wools, plain-weave cotton, cotton sateen • 75 × 81 • David Pottinger

121

begin to pick out small details that identify these quilts, and to develop a larger sense of color, craftsmanship and design differences.

Patterns

Many of the same patterns are found in both Ohio and Indiana quilts. The block design Shooflys and Nine Patches, typical in Ohio, are equally common in Indiana. In fact, the overall appearance of the Indiana examples is frequently indistinguishable from examples made in Ohio or other midwestern communities. On the other hand, certain patterns such as the early Ohio Double Inside Border Plain quilts, the Lancaster Diamond in the Squares and the classic Ohio pattern, Railroad Crossing, are only rarely found in Indiana.

As noted, in any Amish community there are certain patterns that achieved particular popularity at different periods and among different church districts or families. The Amish travel extensively from one community to another for visiting and family ceremonies such as weddings and funerals. This was as true in the late 19th and early 20th centuries as it is today. There were many opportunities to see quilts made in other communities, and the occasional and exceptional use of particular patterns can perhaps be linked to these inter-community travels. For example, a few Center Diamond quilts have been found in Indiana. These were made from cottons, not commonly used in Lancaster, and the quilting is different from a Lancaster Diamond. This is not a pattern "native" to Indiana, but rather a rare exception, most likely the work of a woman who visited with family or friends in Lancaster.

In one group of communities in Indiana, pattern trading had no effect on quiltmaking. Among the Old Order Amish of Allen, Adams and Daviess counties, church rules mandated the making of entirely plain quilts until the

(above) **Double Nine-Patch Variation**
Indiana, dated "1920"; initialed "P.J.Y."
Plain- and twill-weave wools • 68 × 74 • Stella Rubin
(below) **Jacob's Ladder**
Indiana, circa 1935–45 • Plain-weave cotton percale, muslin, broadcloth, cotton sateen, creped cotton, cotton/rayon blends • 80 × 87 • Michael Oruch

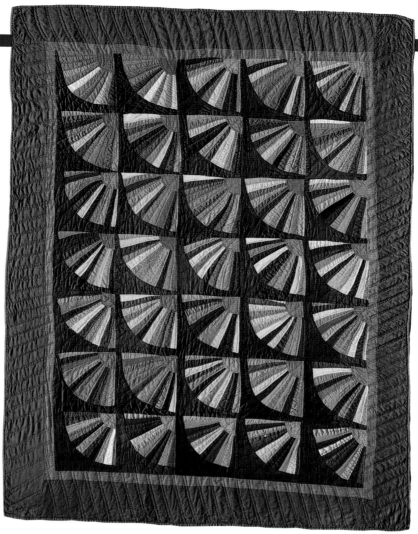

1960s. The families in these counties are the descendants of those 19th-century immigrants who chose to align themselves with the Old Order Amish rather than the Amish Mennonites. They brought with them from Europe particular cultural traditions, and they applied the strictest interpretations of the *Ordnung* to their lives, maintaining conservative, closed communities much like the Nebraska Amish of Mifflin County.

The majority of quilts made in Elkhart and LaGrange counties in Indiana were like those made in other midwestern communities: various block designs created by the arrangement of square and triangular pieces. Among some of the most popular patterns were Shoofly and Nine-Patch variations, Rolling Stone, Baskets, Bow Ties, Swallow Tail, Variable Stars, Double T and Hole in the Barn Door.

More complex overall patterns were also used, but fewer of these designs were made, probably because they require a great deal of cutting, piecing and rather exact sewing work to put them together. Among the most popular of the eye-dazzling overall designs were Streak of Lightning, Corn and Beans, Ocean Waves, Zigzags, Wild Goose Chase, Lone and Broken Stars, Indiana Puzzle, Drunkard's Path and Garden Maze. All of these patterns were favorites in Indiana and other midwestern communities.

One pattern that seems to have been particularly distinctive to the Indiana community is the Fan design. Although Fan quilts are found occasionally in Lancaster or Ohio, the design apparently gained special popularity in Indiana during the first 30 years of the 20th century. There are several variations, but the most common arrangement created a twisting path of fans across the diagonal of the quilt. In keeping with the Victorian influence on Amish quiltmaking at this time, quilters frequently applied

Fans
Indiana, circa 1930–40 • Plain- and twill-weave wools, velvet, rayon, creped wool, cotton sateen • 61 × 80½ • Norma J. Wangel

turkey track embroidery stitching to the edges of the pieces.

Log Cabin quilts were popular with Amish women everywhere, particularly during the first decades of the 20th century. These quilts were usually made in wool fabrics and constructed by a traditional logwork method. Each block was pieced on a square of foundation fabric. The center of the block was sewn on first and the quilter added one log at a time, sewing the fabric from the back and turning it over. The edge of each log strip was then covered by the next row of logs. Often these quilts were knotted instead of quilted, or they were quilted sparsely, only in the outside border area. Although this traditional log cabin construction method can be found on Indiana quilts made in wool at the turn of the century, many more such quilts were created in Ohio and Pennsylvania.

The Log Cabin quilts that are more distinctly identifiable as the products of Indiana quilt-making began to appear in the 1920s. These were most typically a Barn Raising variation, made out of simple piecework blocks. The use of cottons or a mixture of cottons and wools, and the shape, size and number of blocks give these quilts an appearance that is distinctive and different from earlier Log Cabin formats.

Fabric

The fabrics chosen for a quilt often provide interesting information about the economic status of the quiltmaker and of the community in which she lived. Though life was hard in the early years in Indiana, by the time quiltmaking began to develop in the 1880s and '90s, the farms around Elkhart and LaGrange counties had grown into prosperous operations, and the community was flourishing, despite various religious rifts. For the most part, the types and qualities of fabric found in the quilts made in Elkhart and LaGrange counties indicate that Amish women were quality conscious, and also

(above) **Fans** • LaGrange County, Indiana
Dated "Feb 28, 1924"; initialed "MY," [Mary J. Yoder]
Twill-weave wools • 67 × 78 • David Pottinger
(below) **Monkey Wrench**
Nappanee, Indiana, circa 1920–30 • Plain-weave cotton percale, cotton sateen • 61½ × 81½ • Michael Oruch

124

Log Cabin, Barn Raising
Indiana, circa 1930–40 • Plain-weave cotton percale, muslin, chambray, some printed fabrics
77 × 85 • Joan Fenton and Albie Tabackman, Quilts Unlimited

125

had the means to purchase fabrics specifically for quiltmaking. That practice was evident in other communities as well, most notably in Lancaster, Pennsylvania, in the Holmes County area of Ohio and in the Arthur, Illinois, settlement. In each of these communities, the selection of good fabric was an important element in quiltmaking.

In Indiana, as in Ohio, the use of wools in quiltmaking occurred primarily in the late 19th and early 20th centuries. (Cotton was equally important as wool in the late 19th century.) From 1900 to 1920, wool declined steadily in popularity for quiltmaking, and by the 1920s cotton was the most common choice of fabric.

Three varieties of wools are found in Indiana quilts. The first and earliest type was known by Amish women as "homespun." This was a loosely woven, coarse and fairly heavy wool. The warp and weft threads were often of two different colors, such as red and blue or green and brown. This fabric is found in the earliest known examples from Indiana and it is a material distinctive to 19th-century quilts. Whether it is actually a homespun wool is questionable. Several Amish women have described this fabric as homemade material, but it seems more likely that it was produced from home-grown wools which were processed and woven by local craftsmen. Evidence points to an almost exclusive reliance on factory-produced goods after the 1870s. Any examples of homespun wool in quilts must therefore be either the last remnants of earlier homemade fabric or the product of local fullers and weavers.

The second type of wool, found infrequently in pieced quilts, is the heavy, densely woven flannel and suiting wool. These wools were more commonly used to make comforts, but there are also some simple block design quilts from the late 19th and early 20th centuries that include them.

The most commonly found wools are the

(top) **Nine-Patch** • Date quilted in border, "1920" • Twill-weave dress-weight wools
(center) **Blue and White Nine-Patch** • Chambray and muslin
(below) **Backs, Bindings and Quilting** • Commonly found on Indiana quilts

126

dress wools: challis, alpaca, brilliantine, serge, broadcloth, cashmere and batiste. These wools appear in quilts from the late 19th century and into the early 1920s. The Fan design, as well as the simpler block patterns, were frequently pieced in these wools.

The cottons used in Indiana quilts were the same as those found elsewhere: plain-weave percales and "calico," chambrays and sateens. All of these continued in heavy use until the 1940s. During the 1940s and 1950s more and more synthetic goods were introduced into Amish clothing and quilts. In the late 1950s and early 1960s, polyester fabrics and quilt battings were well-established materials among the Indiana Amish communities.

Backing or Lining

Plain, solid colored cottons were the most commonly used fabrics for the quilt backing. A few examples with printed materials exist, but they were likely the work of quiltmakers with a more liberal church affiliation.

Bindings

The bindings on Indiana quilts are very similar in width and application to those found in Ohio. The practice of turning the backing material over to make the binding does seem to have been a bit more widespread in the Indiana communities, but there are also many examples of the more finely applied bindings. Scalloped edges appeared at roughly the same time in Indiana as they did in Ohio, beginning in the late 1930s and gaining more widespread favor during the 1940s and 1950s.

Quilting

A great variety of quilting motifs cover Indiana quilts, from the most common straight quilting to rare examples of quilted animals, hearts, stars and birds. The motifs on Indiana quilts are usually quite similar to those found in

Ohio and in other midwestern settlements. Rope or twist is one of the most common outer border designs. Floral and leaf patterns were popular during the late 19th century and throughout the 20th century. Another standard quilting design was a double row of straight or diagonal lines in the outer border and a grid of lines stitched into the fill or unpieced blocks.

As in Ohio or Lancaster or anywhere else, the finest and most profuse quilting tended to appear in the earlier examples.

Embroidery

Embroidery work is usually found in two places on Indiana quilts. It appears as turkey track stitching on Fan quilts, and it is used for stitching initials and dates onto quilts. Embroidered initials were most frequently stitched on friendship quilts. On the earliest examples, the initials of the person making the block, and perhaps the date of the project, appeared on the pieced blocks making up the quilt. In later quilts, from the 1930s on, a small floral design or even a few words were stitched in embroidery thread, in addition to the initials or names of the various friends and relatives making the quilt. During the 1920s and 1930s embroidered quilts were permitted in some of the more liberal church districts, but apparently this quilt fashion never became particularly popular among women in Elkhart and LaGrange counties.

Color

As in Ohio and elsewhere, color plays an important role in the appearance of Indiana quilts. Indiana women selected colors not radically different from those chosen by Ohio women and used certain colors and color combinations that followed the trends in other Amish communities from the late 19th through the mid-20th centuries.

Some of the earliest quilts made by Amish women in Indiana were quite simple. It was the

choice of colors that added such a striking dimension to the basic patterns. The most commonly used colors in these early examples were part of a saturated palette of blues, browns, tans and greens. More peculiar to Indiana quiltmakers was the use of rich burgundy reds, deeper golden yellows and some oranges. Indigo blue was also extremely popular and used for everything from shirts to dress linings and from dresses to quilts.

Shortly after the turn of the century, the use of black, particularly for a background material, achieved some popularity in Indiana as it did in other Amish communities. This color choice appears to have been the delayed adaptation of Victorian ideas to Amish-style fabrics and designs. Yet even in the years when Amish women were making black and blue, black and red, and black and multicolored patchwork, they still included a wide variety of blues, greens, lavenders, reds, grays and browns as major elements of their designs.

In contrast to some other communities, quilts in Indiana often included a strong red. In the Elkhart and LaGrange communities, women purchased this bright red specifically for quiltmaking. The color was not permissible for dresses.

Blue and white quilts, similar to those made in Mifflin County and in Ohio, can also be found among the Indiana Amish. These quilts generally date from the middle and late 1920s through the 1940s. Although blue and white quilts were acceptable in more liberal church districts, they were not as popular or widespread in Indiana as in some other areas of the country.

The occasional use of some printed fabrics is another notable aspect of quiltmaking among the Indiana Amish. The overwhelming majority of quilts contain only solid colored materials, but there does seem to have been a certain acceptance of the use of small amounts of

Box and Cross Variation
Indiana, circa 1920 – 30 • Plain-weave cotton percale and muslin • 65 × 74
Joan Fenton and Albie Tabackman, Quilts Unlimited

printed goods. Dotted, plaid and striped design materials were occasionally interspersed among the solid colors. Figured materials appear in both 19th and 20th century examples.

The occasional use of printed fabrics in otherwise solid-colored quilts illustrates the latitude and boundary stretching permitted in most Amish communities. Although the standards called for solid-colored materials, some women apparently felt that a slight bending of the rules was permissible. In certain communities the standards for quiltmaking were formal and strict. In the Elkhart and LaGrange settlements the rules were less clearly defined. The regulations existed, but the women in this large, stable and prosperous community were free to choose from a wide variety of patterns and colors.

Overview

Although the quilt traditions of Ohio and Indiana were not that dissimilar, practices developed in these two large settlements that reflect the different experiences of the Indiana and Ohio Amish. Community stability and economic prosperity affected quiltmaking practices in Indiana just as in other communities. Family migrations throughout the Middle West and "English" and Mennonite influences were also factors in the appearance and style of Amish quilts made in Indiana.

As in other settlements, Indiana quiltmaking can be divided into various time periods. The first quilts were distinctive for their simplicity, rich color and fine quilting. These elements are present in early Ohio examples as well, and the late 19th century quilts from these two communities are similar. In the 1850s and 1860s, however, settlements in Indiana were smaller and newer than those in Ohio. Written evidence suggests that there was some quiltmaking activity in Ohio during that time, but no written or material evidence of quiltmaking in Indiana exists before the 1870s. It was in the years

Young Man's Fancy
Goshen, Indiana, circa 1900–1910 • Made by Melinda Chupp
Plain- and twill-weave cotton • 66 × 77½ • Eve Granick and David Wheatcroft

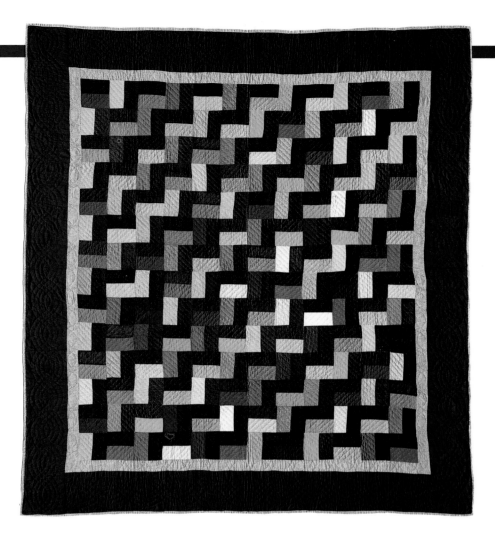

between the 1870s and the last decade of the 19th century that Indiana Amish women embraced quiltmaking with the same enthusiasm as women in other Amish settlements.

It is vital to remember Amish population figures from the turn of the century in order to understand why so few quilts remain from before 1900. National and religious census data indicate that between 1890 and 1910 the number of church districts and families in the Elkhart-LaGrange area doubled from four districts to eight. Four districts represent at most about 80 families living in the area in 1890. By 1910 the community had grown to about 160 families, and in just one more decade the population doubled again to 16 districts with some 300 families.[13]

During the 20th century the Indiana communities grew and prospered, and quiltmaking changed gradually in these years as it did elsewhere in Ohio and Pennsylvania. New patterns and quilting designs evolved, and the selection of colors and fabrics changed. Black backgrounds, two-color blockwork and multicolored patterns were all popular in the years between 1900 and the 1930s and the 1940s. Pastels and a variety of bright, harsh colors gained widespread use through the 1940s, 1950s and 1960s. The frequent use of wool in 19th-century quilts was replaced almost completely by the use of cottons and sateens in the early 20th century, and these fabrics were in turn replaced by synthetics like rayon and polyester in the 1940s, 1950s and 1960s.

In comparing the quilts made in Pennsylvania and Ohio to those produced in Indiana and farther west it is important to note a certain general decline in craftsmanship. The attention to careful and elaborate quilting in Lancaster was largely abandoned by Ohio quiltmakers in favor of careful and elaborate piecework. In Indiana both the quilting and piecing are of a generally cruder quality than in either Ohio or Pennsylvania. Fewer and broader quilting

Brick Wall
Nappanee, Indiana, circa 1930–40 • Plain-weave cotton percale, chambray, cotton sateen
74 × 84 • Michael Oruch

Paving Blocks Variation
LaGrange County, Indiana, circa 1925–35 • Plain- and twill-weave wool, wool crepe
75 × 84 • Eve Granick and David Wheatcroft

131

stitches are found on Indiana quilts and their size and scale of piecework is often larger. The attention given to careful construction of seams and even piecework, as well as the quality of such small details as bindings, indicate that, in general, women in Indiana concentrated less on fine craftsmanship and needlework.

The reasons for this general trend can only be guessed.[14] Quilting and sewing are learned skills, passed from one generation to the next. Women learn the standards for good work from their mothers and grandmothers. As Amish families moved farther and farther west during the 19th century, women in the frontier communities were faced with endless amounts of farm and housework. They left behind in the East established and comfortable homes and easy access to a wide variety of ready-made items. On the frontier they lived in crude structures and were required in the earliest years to produce nearly all of their own household goods. There was little or no time for practice at refined sewing.

Although Indiana was no longer a frontier when substantial numbers of Amish women began quiltmaking there, the general quality of life for the Indiana Amish was still less refined than that of their more eastern cousins. The traditions of elaborate needlework, handed down in Lancaster County in an unbroken chain from mothers to daughters, were simply not present on the Indiana prairie.

Despite the lack of refinement or elegance, there are many simple, ordinary, and beautiful examples and a number of extraordinary and unique works of quiltmaking to be found among the Indiana Amish. Like the quilts of Ohio Amish women, the handiwork and traditions of quiltmaking were carried from Indiana to communities in Iowa, Kansas, Illinois, Oklahoma, Michigan and Wisconsin, where new Amish settlements were founded in the 19th and 20th centuries.

Communities Beyond Pennsylvania, Ohio and Indiana

From a few colonial families and a small group of about 8,000 people at the turn of the 20th century, the Amish population has grown to some 100,000 people living today in 21 different states and Canada. Although 75 percent of the Amish live in Ohio, Pennsylvania or Indiana, there are well-established communities elsewhere throughout the Midwest and Canada.

During the 19th century, communities were founded in Iowa (1846), Illinois (1864), Maryland (1850), Kansas (1883) and Oklahoma (1893). A settlement was also begun in 1824 in Ontario, Canada, by some of the newly arrived European Amish. These communities have all flourished over the years, but their growth has never approached that of the three major early settlements in Pennsylvania, Ohio and Indiana.

The Amish population grew rapidly during the early and middle years of the 20th century. New settlements were established almost every year throughout North America. Many of these efforts failed and families moved away after a few years to begin in new areas or return to the original communities. Of the settlements begun in the early 20th century, the communities in Wisconsin (1925), Michigan (1900), Delaware (1915) and Florida (1927) survived and flourished. Since World War II, communities have also been started in New York State (1949), Tennessee (1944), Kentucky (1958) and Missouri (1947).

Especially in the early 20th century, many midwestern families did a lot of moving. Many families lived in two or three states, and their families were quite spread out, with aunts, uncles, grandparents and cousins living in various communities in different states. When an

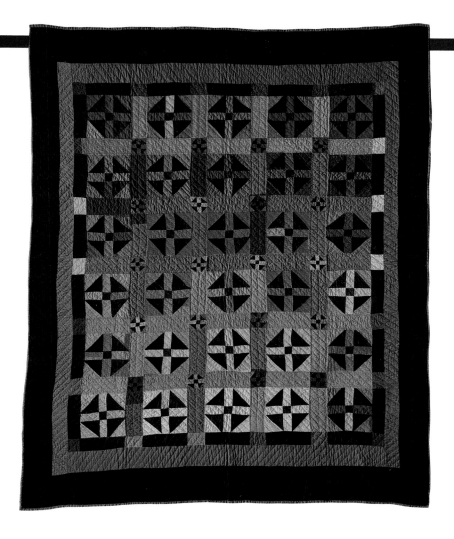

Amishwoman is asked about the origins of a quilt, the response is frequently, "I'm not sure; maybe we made that in Indiana; no, maybe when we were in Iowa" (or Kansas or Missouri or Wisconsin).[15] Quilts made in Indiana may have traveled from Elkhart County to Iowa to Kansas and sometimes back again. Thus, quilts found in all of the different communities outside of the "Big Three" are, in general, more difficult to identify by the community in which they were made, because most of the standardized quilt-design rules were brought from the mother communities to the new settlements.

Quilts made in the largest settlements in Pennsylvania, Ohio and Indiana were among the earliest collected by outsiders and the most publicized. However, in some communities beyond the largest settlements — particularly in some of the older communities, such as Arthur, Illinois; Kalona, Iowa; and Reno County, Kansas — there were some distinguishing

aspects to quiltmaking and some very distinctive quilts which are noteworthy.

Iowa

In 1846 several Amish families settled in Johnson County near Kalona. They came from the established settlements in Ohio, as was common, primarily in search of new land. The first years in Iowa were difficult, but by 1851 there were enough families and farms established to formally organize a church in the Kalona area.

From the beginning, disagreements concerning practices and church policies plagued the Iowa Amish community. A number of members believed that the rules were too liberal and sought a stricter adherence to traditional Amish disciplines. Debates concerned even small issues, such as the use of colored or decorated dishes, which one church elder believed to

Double Shoofly
Dover, Delaware, circa 1930–40
Plain- and twill-weave cotton, cotton sateen, twill-weave wool, flannel backing • 64 × 78½
Eve Granick and David Wheatcroft

be too fancy. The disagreements were periodically smoothed over and the settlement around Kalona did continue to grow steadily throughout the second half of the 19th century. In the 1860s the single church district was divided to accommodate the growing membership; new church districts were created in the late 1870s as well. As the years progressed, however, the disagreements between the liberal and conservative factions continued to surface over and over again, and they grew more and more difficult to resolve.

In 1914 several families of the conservative group finally decided to leave Kalona to begin a new settlement in Buchanan County. They were joined there by other families from Kansas, Indiana and Ohio, and they established a successful community near Hazelton.

Despite all of the divisions and dissension the Johnson County Amish have experienced over the years, theirs is among the most prosperous and growing settlements in the Midwest.

Today a wide range of groups, both Amish and Mennonites, live in and around Kalona. All have grown in number and sent out families to settle in other areas of the state. In addition, they have contributed to the membership of communities in Wisconsin, Illinois, Missouri, Tennessee, Kentucky and Minnesota. The three centers of Old Order Amish life in Iowa today are at Kalona in Johnson County, at Hazelton in Buchanan County and in three smaller "daughter" communities at Milton (Van Buren County), Bloomfield (Davis County), and McIntire-Riceville (Mitchell County).

For the most part, the quiltmaking traditions of Iowa are similar to those of Indiana and Ohio. There are, however, a few aspects of quiltmaking in Iowa which are notable, and an understanding of these may be useful in helping to identify a quilt made in one of the Iowa communities.

Ocean Wave
Cashton, Wisconsin; probably made in Indiana, circa 1925–35
Plain- and twill-weave cottons • 63 × 81 • Michael Oruch

Patterns

Iowa quiltmakers used the same block patterns found in other midwestern Amish communities. A variety of designs, both traditional versions and their variations, were made by Amish women, but Shooflys, Nine Patches and Bow Ties were among some of the most commonly used. Overall patterns (in contrast to those worked in blocks) like Ocean Waves, Log Cabins or Tumbling Blocks were rare in the Kalona communities. (Only in the mid-20th century did more complicated overall designs gain any real popularity. Weddings Rings, Broken and Lone Stars became favorites in those later years.) Several Medallion-style quilts were also made in the Kalona area, although only a few examples exist as evidence. The Medallion pattern, typical to Lancaster County, was uncommon to midwestern Amish quiltmakers.

In size and proportions, Iowa quilts are generally similar to those made in other midwestern communities. The most typical arrangement included pieced blockwork set on the point and interspersed with fill or "off" blocks. This grouping was surrounded by a small inside border and a wider outside border. In Iowa, as in some other communities, such as Somerset, Pennsylvania, and Arthur, Illinois, it was not unusual to eliminate the small inside border or to use it only on two sides.

In general, the patterns found in Iowa quilts tend to be less complex than those in other communities. The blocks were often made on a larger scale than those found in Ohio or even Indiana, and the piecework was also larger and less elegant. Although quiltmaking was an important and widespread activity among Amish women in Iowa, it never achieved the kind of artistic intensity evident particularly in Ohio quilts.

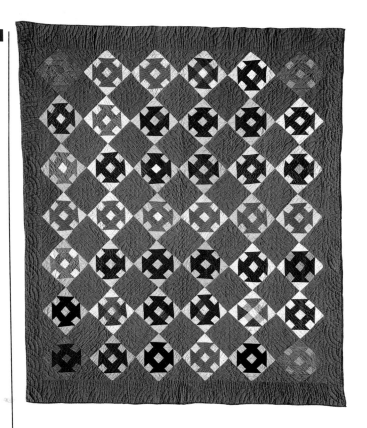

(above) **Monkey Wrench**
Kalona, Iowa, circa 1930–40, Helmuth family
Plain-weave cotton percale, cotton crepe, wool crepe,
rayon; some printed fabric on front • 69½ × 84½
Woodin Wheel, Kalona, Iowa
(below) **Monkey Wrench**
Kalona, Iowa, circa 1910–20, Helmuth family
Plain-weave cotton percale • 72½ × 85 • Woodin Wheel, Kalona, Iowa
These two quilts were made by two generations of the Helmuth family. The quilt at the top, made in the 1910–20 era, is typical in its materials, quilting and design of the period. The quilt at the bottom, made a generation later by the daughter, exhibits the mixed materials and changes in quilting and design proportion of that period.

Fabrics

Like other midwestern Amish, the women in Kalona used both wool and cotton for their quilts in the 19th century. As in other communities, the use of wool in earlier quilts was replaced by a predominant use of cottons by the beginning of the 20th century. Dress wools, suiting wools and flannels can all be found in Iowa quilts through the first decades of this century. In general, Kalona was a plainer and less prosperous community than the large settlements in Pennsylvania, Ohio and Indiana. The quality of fabrics found in the quilts made in Kalona reflects these economic differences. Wools were often coarser and thicker, and cottons were frequently of a cheaper quality. In the years of the Depression and during the Second World War, feedsacking and low-count muslins were widely used.

Quilt Backing

The church districts around Kalona permitted the use of patterned fabrics for quilt linings, a practice similar to the Lancaster, Pennsylvania, area. Checks, plaids, stripes and small prints appear frequently on quilt backs. A type of cotton or light wool outing flannel was also popular for quilt backing in the Kalona area. These fabrics were not acceptable in the Buchanan County settlement, however, where the conservative faction from the Kalona community established stricter and plainer standards.

Bindings and Quilting

Bindings found on the quilts made in Kalona, or any of the other Iowa communities, are no different from those found in other midwestern settlements. The quilting motifs seen on Iowa quilts are also largely the same as those used on quilts made in other midwestern communities. In general, the quilting tends to be simpler and of a cruder quality than those from Ohio or even Indiana, particularly in quilts made after the 1940s.

(above) **Nine Patch**
Kalona, Iowa, dated "1926" • Made by Mrs. Ben E. Miller for her son, Harley.
Twill- and plain-weave wools, cotton sateen • 63½ × 75½ • Private collection
(below) **Detail** — printed and solid materials found commonly on quilts made in Iowa.

Color

Two notable quilting practices occurred in the Iowa communities: the use of a small amount of printed fabric on the quilt top, and the use of white and pastel colors. We usually think of Amish quilts as being made only in solid colors, but in Kalona, throughout both the late 19th and early 20th centuries, the use of pieces of printed fabric was widely permitted. Usually the figure was fairly fine: checks, dots, small stripes or small flowers.

The use of blue and white, pink and white and a variety of pastel colors appeared in other communities at various times, but it was particularly prevalent in the Kalona area. These practices began quite early and became rather widespread after the 1940s. One of the oldest women interviewed described the quilts she received from home when she married in 1912. "Each of us had a white quilt with pink for good and dark quilts for everyday use, greens and blues. I had a Basket quilt made from cotton 'calico.' It was pink with different colors and the lining was white with black dots. My husband had one that was blue and pink."[16]

The families who left Kalona for the Buchanan County settlement disagreed strongly with those worldly and untraditional practices; consequently, the quilts from that community reflect a much stricter interpretation of the *Ordnung*. Black, blues, greens and some purples were the choice of colors for quilts made around Hazelton. A few pastel shades do appear in quilts made after the 1940s, but women in this settlement still make the same patterns and use the same color schemes today as they did in the early 20th century.

In the other small "daughter" communities like Milton, where the majority of families were often younger, the rules surrounding quiltmaking appear to have been comparatively relaxed. Most of the women in such communities were married in the post-World War II period. Aside from the use of rather strong colors and typi-

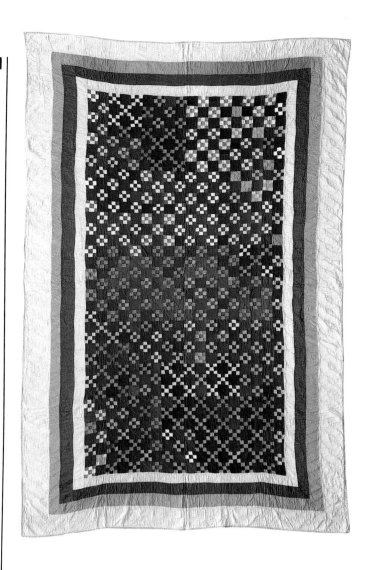

Nine Patch
Kalona, Iowa, circa 1930–40
Plain- and twill-weave cottons • 54 × 85 • Private collection

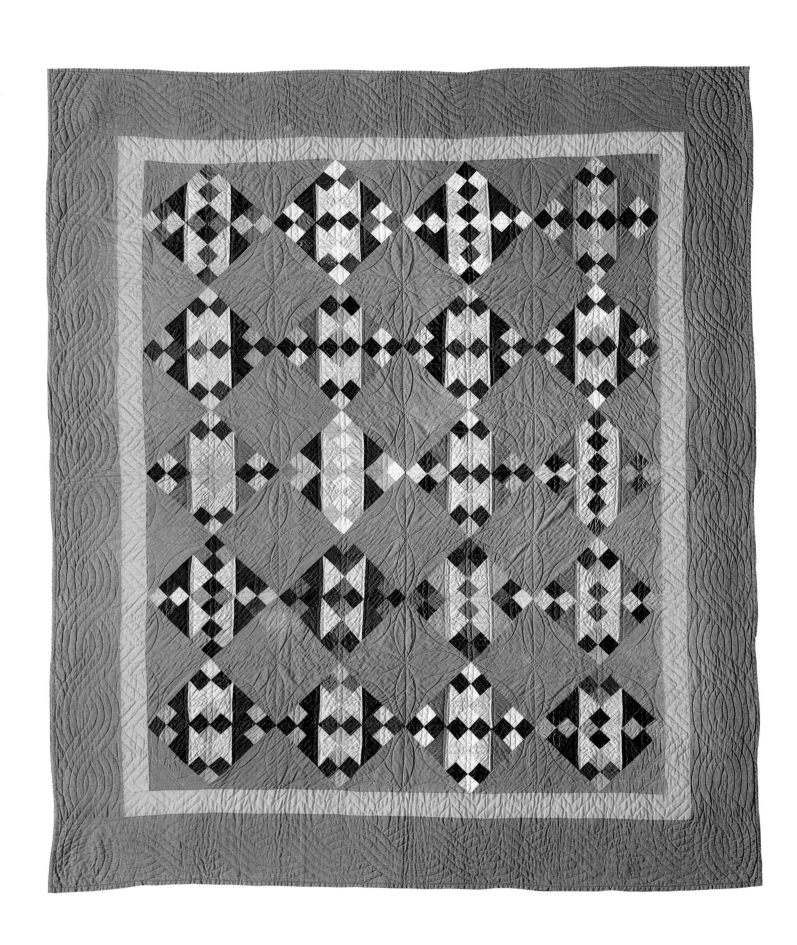

Jacob's Ladder
Kalona, Iowa, dated "1927," initialed "S.Y.M."
Cotton chambray, percale, polished cotton • 66 × 80 • Michael Oruch

138

cally Amish color combinations, the white background quilts made in this community are largely indistinguishable from quilts made by any other American woman of the period.

Overview

In general, the quilts made in Kalona and in the smaller Iowa communities followed the trends in the Amish settlements further east. Quilts from the earliest years were often fashioned in darker colors and made of both cotton and wools. In contrast to other communities, Kalona permitted white, lighter colors and printed materials to be used, even in the early years. Simple block patterns were the most common designs in Iowa, though a few Medallion-style quilts were made. As in other communities, new patterns were added to the quilters' repertoires as the 20th century progressed.

The quality and craftsmanship of piecing, sewing and quilting has generally declined during the 20th century in all Amish communities. In Iowa, even in the earliest days, the standards were never as high as in the eastern settlements. Even early quilts are usually a little heavier with less refined materials and sewing work. There were, of course, exceptional quilts and quiltmakers in Kalona, as there were in almost every Amish settlement, but the overall standards for both sewing and design were lower in Iowa than they were in either Indiana or Ohio.

Every Amish community achieves varying degrees of stability, both economic and social. Often the two elements are closely linked, and they directly affect quiltmaking. The trend of declining craftsmanship as the Amish moved their communities farther west seems inextricably linked to economics. In communities where religious and social dissensions were strong, quiltmaking appears to have been less an arena for personal expression or artistic experimentation and more a standardized form.

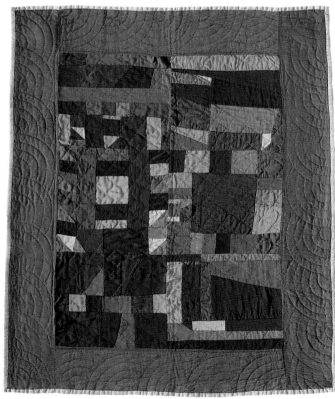

(above) **Chinese Coin**
Buchanan County, Iowa, circa 1930 – 40
Plain-weave cotton muslin, feedsacking, chambray, cotton sateen • 34 × 49 • Michael Oruch
(below) **Crazy Quilt**
Iowa, circa 1920 – 30
Plain- and twill-weave wool, cotton sateen • 36½ × 45½ • Judi Boisson

Illinois

The Old Order Amish founded two settlements in the state of Illinois during the 19th century. In 1872 a group of 17 families, mostly from Indiana, started a district near Shelby City, about 20 miles southwest of Arthur. They lived there until the 1880s, when virtually the entire group moved together to Reno County, Kansas.

An earlier settlement, begun in 1865 in the Douglas-Moultrie County area near Arthur, was much more successful. These families came from Somerset and Lancaster in Pennsylvania and from different communities in Ohio, Indiana and Iowa. Joseph N. Keim of Goshen, Indiana, was the first bishop for the settlement. The choice of the Arthur area was a happy coincidence: a party of men who were on a land search trip through the Midwest passed through Arthur on their return trip east and decided that the inexpensive and flat farmlands would make a good location for a settlement. Their judgment was excellent and from the beginning this community was stable and prosperous. By 1888 the population had grown sufficiently to divide into two church districts. By the 1920s there were five districts; presently there are 14 districts and almost 300 families.

The community in and around Arthur is a striking example of a settlement developed by families coming from various eastern and midwestern states in search of new land, and peacefully agreeing on rules for living. For the most part, the quilts made there reflect both the diversity of the families and the "mother" communities from which they came, and the stability and economic success of the new community which they formed. Some quilts made in Arthur illustrate the ties to Pennsylvania; others are directly linked to Indiana and Ohio traditions.

Overview

In almost every element of quiltmaking — the patterns, proportions, backing, binding and quilting — the women in Arthur followed closely the standards that evolved in the Ohio and Indiana communities. The vast majority of quilts made in this community were the usual block patterns: Shoofly, Bow Tie, One-, Four-, and Nine-Patch variations, Baskets and Variable Stars. These quilts exemplify the general standards of the community in various time spans. These periods are generally equivalent to those found elsewhere: the late 19th and very early 20th centuries; 1910–1940; and the post-1940 era. Although quilts from Arthur are quite similar to those made in other midwestern communities, the choice of materials and often the sense of color, design and craftsmanship do distinguish them from those made in other settlements.

Fine quality fabrics were quite important in Arthur. Joyce Brown, the granddaughter of Sam

Double Inside Border Plain Quilt
Arthur, Illinois, circa 1900–10 • Twill-weave wool challis • 69 × 78 • Michael Oruch

Greenburg, described the Arthur, Holmes and Lancaster settlements as the "fanciest" of the Amish communities. That these women chose fine materials indicates their more general concern for quality, which extended to the aesthetics of color and design as well. Fine materials, a strong sense of color, good quality quilting and the use of unusual borders or piecing arrangements are elements that mark many of the quilts made in the late 19th and early 20th centuries in Arthur.

Most of the quilts were done in block designs, although a smaller number of atypical and overall patterns were also made. The most unusual and striking quilts from this settlement, however, were the work of a few women who created a group of unique quilts, exceptional not only in the Arthur community but to the entire body of Amish quilts.

As in Ohio, certain economic and social conditions in the Arthur community appear to have heavily influenced quiltmaking practices. Arthur in the 19th century was a fairly hospitable environment for farming and offered enough land for the community to grow. The settlement developed quickly into one of the most prosperous of all the midwestern communities. Furthermore, the church experienced little of the religious dissension which affected other settlements. Even today there are few Mennonite groups in the area, in contrast to the large number and variety of Mennonite affiliations in Iowa, Indiana and Kansas.

The influence of this prosperity and stability permeated all aspects of life in Arthur and helped to foster an atmosphere of unusual creativity. Even the simplest, most ordinary patterns are somehow elevated by the use of fine materials. In the hands of certain women these fabrics were transformed into exceptional and very personal examples of quiltmaking.

(above) **Crazy Quilt**
Arthur, Illinois, circa 1900–10
Plain- and twill-weave wools • Harvey and Rosalyn Pranian
(below) **Stars**
Arthur, Illinois, circa 1915–25
Plain- and twill-weave wool • 68 × 80 • Collection of Bruce McCarty

Crazy Quilt
Arthur, Illinois, circa 1910–20 • Made by Lydia Beachy.
66 × 78 • David Pottinger
142

Kansas and Oklahoma

Old Order communities were established in both Kansas and Oklahoma in the late 19th century. These settlements have always remained small in size and closely connected, both socially and emotionally, to the larger "mother" communities further east. The ties to family and friends in both Iowa and Indiana have had important influences on the quilt-making styles that evolved in these western settlements.

Kansas

Kansas was organized as a territory in 1854 and joined the Union just prior to the Civil War in 1861. This state was heavily settled by Mennonites, particularly those who emigrated as a group in the 1870s from Russia, Poland and Prussia.

The Old Order Amish did not reach Kansas until the 1880s. Since 1883 there have been two small but thriving communities of Old Order families located in Reno County in the area around Yoder, Partridge, Haven and Hutchinson. A small settlement started in 1903 near Garnett in Anderson County has also survived to the present day as an Old Order group. Other Old Order settlements were begun at various times in the 20th century, but these communities gradually disbanded as families joined Mennonite groups. All of the families who located in Kansas in these two areas in the late 19th and early 20th centuries came from the established settlements in Illinois, Iowa and Indiana.

There are a number of quilts from both the 19th and 20th centuries that can be attributed to Amish women living in Kansas. The elements of design, color, proportions and quilting were heavily influenced by traditions brought from the eastern communities when the Amish moved here in the 1880s. The women who came to the Haven and Hutchinson areas were often

newly married and they brought with them their quilts from home and the strong customs of Indiana quiltmaking.

In the choices of color, pattern and fabric, a certain plainness prevailed. Many block patterns were made, as well as the less typical overall designs. Among late 19th and early 20th-century examples, the craftsmanship in piecing and quilting was generally good and the choice of colored plain cottons was standard.

Indigo blue was a dominant color in early quilts and was used along with tans, browns, greens, cranberry and bright reds, and some yellows, oranges and blacks. During the 1930s the Kansas Amish, like Amish women elsewhere, adopted a palette of more pastel colors and began to use white backgrounds.

There are a few examples of wool or sateen fabrics found in Kansas, but the most commonly used material was a plain, solid-colored percale or "calico" cotton. In the 1930s the Depression and the effects of the Dust Bowl made a strong impact on the Kansas Amish communities. During that time, feedsacking, cheap muslins and other inexpensive and low-quality fabrics were widely used.

As elsewhere, Amish women in Kansas followed the same general trends evident in Amish

Nine Patch
Oklahoma, circa 1910–20 • Made by Barbara Chupp
Plain-weave cottons • 90 X 72 • America Hurrah, New York City
Mrs. Chupp lived in communities in both Oklahoma and Kansas. In her later years she moved
to Kalona, Iowa.

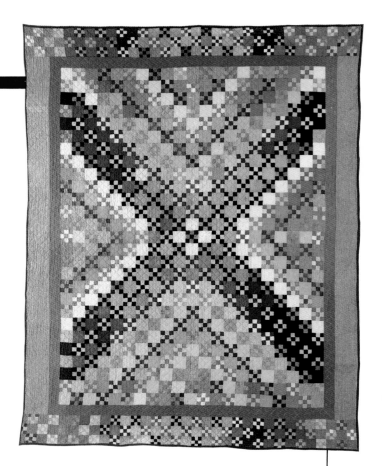

quilts dating from the late 19th century through the 1940s and 1950s. The most noticeable differences between the quilts made in Kansas and those made in other places seem to be related once again to the issues of community prosperity and stability. A general simplicity of designs, materials, quilting and sewing skills accurately reflect the overall lifestyle and group outlook of the Kansas Amish.

Oklahoma

The area now known as Oklahoma was designated largely as Indian territory until the 1890s. Settlement by white pioneers was not permitted until 1892, and then only in limited areas. Within 15 years of the arrival of the first white settlers, however, the Indian territory was merged with the Oklahoma territory to create one state, which joined the Union in 1907.

The Old Order Amish established their first community in Oklahoma in 1893 near Thomas in Custer County. A number of other settlements were also founded in the early 20th century, but only the community started near Chouteau in 1910 has survived to the present day as an Old Order group. (Chouteau is located in Mayes County in the eastern part of the state.)

The families who migrated to Oklahoma at the turn of the century came from Pennsylvania, Ohio, Indiana, Iowa and Kansas. Despite a steady increase in the number of families and communities, the Oklahoma Amish were unable to establish stable communities. With the increased spread of Mennonites into the area and their emphasis on Sunday and Bible schools and English-language worship services, and the effects of evangelism on several of the Old Orders' own community leaders, many Amish families joined more progressive Mennonite fellowships. Almost all of the families who did remain steadfastly in the Old Order chose to return to more stable settlements in Kansas, Indiana and Iowa.

A relatively small number of quilts were made in Oklahoma in the early 20th century. The church there was small and only newly begun. For the most part, traditions were brought from other communities and no truly indigenous style developed. However, among the typical and simple examples of quilts found in Oklahoma are the works of several women — Barbara Chupp, "crippled" Melinda Yoder and Barbara Yoder — whose visual and sewing skills surpassed the average.

Quilts made in Kansas and Oklahoma share certain characteristics for a number of reasons. First, the family ties between these two states were quite strong. Many of the families who settled in Oklahoma came directly from Kansas, and many also returned there in the 20th century when an increasingly liberal church resulted in the demise of most of the Old Order groups in Oklahoma. Second, the two states have similar geography. Just as the experience of pioneering in Ohio or Indiana had been quite different from the settled life in Pennsylvania, homesteading in Kansas and Oklahoma offered a new physical and emotional challenge to the Amish families who left behind established farms and communities in Indiana and Iowa.

Nine Patch Variation
Hutchinson, Kansas • circa 1910–20 • 72 × 90
Cotton • Barbara Chupp • America Hurrah New York City

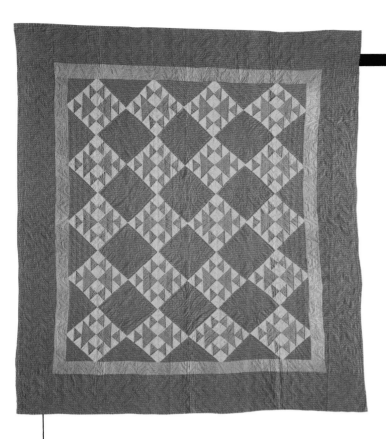

every Amish community, as among any group of people, there have always been men and women who exhibited visual, intellectual or artistic skills which surpassed the normal standards. Such skills are not highly valued or even particularly encouraged in Amish culture. In some communities the expression of these talents is even vigorously discouraged. In church districts where the bishop's interpretation of the *Ordnung* allowed for a certain amount of boundary stretching, unusual and surprising quilts can be found. This was true in the large communities of Ohio and Indiana, and it also applies to the quilts made in the small settlements of Kansas and Oklahoma.

Canada

While the majority of Old Order Amish communities in North America are in the United States, a number of settlements in Canada were founded during both the 19th and 20th centuries. In the most general terms the experiences of the Canadian Amish have been similar to those of the Amish who settled in the United States. The differences that do exist between the stateside Amish communities and those in Canada are a reflection of a different heritage and history.

Among the 18th century Amish immigrants to Pennsylvania there were a limited number of families and family names. The Amish who came to North America in the 19th century, including those who settled immediately in Canada, brought new names, new blood lines and new interpretations of church life. The first Amish immigrant to Canada was a Bavarian by the name of Christian Nafziger. He arrived in Waterloo County, Ontario, in 1822 after a long and arduous trip from Bavaria via Amsterdam, New Orleans and Lancaster, Pennsylvania.

Nafziger and the other European Amish families who began settling in Canada in 1824 were

Their similar pioneering experience became a bond between the Oklahoma Amish and their Kansas relatives.

The economic and social stability of these prairie settlements had a strong impact on quiltmaking in both states. In the 1890s an Amish woman in LaGrange, Indiana, lived on an established farm. Although there was always a great deal of work to be done, she did have time, money and energy to devote to quiltmaking; in some church districts she also had tacit permission to exercise personal creativity in her quilt designs. In Kansas, and even more so in Oklahoma, families were faced with the task of developing new land. Quiltmaking was still an important tradition, but time and money were directed primarily toward the goal of establishing farms. A concern for refined quiltmaking or home decoration was secondary at best. Even in the 20th century, as these communities gained in strength, the issue of economics remained important. These were small settlements in a harsh environment, and they simply never achieved the same level of prosperity that communities in Ohio or Indiana or Illinois did.

Beyond economics, the social stability and intricacies of interpreting the *Ordnung* played perhaps an even greater role in quiltmaking. In

Double Bow Tie • Crosses and Losses
Thomas, Oklahoma, circa 1910–20
Plain-weave cotton chambray, polished cotton • 75 × 87½
Darwin D. Bearley collection

145

part of what is considered the second wave of large scale immigration to North America by Europeans. This wave was spawned by the social and economic unrest that gripped Europe in the years following the Napoleonic Wars (1803 – 1815). Political turmoil and a growing sense of militarism created great concern for European Amish and Mennonite families. The New World's peace and promise of new opportunities that especially emerged following the War of 1812 helped to create an immigration fever. Europeans of every extraction, including members of the Mennonite and Amish faiths, made their way to North America.

At the same time that Europeans were looking to North America for new opportunities, Americans were also on the move. Amish and Mennonite families were part of the national trend westward in search of land and prosperity. By the 1820s, the earliest eastern Amish settlements were almost 80 years old. With little room for additional growth on affordable land, young families and the new European immigrants looked to the West and to Canada.

The first white settlers to the southern Ontario area were Pennsylvania Mennonites who began moving into Waterloo township in 1800. The difficulties endured by pacifist church groups during the Revolution and the instability of the new American government in the early years may have contributed to the Mennonite decision to immigrate and settle in "Upper" Canada.[17] The Canadian government offered a promise of military exemption and land at inexpensive prices. By 1822 when Christian Nafziger arrived in search of land for the European Amish, the Mennonites had established a community which would form the base for further settlement by the Amish and by other German immigrants as well.

Nafziger found the Canadian Mennonites ready and willing to assist him. After arranging with the authorities for land, Nafziger returned

to Europe to spread the news of his efforts. In 1823 the "German Block" was formally surveyed and 200-acre plots were laid out to form the new Wilmot Township. Directly west of the Mennonite settlement in Waterloo, this land was a vast tract of untouched forest. The first families claimed land in 1824, and by 1825 the flow of immigrants was quite steady.

Both Amish and Mennonite families arrived in Ontario, along with Lutheran and Catholic settlers from the Alsace-Lorraine region and South Germany. The first years were filled with the difficult work of clearing the land for cultivation and building simple structures to house animals and families. There appears to have been a fair amount of social interaction among all of the Canadian Germans, regardless of their religious faith. This mirrors the experiences of

Baskets
Milverton, Ontario, Canada, circa 1940 – 50
Plain- and twill-weave cotton, cotton rayon, creped wool, plain- and twill-weave wool,
brocaded fabric, cotton sateen, flannel back • 75 × 88 • Private collection

the American Amish community as well. While the lines between "sectarian" groups — the Amish and Mennonites — and the "church" people — Lutherans and Reformed — were very distinct in the later 19th century and are even more sharply drawn today, in the early 19th century the common language and culture shared by all of these Germans permeated daily life. Theron F. Schlabach writes in *Peace, Faith, Nation* that "intermarriage was extensive with intricate family networks across church and sectarian lines. In daily life Mennonites and Amish constantly mixed with their neighbors in mills, distilleries, markets and shops."[18] In Ontario in the early 19th century there is abundant evidence of mutual aid and friendship between the Mennonites and Amish and among other Germans as well.

Between 1824 and the 1870s the Amish flourished in Canada. Population growth from within and the continuous influx of European immigrants fostered growth in the Ontario Amish community. New congregations were organized in East Zorra in 1837 and in Hay Township in 1848. Wellesley Township was organized in 1859 and Mornington in Perth County was established in 1874.[19]

The Amish who came to North America in the 19th century were from several different areas of Europe and from some diverse cultural and congregational traditions, compared to the 19th century descendants of the colonial Amish. C. Henry Smith writes in the *Story of the Mennonites* that "up until the middle of the 19th century, the whole Amish brotherhood, both the Pennsylvania contingent and the more recent Alsatian immigrants felt themselves to be one body in faith and practice."[20]

While this may have been the case spiritually, the two groups did not mix readily. The majority of 19th century immigrants established their own communities and their own way of doing things. As the 19th century progressed, differ-

ences among these congregations throughout the United States and Canada gradually became sharper and more problematic. The Canadian congregations moved toward a more progressive interpretation of church life. These changes were not made easily, and the divisions and conflicts which resulted in the formation of the Old Order Amish group in the United States between the 1860s and 1880s also took place in Canada.

For the Canadian Amish, the use of English in church and the growing popularity of Sunday schools contributed to a growing dissension. The most important symbolic issue in Canada, however, concerned the building of church houses. Until 1883 the Amish Mennonites in Canada held worship services in homes. When Amish congregations began to build church houses in the mid-1880s, a small number of dissenting families separated themselves and formed a single congregation. One source estimates that only 10 percent of the Waterloo/ Perth County families remained in the Old Order.[21] This is substantiated by the very limited number of family names currently in the settlement. In 1985, among the 149 Old Order families living in the Wellesley and Mornington Township area, six surnames — Kuepfer, Albrect, Jantzi, Wagler, Zehr and Stricher — are attributed to 140 families. The remaining nine households share three different names.[22] Among all of the Canadian Amish Mennonite congregations which existed in the 1880s, only a few of the members of the Wellesley and Mornington districts dissented from the majority. In maintaining the older traditions, including home worship, they became known as the "House Amish" and also as the *Holmesers*. Having only one resident minister and no bishop they maintained both social and religious ties to the Holmes County Old Order group in Ohio.

That the majority of Canadian Amish fami-

lies joined the progressive faction is not surprising. The 19th century European Amish in both Canada and the United States were different from the colonial Amish group. In the earliest years when greater cultural variations were tolerated, the differences did not seem so important. By the 1880s, however, Canadian society as a whole had changed so dramatically that the Amish were forced to scrutinize their rules and practices for membership. The gradations were numerous and often confusing to the outsider, but clear differences between the Old Order and the Amish Mennonite groups emerged at this point. By the end of the 19th century many of the Canadian Amish Mennonite congregations had joined with the organization of Mennonite conferences. From 1886 until the mid-20th century, when Old Order Amish families from the United States began immigrating to Canada, there were only two Old Order Amish congregations in Canada. Located in Wellesley and Mornington townships, these families severed formal religious ties with the Amish Mennonite groups in the area and pursued a more traditional lifestyle. These Old Order communities continued to grow in the early and mid-20th century at a slow but steady rate.

20th Century Settlements in Canada

Just as the 19th century Amish immigrants left Europe for economic and social reasons, a group of 20th century Old Order Amish families moved from the United States to Canada. A number of reasons prompted this move, including a more liberal policy on the part of the Canadian government at that time toward such issues as Social Security pensions, military service and public education. During the 1950s, when the American Amish were embroiled in some difficult disputes with local and national authorities related to the draft and schools, immigration to Canada seemed a viable solu-

(above) **Bars**
Waterloo County, Ontario, Canada, circa 1900–1910
made by Susan Jantzi (1867–1961) before her marriage at age 34
to Daniel Kuepfer of Perth County, Ontario.
Cotton • 62 × 71 • Private collection
(below) **Jacob's Ladder**
Mornington Township, Perth County, Ontario, Canada, circa 1936–37, made during that
winter by Lydia (Nafziger) Jantzi for her son who married in June 1937.
Cotton sateen, twill- and plain-weave wools; back is printed cotton turned over to form a wide binding • 72 × 84 • Private collection

tion for a number of Amish families.

Groups from various settlements in the United States began moving to Canada in 1953. The first new community was started at Aylmer, Ontario, and was followed by others in Sullivan Township in Grey County, Norwich and Lakeside in Oxford County and, more recently, by newer communities in Huron and Bruce counties.

These settlements are made up almost entirely of families who have moved from established communities in the United States, seeking to organize settlements with particular characteristics. They brought with them to Canada their own customs and material culture. Quilts made in Ohio or Indiana were packed up with other family possessions and carried along. Even quilts made in the 1950s and 1960s in Canada represent American customs rather than indigenous Canadian practices. Only the quilts made in the late 19th and into the 20th centuries in the Mornington and Wellesley area by the descendants of the 19th century European immigrants, can be described as being distinctly Canadian. These quilts share a few characteristics which separate them from the work of American Amish women.

Because the early Old Order Canadian community was so small we do not have a great number of accurately placed examples to examine. Until the 1880s Old Order families were indistinguishable from the rest of the Canadian Amish Mennonite community. The problem of identifying Canadian Old Order Amish quilts is further compounded by the way in which these quilts arrived in the hands of dealers and collectors. In discussions with pickers who bought most of the quilts out of Canadian homes, there seems to be a general confusion about the differences between the Old Order Amish, Old Order Mennonites and more mainstream Mennonite families. Because the Mennonite community is much larger than the Amish commu-

nity in Canada, the interest in Old Order quilts was much less developed than in the United States. As quilts were picked out of the homes there appears to have been a fair amount of mislabeling. In this case the power of the marketplace and the greater interest in Mennonite culture have obliterated much of the opportunity for scholarship or accuracy. The lack of a striking difference between late 19th century Amish and Mennonite quilts does, however, illustrate the cultural similarity between these two groups in Canada.

Among the early 20th century examples of Old Order Amish quilts, differences do appear more clearly. The prohibition against any widespread use of printed fabrics and the preference for block designs link the Canadian community to American Amish traditions.

Two elements stand out as distinctive features of Canadian Old Order Amish quilts. The first is the choice of fabrics. While plain-weave cottons and plain- and twill-weave dress wools are found in early examples, a more varied assortment of fabrics is evident early in the 20th century. The presence of brocades, rayons and decorative-weave fabrics, as well as a general lack of concern for any unified fabric selection, is striking. A single quilt may combine several different weights and types of material. The overall effect of this choice creates a less refined or less carefully crafted appearance. The quilting, although satisfactory, is more sparse than many American examples made in the same time period.

The second distinctive aspect of Canadian quilts is their frequent use of patterned fabrics for backings and occasional use of those fabrics on quilt tops as well. This practice exists in a few American communities, such as Kalona, Iowa, and in Lancaster, Pennsylvania.

By comparing the quilts of the Canadian Amish with those of their American cousins, one sees evidence that a shared tradition exists.

Quiltmaking in the Canadian communities, however, never seems to have reached the importance that it attained in the larger United States settlements. Like many of the smaller and less stable American communities the Canadians rarely moved beyond the most pragmatic and economical choices in quiltmaking.

Communities Founded in the 20th Century

New Amish settlements began in four different states during the first half of the 20th century. In the post-World War II era and again in the 1970s, the Amish population and the number of new settlements and church districts in existing communities throughout the United States jumped dramatically. Communities were begun in Missouri, Tennessee, Minnesota, Kentucky and New York, and many new settlements were also founded in different areas of Pennsylvania, Ohio, Indiana and Iowa.

For the most part, these new settlements were small and sometimes isolated communities which maintained strong ties to older, more established settlements. The community members brought with them to the new locations the social and symbolic practices of their "mother" communities. Many of the quilts found in these areas were actually made "at home" in Ohio or Indiana or Pennsylvania. In the 1920s and 1930s quiltmaking in these settlements was largely indistinguishable from that being done in the largest midwestern communities.

In 1910 a few Amish families established farms and a church district in Michigan. St. Joseph's County, which lies just across the state line from Indiana, was settled by families from LaGrange and Elkhart counties. The Michigan settlements were simply an outgrowth and extension of those in Indiana, and the quilts made here reflected the social and symbolic practices and the basic visual and cultural traditions of the Indiana Amish.

Diamonds in a Grid
Guthrie, Kentucky, circa 1940–50
Plain-weave cotton, cotton/rayon; backing is printed stripes • 75 × 87½ • Michael Oruch

Lady of the Lake
Wilton, Wisconsin, circa 1940 – 50, Mrs. John Yoder
Cotton sateen, cotton/rayon challis, cotton plain-weave • 63 × 71 • Eve Granick and
David Wheatcroft

151

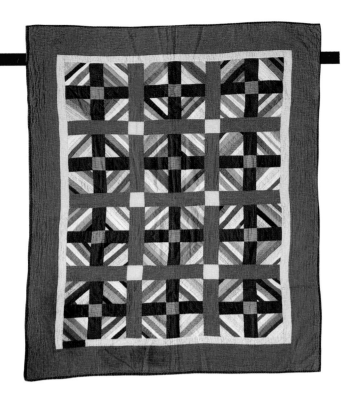

In 1915 a small community was founded in the area around Dover, Delaware. Over the years this settlement achieved a fair amount of growth as families from a variety of midwestern communities moved to Delaware and established farms. The standards for dress, buggy color and house styles found here are all related to midwestern practices. Quilts found in this community appear to be most strongly related to midwestern traditions of block and overall patterns.

In 1927 a small Amish settlement was started in Pinecraft, Florida. Considered primarily as a winter resort for older couples who wished to avoid the harsh weather of the North, the Florida community served as a seasonal retreat and provided opportunities for a great deal of socializing. Some rather un-Amish traditions developed in this winter settlement, such as eating out in restaurants and playing recreational games, but the primary bonds of the men and women who came here were to their home communities in Ohio, Indiana or Pennsylvania. Quiltmaking was practiced here solely as a social rather than a functional activity, and there was a great deal of interaction between Mennonite and Amish Mennonite women.

The fourth of the new settlements made in the early part of this century was in Wisconsin in 1925. Located near Medford in Taylor County, it was the only Old Order settlement in the state until the 1960s and '70s, when land at reasonable costs and a preference for isolated rural settings spurred a tremendous growth of Amish settlements in Wisconsin. Since 1960, 13 new communities have been started in various parts of the state. The Amish in Wisconsin are perhaps best known for their involvement in the historic Supreme Court case of 1972, *Wisconsin v. Yoder,* which determined that no state could require Amish children to attend public high school.

The settlement near Medford was founded in 1925 by families from various states who moved to Wisconsin in the 1920s and 1930s to establish a more traditional church. The first bishop of the community was from Haven, Kansas, and the founding families came from many of the states in the Midwest.

The quilts found in Medford and in the other areas of Wisconsin settled since 1960 (Cashton, Amherst, Wilton, Blair) were most often made in Ohio, Iowa or Indiana. Even those quilts that were made in Wisconsin during the 1930s, 1940s and 1950s are often difficult, if not impossible, to distinguish stylistically from those made elsewhere. Patterns, proportions and color all mirror the styles of the larger and earlier settlements. Only the quality of fabrics and sometimes the poorer quality of quilting really distinguish these Wisconsin quilts. No general or distinctive style developed in Medford; rather, this settlement and the communities which were founded later in the 1960s sought to preserve some of the most traditional values.

Despite the general conformity to plain sewing and simple quiltmaking styles in this community, a few particular women made quilts that are noteworthy examples of individual variation and personal expression.

Roman Stripe Variation
Wisconsin, circa 1940–50
Cottons • ESPRIT collection, San Francisco

152

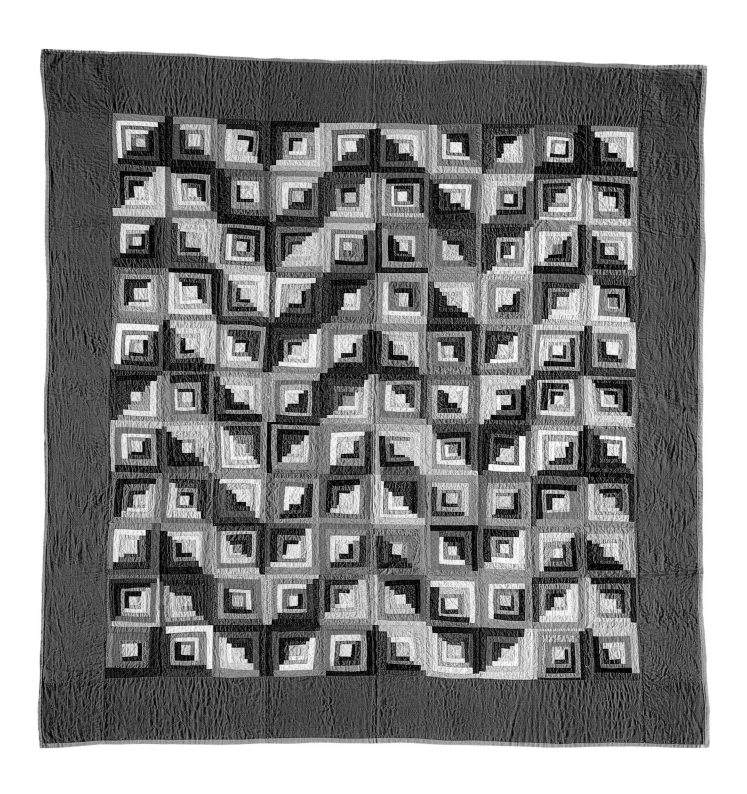

Log Cabin
Medford, Wisconsin, circa 1930–40, made by Mrs. Yost Miller (Barbara)
Plain- and twill-weave cottons, twill-weave wool • 61 × 65 • Eve Granick and David Wheatcroft

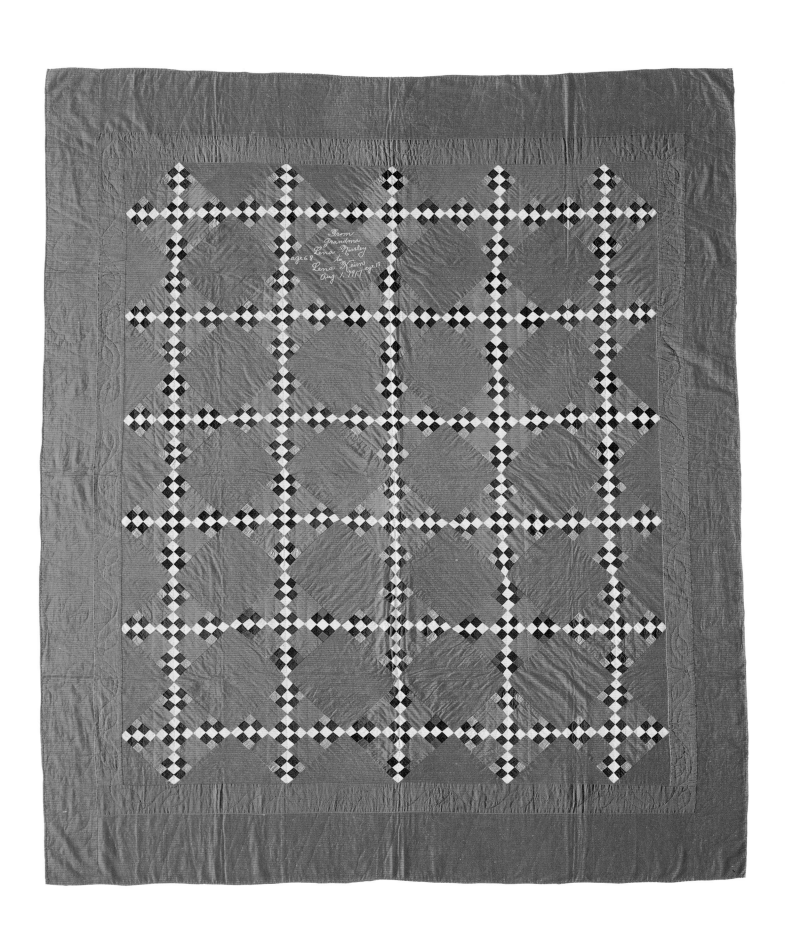

Miniature Nine-Patch Chain Variation
Hutchinson, Kansas, dated "August 1, 1917" • Signed: "from Grandma Lena Nissley age 68
to Lena Keim age 18" • Plain-weave cotton percale, polished cotton • 69 × 83
Eve Granick and David Wheatcroft

Quiltmaking: Its Part In Amish Women's Lives

Occasions for Quiltmaking

Since the late 19th century, Amish women have made and used quilts for a variety of reasons, and they have given or received quilts as gifts on different occasions. Traditionally, quilts were made for sons and daughters as part of their wedding portion. Most men and women were given at least one quilt as a gift, and many received two or three quilts at the time of their marriage. Occasionally a quilt was given to a young woman as a "namesake" gift —from an aunt or grandmother to a girl who shared her name. Namesake gifts were more often smaller remembrances such as a dress, a piece of china or a pincushion, but quilts, too, were passed from one generation to the next as tokens of affection.

Quilts made for everyday family use were often done quickly and simply, in some cases not even quilted but tied or knotted into comforts. Crib quilts were made for new family members and doll quilts for girls to use in their play.

In the 20th century the Amish adopted the "English" custom of giving quilt blocks or sometimes a finished quilt to a woman moving away from a community. Friendship quilts were usually made out of block designs with initials or perhaps a name embroidered in each block. In some of the more liberal church groups, embroidered floral designs or even Bible quotations were added. The embroidering of each friend's name and mailing address (including zip code) onto the blocks has been a clever and popular friendship quilt tradition since the 1950s.

Today Amish women continue to make quilts for weddings, babies and children; as a show of friendship; and for their own everyday use. In addition to these traditional reasons, they also make quilts for community fund-raising events, such as school sales or relief work. Finally, Amish women today make a vast number of quilts for a growing commercial market. Those women who undertake this work usually do so as a means of earning additional income for their families.

Among the Amish, quiltmaking has always been an activity for every age group. Young girls begin by piecing doll quilts. Teenagers usually piece their first full-size quilts and learn more of the rudiments of quilting. Before their weddings most Amish women produce at least one quilt to bring to their new homes. The quilts received at the time of a marriage are often a cooperative effort by the young bride herself and the other women of her family.

During the years when women are giving birth to children and raising their families, new quilts are necessary to replace those worn out by heavy use and repeated washings. Often at least one quilt is reserved for Sundays and guest use only. Some of the oldest quilts we have today exist because of this custom. They were special quilts made with extra care and given special

attention.

In the later years of an Amish woman's life, when her children are grown and settled, she has time again to devote to sewing and quiltmaking. Quilt tops, quilt patches and finished quilts are often produced in great numbers by grandmothers. Even a few men, when they retire from farming, have found satisfaction in different aspects of quiltmaking, from building frames to cutting templates to cutting and sorting piecework and, in some rare cases, to piecing and sewing quilts.

For Amish women, quiltmaking can be either a group activity or a job done individually. Quilting is a popular social activity and most women have fond memories of the quilting parties they have attended over the years:

> It was a really special day when mother had her sisters over for quilting. We girls did the cooking and we loved having all the aunts to visit.[1]

A quilting party is generally organized by a woman who has a finished quilt top that is ready to be quilted. About 12 people are needed to start the quilting on a full-sized top, and as the work progresses, fewer hands are used. To begin, the quilters sit around the four sides of the frame and work from the outer edges toward the center. When the women seated along the top and bottom have quilted as far as they can reach, the quilt is rolled and the number of spaces for workers along the sides of the frame decreases.

In general, a quilting requires "more than a day but less than two days."[2] One woman noted that, "if I do it myself it takes about two weeks of pretty steady work."[3] On the day of a quilting, the women arrive around nine o'clock in the morning and stay until about four o'clock in the afternoon. A dinner at noon is the obligation of the hostess. Another woman remembered quite fondly that in Iowa a popular quilt meal was cooked rice with raisin and ham.[4]

(above) **Log Cabin**
Indiana, circa 1900–20 • Plain- and twill-weave wool, cotton sateen
31½ × 37 • Eve Granick and David Wheatcroft
(below) **Ocean Wave with Star**
Topeka, Indiana, circa 1900–1910
Plain-weave cotton percale, muslin • 16 × 20 • Michael Oruch

Most of the women interviewed said that they usually attended only one or two quiltings a year. The choice of guests for a quilting can be organized along several different lines. On some occasions women invite only their sisters or cousins; at other times they extend the party to include neighbors and family. Only rarely are "English" neighbors invited to Amish quiltings, and in the early and mid-20th century Amish women generally did not attend "English" quilting parties. Quiltings are mentioned frequently in both *The Budget* and *Die Botschaft* (another national weekly newspaper for the Amish and Old Order Mennonite communities) with careful note of who attended and what work was accomplished.

Quilting is not the only traditional group activity among women in the Amish community. They also get together to do other sewing work and to help each other with moving preparations or major housecleaning jobs. Barnraisings and butchering are additional occasions for women to gather for work and social activity. At these affairs there are meals to prepare and children to supervise, as well as the opportunity to visit and catch up on small talk.

In addition to these family and neighbor gatherings, some communities have loosely organized widows' groups. Widows get together for sewing work or simply to visit. In the Nappanee, Indiana, area each woman in the widows' group has a "secret sister." At the beginning of the year each draws the name of another member of the group. During the coming year each woman is a special and secret friend to the one whose name she has drawn, giving gifts at holidays and on her birthday. At the end of the year, the name of each secret sister is revealed at a small party. One woman who spoke about this tradition had a tablecloth embroidered with the names of all of the women in her group.

These social activities are important ele-

ments in the lives of Amish women. They intertwine the pleasures of friendship and a sense of community with the principles of work and mutual support which are so important in Amish culture.

The Daily Life of Women

Every culture has certain expectations and obligations for both men and women. For Amish women, these specific expectations and standards determine their vocations, appearance, attitudes and aspirations for their entire lives.

By the standards of late 20th-century American life, the world of these women may seem limited and restricted. They have few personal choices to make aside from their decision to join the church. Nearly all other major issues are decided by the church and group norms. Women are wives, mothers or maiden aunts. They dress according to the stylistic choices of the community, whose rules are usually made by men. They learn about the care and maintenance of homes, cooking, cleaning, children and gardens. All of these skills are taught at a young age. The importance of hard work and willing submission to patriarchal authority are attitudes that are instilled by adult example into Amish children from early childhood.

There are many restrictions on the lives of Amish men as well, for Amish culture and community finds its strength in conformity and the maintenance of a traditional, agrarian and family-oriented lifestyle. The lives of Amish women and men are shaped by their individual submission to the group. Those who are unable to conform to this basic standard cannot stay in the community. Although these rules may seem highly restrictive to the outsider, the strength of group life provides real satisfaction and fulfillment for the Amish person. Life is tied closely to the cycle of seasons and work and to a large extended family and a supportive community.

In religious life, women are viewed as individuals with "an equal vote but not an equal voice."[5] A woman makes her own choice in joining the church, and she is considered an individual member. If her husband transgresses, is shunned or leaves the church, the wife is still considered a member in good standing unless she chooses to go along with her husband's actions.

In the sphere of daily life, women manage the family, seeing to all of the household affairs, including the care of children, cleaning, cooking, gardening, preparing produce for market, preserving and canning food and making clothing for all family members. Women and young adolescent girls also frequently help with the harvest and planting of crops. Women are responsible for the care and appearance of the lawn and the area around the house, including fences, walkways, grape arbors and flower beds. Many women put a great deal of effort and energy into this work. The sense of simple design and careful organization which is evident in Amish quilts extends to the arrangement of both the interior and exterior of Amish homes.

The yearly cycle of seasons governs the flow of work in an Amish household and farm. The winter months are the slowest time, since there is little farm work other than the care of animals. Women usually concentrate heavily on sewing and quilting during those months. As soon as the ground is ready to work in the early spring, gardens are planted. For women, spring also means a major housecleaning, and being on call to help in the fields with the planting of crops.

The late spring and early summer are times for tending gardens and yards, and when the garden produce begins to ripen, canning and preserving are done. This is the major work of the summer and requires much time and effort. Sewing is also done during the summer, and most women do a fair amount in preparation for the school year, which usually begins in late August. Canning continues until the first frost.

In the late fall, women do a second major housecleaning and prepare the gardens and houses for the winter months. November is the traditional time for weddings among the Amish; many couples attend four or five weddings in the space of a month. The Amish celebrate Thanksgiving and Christmas, although on a much different scale than most other North Americans. Both holidays are occasions for visiting, feasting and being with family. The Amish give few gifts at Christmas, and traditionally those are limited to young children. When the holidays end, sewing work resumes, filling the winter months until spring returns again.

Quilt Construction and Tools

The treadle sewing machine is a vitally important fixture in every Amish home. Even women who own the most modern sewing machine models operate them solely by foot power. Quilt tops are pieced most often on the sewing machine. When a top is finished and ready to quilt, the backing or lining material is prepared and laid on the quilting frame. Batting is laid over the backing, and the quilt top is placed over it. The three layers are then stretched into place on the frame and quilting can begin. Quilting serves both a functional and decorative purpose. It holds the three layers of the quilt firmly together, at the same time it provides dimension and design to the finished quilt.

Chalk, soap or pencil are used to mark the quilting pattern. Women usually have a collection of templates, generally made out of cardboard. Other quilting pattern tools can include kitchen utensils such as cups or bowls, coins or simply a ruler.

Many women prepare yard lengths of thread before starting to quilt. The thread is cut and laid aside until needed. Quilting begins by bringing the needle and thread through the back to the front, then pulling the end knot into the space between the batting and quilt top. Good quilters work rapidly, picking up the fabric with four or five stitches in one movement. The choice of needles varies: some women prefer "shorts"; others insist that "longs" make better quilting needles. Thimbles are useful, as is an emery bag to keep the needles smooth.

When the quilting is finished, the quilt is taken out of the frame and the binding is applied, either by hand, by machine or by some combination of the two methods.

Adaptive Behavior and Quiltmaking

In his writings on Amish life, John Hostetler identifies various ways in which individuals deal with the difficult goals of the Amish community and how they adapt to the Amish way of life. He writes:

> As in any community, rules and expectations vary among Amish members. Rules are not understood by all individuals in the same way nor are they emphasized with equal intensity in various districts.[6]

There are several different modes of behavior described in sociological models which illustrate different types of adaptation.[7] Three of the most common behaviors — conformity, ritualism and innovation — seem to apply very distinctly to the practice of quiltmaking among Amish women. These different behaviors can also help to explain why there are differences in quilts made in various communities, and why certain quiltmakers were acceptably exceptional in a culture which generally disdains individual achievement.

Conformity is the most common form of adaptive behavior in both Amish and non-Amish society. It describes the basic behavior of the majority of individuals who accept the expressed norms of the culture. Conformity also aptly describes the vast majority of Amish quilts. Throughout the United States, most Amish women in most communities used very standard patterns, colors and forms. The quilts they produced are beautiful examples of the typical Amish sensibilities of each era and of each community. These quilts are important additions to any comprehensive collection, and they are critically important to our understanding of Amish textiles.

The great variety that appears in Amish quiltmaking is indicative of the adaptive process. In settlements like Lancaster or Holmes County, where affluence and community stability developed, the acceptable standards for sewing and fabric selection, those to which most women conformed, were quite elegant. In other settlements, where the desire for a "plainer" church or the demands of farming in a more hostile environment were present, the rules called for a conformity to simpler and less refined standards.

The second pattern of behavior described in Hostetler's sociological model is ritualism and a tendency toward overconformity to the rules.[8] Communities that adhere to the very strictest interpretations of the *Ordnung* place great importance on the rigid adherence to ritualistic symbolism in dress, social behavior and even quiltmaking. The Nebraska Amish and the Swartzentruber districts in Ohio are examples of this greater-than-average call to conformity. In one community in Tennessee, ritualism and rule-making have affected quiltmaking dramatically. One woman who moved into the community was required to re-cover a quilt that had some red in it. The minister, in an attempt to return to "old-fashioned" standards, mandated

quilt styles that were far plainer than anything made by Amish women several generations ago.[9] Quilts made in this community use only dark greens, blacks, browns and dark blues in the very simplest patterns.

Though the Amish may appear as a solidly homogeneous culture, they are, in fact, like any group of people. Among them have always been the few individuals with unusual ideas and those who felt a need to create something different or wholly personal. While innovators accept the standards of Amish life and live easily in the community, they also feel compelled to use nonstandard methods to achieve their goals. Innovation plays an important role in the Amish community and the personal character of the innovator has a great deal to do with whether the innovation is deemed too radical or threatening, and therefore unacceptable. If the wife of the bishop in a community institutes a small change in the use of different fabrics or the use of a new pattern, it may then be judged

acceptable for other community members. In many communities, any woman whose place in the church is well established and who generally follows all the important rules is able to try something a bit different in the realm of quilt-making. Unlike some other areas of community life, this medium of expression appears in many settlements to have been a relatively uncharged arena. In one Indiana district, a woman mentioned that, "if we wanted to try a new pattern or color, mother wasn't that concerned."[10]

Today, as in the past, certain Amish women are prolific and sometimes innovative quilt-makers. Others are less interested or inclined. The interest and effort applied to quiltmaking seems to have run strongly in certain families and within particular communities. Quilts that rise above simple bed coverings or the general standards of Amish quiltmaking come in many forms. Some are very plain with slight but unique variations on an ordinary pattern. Others employ an unusually rich or subtle color

Unnamed Pattern
Tennessee, 1960s
Rayon, polyester, denim • 70 × 73 • Michael Oruch

scheme. Some extraordinary quilts express a strong measure of compulsiveness on the part of the quiltmaker, with the cutting and piecing of hundreds or even thousands of tiny scraps. The rarest of Amish quilts are those whose designs are the complete invention of the quiltmaker. Although they may depend upon traditional geometric elements, the final overall design is a unique and innovative creation.

Trends in Amish Quiltmaking

In most aspects of life the Amish have deliberately and consciously remained out of step with the general American culture, adopting customs and objects that have been abandoned and maintaining older forms many years after their disappearance from the larger cultural scene. Quiltmaking appears to be a striking example of this chosen cultural lag. In comparing Amish and "English," or American, quiltmaking over the last 100 years, definite trends emerge.

As already noted, we have no documentation of pieced quiltmaking by Amish women before the 1870s, and the evidence for any production of quilts in quantity only begins in the 1880s. By the time Amish women began making pieced

(above) **Bars and Nine Patch** • circa 1830–40
Cotton, chintz border • America Hurrah, New York City
(below) **Applique**
Somerset County, Pennsylvania, dated "1862," signed "Hannah Custer, Nancy Lehman"
Plain-weave cotton • 68½ × 85

Log Cabin
Massachussetts, circa 1880
America Hurrah, New York City

quilts in any numbers during the 1880s, other American women had been producing both pieced and appliqued works for decades. Other Pennsylvania Germans, including the Mennonites, embraced quiltmaking at least a decade or more before the Amish, revealing once again the inherent conservatism of Amish culture.

In the 1880s the Victorian age was in full bloom. In many American homes, simple traditional piecework quilts had been replaced by in-vogue Victorian-style crazy quilts, appliques and more complex piecework. The arbiters of American culture and good taste judged simple patchwork to be old-fashioned and boring. When the Amish finally embraced pieced quilts they appear to have deliberately chosen outdated and simple styles. In Lancaster, Amish women worked out variations of the Medallion Square. This design had been virtually forgotten after the 1850s by other American women. In areas outside of Lancaster County, Amish women concentrated on the use of simple and

(above) **Diamond in the Square**
Lancaster County, Pennsylvania • circa 1915–25
Plain-weave wool batiste • 74 × 75½ • Jonathan Holstein and Gail Van der Hoof
(below) **Central Medallion**
circa 1830
America Hurrah, New York City

repetitive block designs. This too was a design choice more typical of mid-19th century tastes than of the prevalent "English" styles of the 1870s and 1880s, when many women were experimenting with complex geometrics and embellished crazy patchwork. The Amish quiltmaker of the 1880s and 1890s generally selected fairly basic patterns, a simple geometry and a rich but muted color scheme.

These choices appear to be purposeful ones on the part of Amish women, not the result of isolation or lack of knowledge about the fashions of the day. Many Amish families received a variety of farm publications, catalogues from Sears and Roebuck or Montgomery Ward, and local newspapers and magazines like *Farmer's Wife*. These newspapers and journals all advertised fabrics and offered quilting patterns and even precut quilting kits. In many communities, Amish women also had at least some contact with their "English" neighbors and they were quite aware of the types of quilts being made by these women.

Like the fashions for clothing, certain patterns in quiltmaking achieved tremendous popularity among the general American public for a period of years. Patterns came into vogue and then lost favor and were replaced by new preferences. These trends moved at various rates of speed in different urban and rural areas of the country, but the Amish quiltmaker tended to lag behind everyone by at least a decade or two. Log Cabin quilts, so admired by the general public from the 1860s until the 1880s, were not popular among Amish quiltmakers until the 1890s and the first decades of the 20th century. The rage for Victorian crazy quilts which swept America in the 1870s and 1880s was not in evidence among Amish quiltmakers until the early part of the 20th century. Even then, it was so muted in comparison that it is only a suggestion of the Victorian style. The increased use of black, particularly as a background, would seem

to be influenced by Victorian sensibilities.[11] Black cotton or wool was used for borders and backgrounds in place of the black velvet and silk materials so favored in American crazy quilts. Turkey track stitching appears in Amish quilts around the turn of the century, again an adaptation by Amish women of one element of the 19th-century Victorian quilt.

Other decorative textiles made by Amish women, such as pincushions, sewing favors and seat covers, also reflect the Amish woman's fascination with a style that had already been largely discarded by other American women.

In the years between the turn of the century and the 1920s, the sewing skills of many American women declined sharply. The ready-made fashion industry blossomed in this period and quiltmaking lost much of its traditional appeal and respect. New political and social issues diverted the attention of American women from the time-honored tradition of needlework.[12] Amish women, on the other hand, continued to sew great quantities of clothing and had little interest in gaining the right to vote or stopping the flow of alcoholic beverages. In these years the advances in the textile and

Four Patch Variation
Mifflin County, Pennsylvania • circa 1920–30
America Hurrah, New York City

chemical industries that resulted in the expansion of colors and types of fabrics available to the Amish seamstress spawned a burst of creativity in quiltmaking. Amish women continued to rely heavily on older, established design traditions through the 1920s and even into the 1930s, but they also elaborated on the old patterns with increasing attention to more complex designs and the use of new, richer and brighter colors.

In contrast to Amish quiltmakers, other American women in the post-World War I years turned to the use of pastel colors and increasingly modern designs, some of which were influenced by the Art Deco and Decorative Arts movements. Appliques also came back into fashion in these years and the use of quilting kits was extremely popular. Despite the huge popularity of these quilt kits and the successful marketing of patterns, Amish quiltmakers by and large ignored most of the national trends and continued to repeat family traditions and to rely on the old styles as a source of pattern design.

Quiltmakers in Lancaster were the most persistent of all Amish women. The use of a set group of patterns continued virtually unchanged in this community well into the 1960s. In other Amish communities less dedicated to tradition than Lancaster, or in those without explicit rules on quiltmaking, experimentation with pattern, color and fabrics began to appear in the 1930s.

It was during the late 1930s and in the 1940s that a number of substantial changes began to take place in Amish quiltmaking. The pastel shades so popular with American women in the 1920s began to appear in Amish quilts, and by the 1940s and early 1950s became widespread. The Depression of the 1930s and the shortages of fabric during World War II affected the quality of materials and indirectly the craftsmanship in Amish quiltmaking. Even in Lancaster, where traditions had remained so steadfast, these years marked a turning point. New materials, new colors and new quilting patterns with

Jacob's Ladder
Ohio, dated "Feb 14 1955"
Cottons • America Hurrah, New York City

fewer stitches came into use.

Following World War II, quiltmaking was virtually abandoned by most American women. But during these years the colors and quilt patterns that had been fashionable in American homes throughout the previous three decades became a part of the Amish quiltmaker's vocabulary. Even in these years, however, the traditional patterns continued to be used widely in many Amish communities, and in the most conservative settlements styles barely changed at all.

Though the art and craftsmanship of quiltmaking suffered somewhat of a decline among the Amish during the 1940s and 1950s, the basic traditions were maintained and many exceptional quilts were made, even in these years. During the 1950s and early 1960s, when quiltmaking was considered too old-fashioned and time consuming by most women, it still remained an integral part of Amish life.

There are, of course, exceptions to all of these general guidelines, but the tradition of quiltmaking among the Amish does appear to have progressed along a recognizable course during the past 100 years. The changes in Amish quilts are inseparable from the changes in Amish culture, and they are linked as well to the larger world of American cultural life. The vision and persistence of the Amish has helped to sustain and enrich the art of American quiltmaking and in recent years has played a large part in our renewed interest in quilts. Despite their small numbers and their restricted lifestyles, the contribution of Amish women to the art of American quiltmaking has been unique and far-reaching.

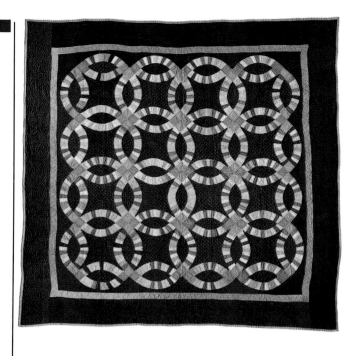

(above) **Double Wedding Ring**
Holmes County, Ohio • This quilt was made for Mrs. Homer Miller by her mother.
Plain-weave cotton percale, muslin, chambray, broadcloth, cotton sateen • 83 × 85 • Eve Granick and David Wheatcroft
Bars Variation-Crazy Chinese Coins
Wayne County, Ohio, circa 1930–40 • Made by Mrs. Valentine Shetler.
Plain-weave cotton, cotton sateen • 63 × 83 • Judi Boisson

Amish Quilts in Different Periods: A Summary

Pre–1870: Characterized by early fabrics. No pieced design. Extremely rare — perhaps less than five to ten known examples. Colors are "natural" browns, blues, rusts, blacks. Look for evidence of machine-sewing to help determine age.

1870–1890: Characterized by early fabrics, cottons, wools. Simple designs in piecing. Simple but saturated color schemes. Careful attention to quilting; increased use of intricate quilting patterns with many stitches.

1890–1920: Characterized by increased use of color and more complex designs; Log Cabin and geometric patterns popular. Fine materials and good to excellent quilting.

1920–1930: Characterized by further expansion of color and design elements; blue and white quilts in many communities. In midwestern communities an increased number of patterns and colors are used. Sateen fabric popular during these years.

1930–1940: Characterized by more liberalization in quiltmaking, more variety in color, patterns and choice of materials. Depression forces many women to use lower-quality materials.

Colors begin to lighten toward the end of the decade to pastel shades.

1940–1950: Pastels, new fabrics used; the war again forces Amish women to use new types of materials — rayons and other synthetic substitutions. Quilting is noticeably changed from earlier years, with fewer stitches and different, less complex designs.

1950–mid 1960s: Characterized by the use of polyester materials, larger piecework. Quilts are larger with less quilting. Quilts are still made for personal use in the home and still truly represent the Amish way of doing things. However, quilting skills have declined considerably since the earlier years.

1970–present: Quilt market expands greatly, creating a major effect on Amish quiltmaking. Amish women become heavily involved in the production of quilts for sale. Quilts made for the home vary a great deal depending upon the plainness of the church group. Many of the more conservative groups continue to make quilts in the old styles, using traditional patterns and colors; others use more up-to-date "English" styles.

Conversations with Amish Women

Much of the information for **The Amish Quilt** was developed from interviews with older women and men in different Amish communities. These oral histories are fascinating in themselves, but they also provide an expanded and personal picture of Amish lives in various communities during several periods. Each woman's story is both an individual one, as well as the story of the group. Here I present some of the information that surfaced in my interviews. These are excerpts from conversations in Pennsylvania, Ohio, Indiana and Iowa. I have indicated only a first name, as these women do not wish to be identified specifically.

Rachel — Born 1924 in Lancaster, Pennsylvania; married in 1944.

Katie — Born 1903 in Mifflin County, Pennsylvania; married in 1928.

Lizzie — Born 1894 in Holmes County, Ohio; married in 1921; moved to Geauga County, Ohio, in 1921.

Maude — Born 1903 in Elkhart County, Indiana; married in 1922.

Anna — Born 1918 in Geauga County, Ohio; married in 1942; moved to Lawrence County, Pennsylvania, in 1928.

Sarah — Born 1933 in Kokomo, Indiana; never married; family moved to Kalona, Iowa, in 1952.

Fannie — Born 1892 in Reno County, Kansas; married in 1912; moved to Shipshewana, Indiana, in 1937; remarried in 1967.

Mary — Born 1910 in Oklahoma; married in 1933; moved to Lagrange County, Indiana, in 1950s.

Lena — Born 1891 in Kalona, Iowa; married in 1912.

At what age did you learn to sew? Who taught you? How old were you when you began quilting?

Rachel: I learned to sew about the time I finished school, at age 12 or 14. My mother taught me. I started quilting around age 16 or so. I started on everyday quilts under Mother's instructions. She was particular about quilting and wouldn't let us girls work on good quilts until we were good at it.

Katie: I started sewing when I was in my teens. My grandmother taught me. I began quilting in my 20s.

Lizzie: I made a little quilt block at age four. I sat on a little rocker and sewed by hand. My mother pinned it for me. I was a proud little girl. I began quilting in my teens.

Maude: I learned about age eight or nine years old. I was so proud I could sew. My mother taught me. I was the oldest girl so we made all the clothing for my younger sisters and brothers. I remember Mom said, "You're big enough; you have to start making your dresses." She cut it and I sewed it [age 13]. I began quilting about age 16 or 17.

Anna: My stepmother taught me to sew when I was about 12. I began quilting in my teens, 17 or 18. I made all my quilts before I was 21 [five quilts]. There were five boys in the family and I helped make quilts for them, two each.

Sarah: I was in grade school when I learned to sew. My mother taught me. I learned to quilt before I learned to piece. I was so much a tomboy, Mom had to use strategy to get me to piece a quilt, so she let me use the light colors. I pieced my first quilt sometime in grade school and made all my quilts before age 21. I didn't sew dresses for myself as early as others.

Fannie: I learned to sew just about age 12. I was sickly as a little girl, so I didn't go to school at first. I was about 13 or 14 when I began quilting, and maybe 16 or 17 when I pieced my quilt tops. There were eight children in the family. I was in the middle and I helped on lots of those quilts too.

Mary: I was six or seven when I first started on little things. My mother helped me. I was 15 or 16 when I began quilting. The first dress I made around age 14 didn't fit too well. I had to tear it apart quite a bit to get it right.

Lena: I was just a young girl. Mother made me sit on a little bench by her rocking chair and practice buttonholes. She cut out the hole and then gave it to me to finish. When I was done she looked at it and then gave me a little bop on the cap saying, "That looks like a hog's ear!" Then she made me try again. I never cared too much for sewing. I learned to quilt about age 16 or 17.

Where did you purchase your fabrics, thread and batting for quiltmaking and clothing?

Rachel: We bought from Sam Greenburg when he came door to door. Also Isaac Korsh. Sam Greenburg had really nice colors for wedding dresses. We bought thread, batting and material from Sam Rubinson. The batting came in blue wrappers. Mom bought it from W.L. Zimmerman in Intercourse, too.

Katie: We mostly bought from Watts store in Belleville. Some from Greenburg and the others who came door to door. We bought by mail order from Montgomery Wards and Sears too.

Lizzie: We bought materials in Middlefield. We sent to Montgomery Wards for needles. Also Sears & Roebuck — they'd send out catalogues after the holidays. I'd wait to buy my goods until after the holidays. Their quilt batting came in sheets and we liked that. There was also the Spector's in town too.

Maude: We bought our things in Nappanee at the old Ringenburg store. We bought from Sears in the '20s and from Garver Brothers in the 1940s and '50s. I've bought from Spector's

Spiderweb Stars
Holmes County, Ohio, dated "1898," initialed "EH"
Plain-weave cotton percale, chambray, cotton sateen, twill-weave wool • 63 × 76
Eve Granick and David Wheatcroft

for the past 25 or 30 years.

Anna: We bought at the general store in New Wilmington; also in New Castle. We'd shop when we went to sell eggs there. When I still lived at home we bought from Spector's. I didn't buy much from Greenburg; he didn't have the goods I wanted. We sent to Garver Brothers and also occasionally to Gohn's. Sears & Roebuck had good percale and shirting goods and we sent to Montgomery Wards sometimes.

Sarah: Mostly we bought our thread and batting in town. Fabric we sent to Spector's and Garver Brothers or Gohn's. When Sam Greenburg came door to door in Indiana we bought from him.

Fannie: In Kansas we bought things at the local store in town — the Roaraboll and Wiley Penny store. Batting was a lot thinner; you just laid it together. You could get dark or white batting but we got white. We bought a lot from Sears and Montgomery Wards. Later on I bought from Spector's after we moved back to Indiana. When Sam Greenburg used to come in the early 1960s my husband would go around with him door to door selling.

Mary: Mom bought a lot from Dembusky and from Garver Brothers. We also bought from Gohn's and from Sam Greenburg. This was all in the 1940s. In the 1950s I know I bought a lot of batting from Mountain Mist Company. I also ordered from Montgomery Wards.

Lena: We bought things in Kalona. I never ordered from mail order.

How many quilts did you and your husband get from home when you married? Who made these quilts and what happened to them?

Rachel: I had four quilts — a Cape (Diamond in the Square), a Bars, a Nine Times Around the World and a rayon spread. My husband had two quilts — a Cape and a Nine Times Around the World. They were made by the mothers and they were used up or sold.

Katie: I had four quilts; my husband had one. One of mine was a striped quilt made of cottons. It was an older quilt and Mom gave it to me. I don't know if she even made it. I also had an embroidered quilt I made in 1928, a Sunshine and Shadow and Grandmother Yoder's quilt. That was red and hair-striped goods. She made one for all us girls when we were teenagers. Those quilts were made by my mom and grandmother. I was too much of a tomboy. I did like the embroidery work; those were popular among the girls then.

My husband's quilt was the same pattern as Grandmother Yoder's but in different colors.

Lizzie: I had four quilts; my husband didn't have any. I had a Nine Patch with all different colors and a gingham blue background. I had one called Toad in the Puddle that was medium blue and pink and one Necktie made out of lots of different colored wools. I also had one spread that I got by selling Larkin goods; that was the premium for selling a certain amount of soap. The quilts were made by my mother and by me. I never had any with black background and for linings I preferred gingham (chambray). I used them up. The Necktie I kept for good and still have.

Maude: Just one; my folks weren't too well-to-do. Mom had 10 children and each child got one. My quilt was a flower basket done in lavender, blue and green. The lining was made of shirting chambray and the quilting was just diamonds and a twist in the border. We were

married in 1922 and it wasn't until 10 years later, in 1932, that my husband got a quilt from his folks. It was a Nine Patch with a lot of different colors made out of cotton. It had a lavender border. My younger sisters had a little more fancy quilts than we had. I helped piece them and quilt. They all got used up or sold.

Anna: I had five quilts, and my husband had three quilted ones and two made out of heavy flannel. My quilts were a Railroad Crossing that came from my mom's family (multicolored, dated 1888), a Star quilt made out of blue and black sateens, a Necktie, a Rocky Road to California and a Cup and Saucer. Joe had a Jacob's Ladder out of blue and black sateen, a blue and lavender cotton star, and one with lots of little pieces put together pretty in percales. The flannel ones were Nine Patches. His mother made his quilts.

For my quilts the stars were really Mom's friendship patches from when we moved from Ohio. After Mom died my stepmother helped me put them together for a quilt. She helped me make all my other quilts too. The Rocky Road pattern I saw at my girl friend's and decided I wanted one like that so we pieced it. We used up the quilts; one of my husband's we gave to our son when he got married. The Cup and Saucer I gave away to a family who had a fire, and I sold a few.

Sarah: I had four quilts: a Four Patch made from feedsacking with a white background, an Album Patch that had a lot of turquoise, a Flower Garden made from dress goods that was multicolored with a green maze, and a yellow and white Maple Leaf. I was the youngest of six kids. In our family the girls could have four quilts if they pieced them, and the boys had three each. I kept all my quilts for good.

Fannie: I had five quilts and my husband had two. We were three girls in our family and five boys. Each one got five quilts. My best quilt was a Ring or Garden Maze. It was blue and green with feather quilting. I had a Plain quilt with three narrow borders; I think a Bear Paw, too, and a Nine Patch. We had a Star and Ocean Wave from his mom, and I made my own quilts. They all were used up.

Mary: I got three quilts and he had four or five. He had a Plain quilt, one that was blue and pink, one that was dark blue and white, and also a Jacob's Ladder that had a bright orange back. The quilts were made by my mother and other relatives and they got used up. Some were sold, too.

Lena: I think I had 10 quilts and my husband had three. Each of us had a white quilt with pink for good and dark quilts for everyday use. They were mostly greens and blues. My best quilt was a Basket. It was pink with different colors and the lining was white with black dots. They were all used up.

In the past, what fabrics and colors did you use for quiltmaking? What did you like best?

Rachel: We used batiste wool and cashmere. Fine wool is best because it sews the nicest. Later on we used rayons and crepes, whatever was available. Crepe and rayon weren't so nice; they faded a lot and the material would shrink in the wash. I liked green, purple and blues.

Katie: We used percale and gingham.

Lizzie: I used broadcloth or anything that was good for quilting. I'd look for something soft. I always had a lot of blue; I liked that best of all. For the quilt linings I preferred gingham.

Maude: Mostly chambrays and cottons, sometimes wool. I liked the Soisette; it was finer and we liked that a lot. I also used lots of feedsacking for shirts, linings — everything. I liked blue,

but we didn't have a lot of choice; we just had to take what was left over [from dressmaking].

Anna: I used straight cotton and feedsacks a lot. I cleaned hundreds and hundreds of those for bedding, towels and clothing. We'd get 10 cents apiece if they were returned [to the company who supplied them] in good condition. I'd send back the good ones and keep the torn ones for sewing. During the war it was really hard to get dry goods. For color I had mostly blue and lavender — just what we wore for clothing. We didn't use much green, orange or pink, nothing too bright. For the backs I liked dark blue percale, or just generally any color percale was good.

Sarah: We used cottons, mostly. For color I used lots of different ones.

Fannie: The best was chambray and ginghams for the linings. Also feedsack for everyday quilts and lots of different cottons. We also used scraps from wool dressmaking sometimes. I liked lavender, blue and green. We didn't use too much black, and when we lived in Kansas you weren't supposed to use too much pink. The bright red we would purchase specially for a quilt. We had lots of blue, too; dress lining was usually blue.

Mary: Indianhead and percale were good quality. They washed well and lasted. We used feedsack and broadcloth and gingham. I liked Indianhead and percale, especially green Indianhead. When I was younger I liked the lighter colors for quilts; now I like the darker ones better.

Lena: We used lots of different things — cotton, gingham, wools and all different colors.

When you made a quilt, how did you decide on the pattern? What quilting patterns did you like? Where did you find the patterns?

Rachel: I like the Cape (Diamond) and Sunshine and Shadow best, and for quilting, feathers or baskets. I really liked the feathers best. The patterns were copied from old quilts, the same patterns my mother used for her quilts. Sometimes we'd get a pattern from a magazine or the paper.

Lizzie: I pieced a lot of different ones — Double T, Stars, Toad in the Puddle. Nine Patches is the easiest. For quilting we used straight lines, and we had a twist at home. For a plain quilt we used a feathered ring. Mother had lots of patterns and sometimes we'd find one in a magazine or the newspaper.

Maude: For sewing, it was easier to use patterns with squares. I liked the Ocean Wave — I thought that was pretty. For quilting, twist was good or diamonds. Later I used some fancier ones like feathers. My patterns I got from my mom's quilts and different ones in my family. I would trade patterns with friends, too. Once my mom saw a pattern in the *Farmer's Guide* and when I was home she got me to make a bigger pattern from the picture in the paper. I went up there one day to visit, and we cut out four or five different patterns and laid them away.

Anna: We had a box with different designs; you just picked out whatever fit for the quilting. Usually you wanted to have all different designs on the quilts. For the quilt patterns I traded some with my friends.

Sarah: I learned to like the same patterns my mother had. I just chose the patterns that appealed to me. Mom liked Maple Leaf and Drunkard's Path and Dresden Plate. We had an "English" neighbor [when we lived] in Indiana. Mom had a pattern from her we always called the "Ella Strebben" pattern. For quilting, we used fiddlehead fern a lot and *fleur de lis*. I used a lot of kitchen utensils for marking off quilting designs — bowls, cups and different kitchen tools. We got some patterns from magazines, too, and from trading with friends.

Fannie: [I chose] from my mom's quilt patterns and sometimes from a newspaper or neighbor. We used feathers and tulips for the quilting. I liked Star quilts and Garden Maze. One of my favorites was an Irish Chain.

Mary: Some of the patterns were from my mother. I got patterns from magazines and the newspaper too. I used to get *Farmer's Wife* and Mountain Mist Quilting Club patterns. I like the Lone Star pattern and Irish Chain.

Lena: I liked the Basket pattern the best. My quilt patterns came from my mom's quilts. We had so many patterns it's hard to remember.

In making a quilt did you purchase new materials, use scraps from other sewing or use goods from old clothing?

Rachel: For the back or larger pieces sometimes you had several yards left over from something else to use for a quilt. Otherwise you had to buy some new goods. We used scraps for the Sun-

Mexican Cross
Holmes County, Ohio • circa 1930–40
Plain-weave cotton, rayon, chambray, sateen
73 × 76½ • Judi Boisson

shine and Shadow quilts. We never used old material, except recently for crib quilts to sell.

Katie: For good quilts we bought percales or gingham goods. Otherwise we'd use scraps from sewing and old goods, especially for comforts.

Lizzie: We bought new material only for the border and backs. I remember Mom bought goods sometimes for the fill blocks too. Otherwise we used scraps, or if old goods weren't too worn out to make an everyday Nine Patch.

Anna: We didn't buy new material very often. I bought enough for a two-color quilt for each of my girls. Mostly we used scraps. We'd put them into a box and pick from there. We never used goods from old clothing.

Sarah: Sometimes we bought new material. My mom loved fabric, and since we lived in Iowa I worked out and had a chance to get blocks and different fabric for her. We used a lot of scraps from sewing work and maybe some old clothing for a comfort.

Fannie: We bought new material for the lining and borders or special colors like red. We used the scraps from dressmaking but not much old clothing; it was too worn out.

Mary: We bought new materials and used scraps.

Lena: We bought new material for the backs. For the blocks we used scraps. For an everyday quilt or comfort without much pattern, we used old clothes to make wool comforts.

Did you ever dye fabrics at home?

Rachel: We used Perfection dyes for redyeing faded clothing.

Katie: We used Perfection dyes for old clothes.

Fans
Lancaster County, Pennsylvania • Dated "1938," initialed, "M.S."
Plain, twill and creped wools, colored embroidery thread • 82 × 83½
Jonathan Holstein and Gail Van der Hoof

Lizzie: At home and later after I got married, I used Perfection Dyes, mostly dark green and blue for feedbags. We'd make quilts and clothes for relief.

Maude: I used Putnam's for clothes that faded. Sometimes if we bought really cheap goods and I didn't like the color, I'd dye them. And sometimes we dyed some white muslin.

Anna: We used Perfection dyes, mostly for feedsacks, to make them dark red or blue, and we'd add salt to hold the color.

Sarah: We used RIT for faded clothes and some for feedsacks.

Fannie: We used Putnam's for old dresses that faded. [Fannie's husband, who added his comments to the interview, noted here that he had heard about his grandmother making home-made dyes.]

Mary: We used Diamond Dyes for faded clothing.

Lena: We used Putnam's for faded clothing.

How many quilts do you think you've made in your life?

Rachel: I had seven boys — I made three for each of them — and one daughter — I made four for her. Also, I made some later after I married, for myself, and probably 20 or 30 quilts in the past years for selling.

Katie: Only really the one embroidered one for myself. I helped with lots of others, but I always said if I ever have a house I'm not making quilts.

Lizzie: I can't even think of how many. Maybe a hundred?

Maude: Maybe 18 or 20. I made five for the children and then some after. Quilt tops I've made over 100. One winter I made 21 tops and gave them away. I made about 10 crib quilts to give away.

Anna: I have two girls and I made each one three quilts out of cotton and two from flannels. For the girls I made a Basket, Sailboat and Necktie. For my son I made the same. In all, maybe 15 or 20 quilts, a half dozen comforts and a few crib quilts.

Sarah: I've made about 12 for myself over the years. I've pieced hundreds of quilt tops to give away and done a lot of quilting for selling.

Fannie: With quilts and quilt tops, maybe not far from 200. I made 30 for the grandchildren.

Mary: I pieced a lot more than I quilted, probably 30 quilts in all — three for myself, one for each of my three sons and three for each of my three girls. And then some others when my first ones wore out.

Lena: I can't remember.

After talking about themselves and quilt-making, the women turned to conversation about their mothers and grandmothers. Each of the women could remember some things, but their answers were more general, and these questions seemed to start them talking about how things were when they were children. Here is summary information from the conversations that relates to quilts and textiles.

Rachel — Her mother was born in 1898 and married in 1918. Her grandmother was born about 1874 and married in 1895. Both lived their entire lives in the Lancaster, Pennsylvania, area. Her mother had a purple batiste wedding dress, and her grandmother's wedding dress was dark blue and plum, also batiste wool. Among her mother's quilts were a Diamond, which was her best Sunday quilt, and a Sunshine and Shadow and an Irish Chain. She also had a Bars quilt, which they used for everyday. Her mother made each of the seven girls in the family four quilts, and the two boys received two quilts each.

Katie — Her mother was born in 1874 in Mifflin County, Pennsylvania. Her two grandmothers were also born in Mifflin County, one in 1839 and one in 1854. She remembered very little about her mother's quilts but did mention one quilt that her grandmother had made of all different colored cottons — red, green, blue, black and gray. Her grandmother had a chair that had been made out of part of a spinning wheel, which she always thought was funny. Her mother had eight girls and she made each of them two or three quilts when they married. When she was a child they had rope beds with chaff ticks on them.

Lizzie — Her mother was born in Holmes County, Ohio, in 1855 and lived on the same farm almost all her life. She married in 1882. Her mother's wedding dress was dark plum cashmere, and Lizzie wore the dress later on. Her mother had many different quilts: one made of stripes of cashmere and serge wool with diamond quilting in it, as well as a Stars quilt and one *debbich* in light blue, dark blue and white. Her family also had a rope bed with a straw tick that they would refill each year. Her mother talked about spinning wheels but never used them. There was a mill near their home in Ohio and they did take wool there for fulling and weaving. This wool was made into a smooth fabric they called homespun. Lizzie recalled that her mother was quite a quilter, and during each winter they always made one or two quilts.

Maude — Her mother was born in 1882 in Nappanee, Indiana, and married in 1900. Her dad's family came from Ohio and moved to Indiana in 1852. When her mother married in the first years of the 20th century, she wore a rust colored cashmere dress. The dress was later given to Maude's sister who made it into a comfort. Her mother didn't have many quilts put away, just the ones she got from home in simple patterns and different colors. They were mostly Nine Patches. Maude's grandmother also had simple quilts made out of scraps into Nine Patches, and they also had a *debbich* with a pattern in blue and dark blue.

Maude remembered her grandmother "dressed sloppy, she wore her cape funny and it was also very big." The bonnets were bigger and quilted for wintertime. The children had navy blue bonnets. "I wore a slip that was homespun — it was scratchy — all red wool and made by my grandmother." Maude noted that her grandmother also had a spinning wheel, though she never saw it used.

Anna — Her mother was born in Holmes County, Ohio, in 1891. She married in 1915 and moved to Geauga County, Ohio, where her husband lived. Her mother died in 1931, when Anna was 12. She remembers only that her mother told her how her grandmother (Anna's great-grandmother) used to make quilts by hand.

Sarah — Her mother was born in Hutchinson, Kansas, in 1892 and married in Kokomo, Indiana, in 1917. Her grandmother was born in Holmes County, Ohio, in 1865 and married there in the 1880s. "Grandpa was a pioneer — he moved to Kansas, then to Minnesota, then to Michigan, to Oregon, and finally back to Kokomo." Sarah's mother wore a gray and blue cashmere wedding dress when she married. One of her mother's quilts that she remembers was a blue and white Wild Goose Chase with "1915" embroidered in the quilting. Her mother and grandmother were both big quiltmakers, and Sarah felt that her mother made a lot more quilts than other women generally did. She mentioned also that her grandmother used tiny printed calico fabrics when she lived in Indiana. "My family was not quite as conservative, but they were Old Order Amish."

Fannie — Her mother and dad were both born in LaGrange County, Indiana, in 1865 and 1862. They were married in 1885 in Kansas. Her mother wore a copen blue cashmere dress for the occasion. She had several quilts, but the only ones Fannie remembers well were a Geese Feet in yellow, green and light blue, and a quilt with small stars and plain blocks in between. Her mother had 11 children and the first ones each had five quilts from home. The youngest ones didn't want quilts, and they had spreads.

Fannie remembered a great many things about her grandmother. Like some of the other women, she also mentioned that her grandmother dressed differently, "really old-fashioned. She always wore her dress cape tied around the back or pinned in a strange way. The aprons were shorter and bonnets were much larger than now. In the summer they wore a blue cotton bonnet instead of black." Fannie also mentioned as an aside that her grandmother smoked a pipe, as did many other older women, and "we thought that was filthy." One of the quilts Fannie remembers seeing at her grandmother's house was blue, brown and green with a little bit of yellow.

Fannie's husband added some of his own comments about the old days, which are reflective of 19th century Indiana Amish life. His grandfather came from Somerset County, Pennsylvania, by walking and hitchhiking during the Civil War. He was trying to avoid registration, something which drove many Amish men further west in the 1860s. Fannie's husband remembers when grown men came to church barefooted, wearing hats with broad brims, wider than anything seen today, and a flat crown.

Mary — Her mother was born in 1878 and married in 1904. Her grandmother was born in 1862, and her great-grandmother in 1832. When her mother married in 1904 she wore a cashmere dress. After their marriage her parents left Indiana and moved to Mississippi. In fact, many of Mary's relatives were involved in the attempt to begin a settlement in Mississippi in 1898. When the settlement failed, they then moved to Kansas.

Mary remembered that her mother had a friendship quilt that was black and multi-colored—a Broken Dish pattern—made for her when she moved to Mississippi. Her grandmother had several quilts and also a handwoven coverlet. One quilt was an Ocean Wave and another was a single large Variable Star made out of red and green wool. Her mother also had a Fan quilt with turkey track embroidery stitches.

Mary's husband described a friendship quilt that his mother had, as well as one that he used as a child that was dated "1916" in the quilting. Mary's mother made three quilts for her when she married, as well as one for each of her three sons and three for the other two girls in the family.

Lena — Her mother was born in the 1850s in Cambria, Pennsylvania (Somerset County). Her father was from Holmes County, Ohio. Her mother moved to Iowa at the time of her marriage in the 1870s and lived there the rest of her life. Lena remembered only one of her mother's quilts, which was simply squares made out of brown and dark green wools. Her grandmother also smoked a pipe and wore great big capes.

Lena's mother learned to spin when she was young, and her grandmother used the spinning wheel and made her own fabric. Her mother had six boys and two girls. She made each child six quilts.

After talking with the women about their families, the interview shifted back again to the community and quilting in the past.

Are there patterns or colors that are not permitted by your church? Were there rules about quilting now or in the past?

Rachel: Not really. We just made quilts like the ones we had at home. Some say you shouldn't use white.

Katie: Just that we couldn't use any print goods when I was little.

Lizzie: Not for quilts, I don't know of any. But for dresses you couldn't use red. Dark red was okay, but not red.

Maude: Nothing too fancy. I remember when some wanted to go into the store and buy material by the yard and cut it up — they said that was wrong; you should just use your scraps. As far as colors, nothing too flashy and never white. In the 1930s and 1940s I remember seeing quilts that were too fancy in some houses. I remember once I just said something about it like, "Well, if you like a quilt like that."

Once a year the ministers had their gathering and discussed different rules. They said you shouldn't make dolls too real to look human. My dad was a preacher and we always obeyed. I remember when pink first came in for the Amish, but we always wore gray, blue, black, dark green and brown. You could use really fine print goods, just for little things like pincushions.

Anna: Just so it wasn't too bright colors. Usually we used what we had for clothing. In Lawrence County we don't use any white, but maybe it's okay in Geauga County.

Sarah: No, I never heard of any — well, maybe in some areas. There was a family here who moved to Canada and they had to get rid of an embroidered quilt.

Fannie: We were not to use too bright colors. My mother had a nice quilt with some bright yellow she had to sell 'cause it was too bright. This was in Kansas [before 1937]. Also, no print goods. My dad was a bishop and we were not to have things that weren't allowed — no pink, yellow or lavender dresses.

Mary: No real rules. Just certain things are liked and not liked. There are always some complaints about brighter colors and whites.

Lena: Not here in Iowa.

When you moved from one community to another did you ever have a quilt that had to be put away because it didn't fit in with the new community's rules?

Maude: There were some people who moved into a district southeast of Nappanee from Ohio. People used to say, "Such quilts as they have," because they were too fancy. But they weren't in our district.

Anna: Well, you would just have to sell it if it wasn't right for the community, or just not use it.

Fannie: This happened to my mother in Kansas.

Did you ever make a friendship quilt?

Rachel: No.

Katie: No.

Maude: Not in the old days.

Anna: Yes, it was a Christmas present for our school teacher. Also, when my brother moved to New York State we made patches. The receiver usually finished them later.

Sarah: No.

Fannie: I had a Basket Friendship quilt.

Mary: We made some for people moving away — just the patches. My mom had one and so did my husband's mother.

Lena: Yes.

Do you quilt and piece all year-round or more during one particular season?

Rachel: We quilt mostly in the winter. In the spring we're too busy in the garden. We also do some in the summer once things are in the ground.

Maude: I piece all year, but maybe it's better to quilt in the winter when there's less other work.

Anna: Only in the winter. In the summer there's not enough time.

Sarah: Just in the winter.

Fannie: I work on quilts usually through the winter and sometimes in the summer when we're not too busy.

What changes have you noticed in quilts and quiltmaking over the years?

Rachel: There is a lot more these days — it's a craze now. We just didn't make so many quilts years ago.

Katie: Now they wouldn't want the kind of quilts we had. They are much fancier today and bigger. We made ours just about two yards wide and two yards long, practically a square.

Lizzie: Quilts are fancier now. My mother disliked fancy things. She said just so it was made well.

Maude: Now they make them just like the outside. The patterns are fancier and they have different styles in the quilting.

Anna: Young people like two or three colors and a design with an overall effect. They don't like the block style — it's too old-fashioned. We didn't use as much black and we used lavender and blues. Today the colors are different, and dacron and polyester is more popular. They don't like the cotton battings.

Sarah: Today the quilts are much larger. Most families go for the lighter colors. When they see old styles they say, What an old ugly quilt. They like the puffy quilts with polyester batting and less quilting.

Fannie: We used more dark colors. Quilts are fancier now, but the quilting is not so fine.

Mary: The quilts are bigger and less quilting now.

Lena: The size is really different. They make them so big nowadays. Also, the quilts are a lot fancier now.

Fabric Glossary

Alpaca: Technically, alpaca is a hair fiber derived from the woolen fleece of Peruvian llamas. The word *alpaca* or "Alapaca" as Amish women often call it, has evolved to describe a particular fabric made from cotton warps and lustrous wool or worsted mohair or lustrous rayon fillings. The fabric is characterized by a plain weave, a lustrous sheen and its wiry or hairlike texture.

Alpaca was a popular fabric throughout the United States beginning in the mid-19th century, and Amish women used this woolen material primarily for dresses. It can also be found in quilts, but early quilts made with alpaca goods are often quite badly damaged, as it is a material that tends to stress and break with age.

Batiste: Named for Jean Baptiste, a French linen weaver, batiste refers to a type of fabric construction rather than a particular fabric. There are cotton, wool and synthetic batistes. The term refers to any fabric constructed in a sheer, fine, plain weave.

Batiste has been popular for many years; among the Amish it has always been a very widely used fabric. Wool batiste was used extensively for dresses and quilts in Lancaster. In the Midwest, both wool and cotton batistes were used for dresses and quilts in the late 19th and early 20th centuries.

Brilliantine: This fabric is described in various sources as a lightweight, smooth, wiry material similar to alpaca. It can be woven in either plain- or twill-weave, and it has a cotton warp and a lustrous wool or mohair filling. A heavier quality brilliantine, popular in the late 19th and early 20th centuries, was called Sicilian cloth. Brilliantine was used by Amish women through the early part of the 20th century for dresses and occasionally in quilts. Like alpaca it is not a fabric that ages well, and quilts with brilliantine are often damaged by brittle cracking and splitting of the material.

Broadcloth: *Broadcloth* refers to a large number of diverse fabrics, since it is a term used to describe fabric woven on a wide loom. The name *broadcloth* was originally applied only to wool fabrics, but today it also refers to cottons as well, principally shirting cottons.

Cotton broadcloth is a plain-weave fabric with a high count (a close, tight weave) and a fine fillingwise rib effect. It is usually mercerized and can be found in several weights and cotton/synthetic blends.

Wool broadcloth comes in both plain- and twill-weave. It is a fine or medium weight material.

After the weaving process, the fabric surface is finished by napping and polishing. This gives the fabric a smooth and lustrous appearance. Amish women have used broadcloth quite extensively for men's suiting, women's and children's clothing and in quilts to a lesser degree. Cotton broadcloth has a tight weave, making it

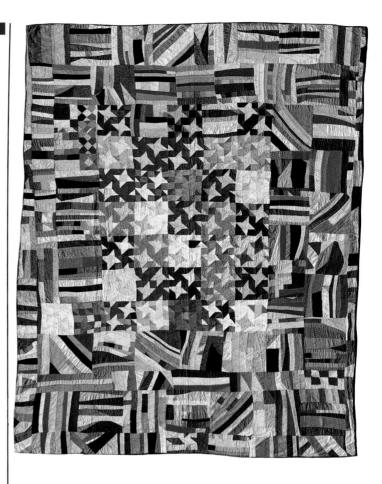

less desirable as a quilting material. Wool broadcloth can be found in quilts, but finer, softer wools were usually preferred for quilt-making.

Calico: Calico has a long and important history in America. It is usually thought of as a printed material, one of the staple goods of the 19th century pioneer woman. In fact, it is a general term for plain-weave cottons manufactured in many grades and varieties. Calico is a lightweight, low-count material, usually sized or finished for crispness.

Older Amish women named calico as one of the most commonly used materials in quilts, and they described it as being "usually not as wide as percale and cheaper." Amish women used plain colored calicoes for a wide variety of purposes. In some communities, printed calicoes were also used as backing material for such small items as pincushions or needle cases. Calico fell out of favor in the 20th century but has been revived as a popular fabric with the renewed interest in quilting and the pioneer way of life.

Cambric: This is another of the lightweight, plain-weave cottons. It is distinguished from batiste or calico by its smooth, soft, well-glazed finish, which is the result of calendering the woven goods. Calendering is the process of passing the cloth under high heat or pressure to

(left) **Nine Patch** • Mifflin County, Pennsylvania, dated "June 1899," initialed "J.T."
Heavy napped wool • 65 × 85 • Joan Fenton
and Albie Tabackman, Quilts Unlimited
Crazy Falling Stars • Indiana, circa 1945–55
Rayon, cotton • 63 × 82 • Judi Boisson

produce a surface texture. This finish washes out with repeated laundering.

Cambric was an inexpensive fabric used largely by Amish women for dress and vest linings. A lining was a necessity in a woolen dress which could otherwise be scratchy on the skin. In the 1930s and 1940s, as the use of wool for dresses became less prevalent among Amish women, the use of dress lining became less important. Other dress materials made of rayon and cotton blends were substituted, and cambric largely disappeared from Amish textiles.

Though cambric can be found in quilts, it was not a particularly strong or desirable material for quiltmaking. It is most commonly found in quilts with highly pieced designs.

Cashmere: True cashmere is a fabric woven from the hair fiber of cashmere goats mixed with other fine wools. The material has a twill weave with a soft finish and is a fine and costly material. The name *cashmere* has been applied incorrectly to many fabrics which are not really cashmere but are made to resemble it.

The material which the Amish have traditionally called "cashmere" is actually a fine soft wool done in a twill weave. This fabric is often also called "batiste wool," but the twill weave of "cashmere" and its slightly heavier appearance help distinguish it from batiste. "Cashmere" was a popular dress and quilt fabric during the late 19th and early 20th centuries. "Cashmere," like other woolen goods, became increasingly difficult for the Amish to obtain after the 1940s. In Lancaster, "cashmere" was heavily preferred for quilts, and it was a favorite for wedding dresses both in Pennsylvania and the Midwest.

Challis: This soft, lightweight fabric can be made of wool, cotton, rayon or a combination of fibers. Challis is made in both plain and twill weaves; it is distinguished from other fabrics by its fluidity and draping quality. Woven with fine yarns, it has a smoother, tighter weave and a more silk-like appearance and feel than batiste or percale. Challis is found more commonly in 20th-century Amish textiles. "Frosted" challis and dress challis made from cotton and rayon blends were particularly popular during the 1940s and 1950s in the Midwest, and these fabrics show up in quilts as well.

"Frosted" fabrics have been popular with many Amish women since the 1940s. Frosting is a way of enhancing a solid-color material by interspersing very small amounts of black, white or a colored thread throughout the fabric. A fabric of this type has the general appearance of a solid color but the frosting makes it just a little fancier.

Chambray: A cotton fabric in plain weave, chambray has a smooth and lustrous finish. Chambray is woven with colored warp yarns and white fillings. It can be made in cotton, rayon or polyesters. The white filling gives it a slightly frosted appearance which has always been popular with the Amish.

Chambray is a sturdy material and a staple fabric in Amish clothing and quilts. In clothing it is used for women's and children's dresses and aprons. In several communities blue chambray is used for men's shirting. In quilts it has been a popular backing or lining material since the 19th century. It is also interspersed in the piecework in quilts from all periods. Chambray was one of the most popular cotton goods available to the Amish seamstress. The most common chambrays were blue, brown, black, green and occasionally red.

Crepe: *Crepe* refers to a variety of fabrics and actually describes a particular fabric treatment or finish. Crepes have pebbly, crinkled or puckered surfaces as a result of treating the weaving yarn, or by using the calendering process on fabrics in finishing. Crepes range from sheer to heavy, but most are lightweight and either hard- or soft-textured. Crepes can be made in any weave but are generally done in the plain-weave pattern.

The Amish began to use crepe (or "creep," as many call it) only after the 1930s and 1940s. It can be found in both clothing and quilts, and the quality of the fiber mixture has a great deal to do with the strength of the material. Wool crepes began to appear in Lancaster quilts in the late 1930s and early 1940s.

Crepe can be recognized by its pebbly surface when compared to batiste or "cashmere." As wool became less available to the Amish, crepes in cotton, rayon and various mixtures eventually replaced the finer wools and wool crepes. The later materials are visually less appealing and less desirable as they did not hold dye colors well, and often the material itself disintegrated. Many Amish women commented that the rayon crepe goods were particularly difficult to wash and ruined easily. There were good quality crepes used in Amish sewing. It is the poorer quality materials, used generally in the 1940s and during the 1950s, that affect the appearance and market value of an Amish quilt. Crepe is less frequently found in quilts outside of Lancaster, where cotton and rayon/cottons were more popular for both dresses and quilts.

Dacron: This is the trademark name of the Dupont company for polyester filaments and staple fibers. Dacron is a condensation polymer obtained from ethylene glycol and terephtalic acid. It is not related chemically to nylon or acrylic fibers. The first commercial production of Dacron began in the early 1950s. Dacron and other polyesters achieved great popularity with the Amish, and by the late 1950s it was a commonly used material in clothing and quilts. Dacron and polyester had many attributes which Amish women liked. It was durable, easily washed, less likely to hold stains, and it resisted wrinkles. The quilt collector may not appreciate its use in quilts, but Amish women found it a superior fabric for their needs.

Flannel: Flannel is a loosely woven cloth of either plain- or twill-weave. There are many types of flannels made in cottons, wools and synthetics. The fulling or napping of the fabric generally obscures the weave on the front side, and flannel is usually identified by its softness and warmth.

The Amish have used flannel materials for a variety of items since the early 19th century. Flannel appears frequently in inventory and estate sale papers. It was an important clothing material, though not so widely used in quilts. Three types of flannel appear in Amish quilts from different time periods. Wool flannel, probably left over from suit- and dress-making, can be found in some of the earlier quilts we know of. These quilts are noticeably heavier in weight and usually quite simple in their design. Cotton flannel was used by Amish quiltmakers occasionally for backing or lining material. This was most common in Lancaster and in Kalona, Iowa, though examples do appear in other communities as well. Finally, cotton flannel sheet blankets were used in place of the batting in quilts from the 1940s onward.

Flax: One of the oldest textile fabrics, flax was a major fiber source until the early 19th century. Linen is the fabric product of flax plants. The growth, harvesting and preparation of flax for textiles was a lengthy process and a vital part of the Pennsylvania German culture. Among rural people, the Amish appear to have clung to this tradition for at least a decade or more after others abandoned it. Flax culture and the use of flax related textiles, even among the Amish, ended with the appearance of inexpensive cottons and wools by the mid-1800s.

Gabardine: This is a twill-weave fabric with a tightly woven and hard finished surface. The cotton and wool constructions are identical with a steeply angled twill. This degree of twill gives the fabric single, fine, close-set diagonal lines which appear only on the face of the material. The back has a flat appearance. Gabardine usually has a lustrous finish and it has a stiffer, more substantial feeling than other wool or cotton materials.

The Amish have long used gabardine for dresses and suiting. Both wool and cotton gabardine can be found in quilts from the late 19th century to the present day.

Gingham: This is another traditional, common and romanticized American fabric. It is a plain-weave cotton textile made in several different weights and qualities. The Amish used primarily the solid color or "novelty" ginghams for clothing and quilts. Traditional checkered gingham can be found frequently as the backing material in Lancaster quilts and, in some cases, as the quilt backing in certain midwestern Amish communities as well. Chambray is a form of gingham.

Glazing: Glazing is a finishing treatment for woven fabric. Starch, glue, paraffin or shellac are applied to the material, and then the fabric is run through a hot friction roller to give it a smooth, polished appearance. The glazing does not withstand washing and eventually washes out. The Amish used glazed cottons for dress and suit linings, and occasionally pieces appear in quilts.

Henrietta: Henrietta cloth was a popular American dress fabric in the late 19th and early 20th centuries. It was used widely to describe a variety of woolen fabrics. Traditionally, henrietta was a cloth of silk warp and woolen weft. By the late 19th century, however, the word had come to describe a number of lightweight, cashmere-like fabrics. It was made in both woolen and worsted woolen cloth. Some henriettas resembled cashmere with a high, shiny finish; others had a more salt-and-pepper appearance due to the different colored warp and weft threads.

The fabric most commonly described in Amish quilts as "henrietta" is the salt-and-pepper variety. This is a type of plain, solid colored fabric which actually had a slightly frosted and fancier appearance so popular with Amish women. This commonly used material disappeared from the market in the 1920s.

Indianhead: Indianhead is the trade name for one of the oldest plain-weave cottons made in America. It was first produced in 1831 by the Nashua Manufacturing Co. Indianhead has a porous plain weave, and the fabric often resembles linen, though it is not as stiff or lustrous. The fabric has a coarser, stiffer feel than either cotton batiste or calico.

The Amish purchased Indianhead goods for use in women's and children's dresses. It can also be found in quilts and seems to have been particularly popular among some Amish women in Indiana and Kansas.

Jean: This name describes a cotton, cotton and wool, or cotton and linen twilled cloth. It is a fabric name that appears everywhere in sources describing early American textiles. Florence Montgomery describes jean in her book, *Textiles in America,* as a linen/cotton twilled cloth of the fustian groups. Fustian is the general term for a large category of linen and cotton or, later, all-cotton textiles. The word "jean" appears frequently in Amish inventories throughout the 19th century.

Linen: Linen describes a wide variety of fabrics of different grades and weaves, all made from the fibers of the flax plant. Among Pennsylvania Germans, linen was the major fabric for household textiles, and it remained so until it was replaced by cotton in the mid-19th century. Linen was an all-purpose material used for every aspect of daily domestic life. The coarsest and simplest tow linens were made into seed and grain bags. Finer weaves were devised for clothing and bedding items such as sheets, pillowcases, bolster cases and curtains. The finest qualities were woven into tablecloths and used as the base for samplers and handiwork such as hand or show towels. All of these items are listed extensively in the inventories of 19th century Amish families.

Mercerizing: Mercerizing is another finishing technique, named after John Mercer who invented the process in 1850. Treatment involves impregnating yarn fibers with cold, concentrated sodium hydroxide solution. This increases the luster, stretch and dyeability of the cotton yarns.

Mohair: Mohair fibers are derived from the long, straight hairs of the Angora goat. These fibers are notable for their receptivity to dyes, their durability and color retention. Mohair fabric is a woolen material made usually from a mix of cotton or woolen warps and mohair fillings. Mohair fabric has a lustrous and silky surface, and it is fairly wrinkle and dirt resistant.

The material which Amish women often describe as mohair is actually quite similar to brilliantine or alpaca. Mohair was a popular dress fabric among Amish women, and it can be found in quilts from the late 19th and early 20th centuries.

Muslin: This is a generic term for a variety of plain-weave cotton fabrics. Muslin can be unbleached, bleached or dyed in various colors or prints. It is an all-purpose material with a long history in American domestic textiles.

Among the Amish, muslin appears frequently in 19th century inventories, particularly after the mid-century. Throughout the 20th century, muslin has been an important textile staple for Amish women. Particularly in the 1930s and 1940s, women depended heavily on such low-quality muslins as feedsacking, which was cheap (or free) and readily available. In quiltmaking, muslin has been used extensively throughout the 20th century.

Organdy: Organdy is not found in Amish quilts, but it is an important fabric for the Amish. Organdy is a plain-weave material woven with fine and tightly twisted yarns into a crisp, hard finished and transparent fabric. It is used by Amish women to make their prayer caps and in some communities for dress aprons.

Percale: This smooth surfaced and strong fabric is done in plain weave from medium-weight yarns. The finished material is usually slightly starched. Percale differs from muslin because of its high count, giving it a much finer, tighter appearance. It is also similar to cambric and calico but lacks the shiny finish or more loosely woven lightweight quality of calico. Percale was widely used by Amish women for quilts and dresses throughout the 20th century.

Polyester: This is the generic name for any manufactured fiber in which the fiber-forming substance is a long-chain, synthetic polymer. Fibers are made from coal, air, water and petroleum, which are cooked in a vacuum at a high temperature to a porcelain-like substance, then melted down to a liquid and forced through holes of a spinneret, which creates the filament yarns. The research to create polyester was begun in 1926 by the Dupont company. By 1946 Dupont had claimed exclusive American rights to the production of polyester filaments. The first major plant for filament production opened in 1950 in England, and by the mid-1950s Dupont owned the world rights for polyester production. The first uses for polyester were in men's clothing, but it was quickly incorporated in a wide variety of fabrics for use in blending and as a single-fiber fabric.

The Amish began using polyester materials in the late 1950s, and the fabrics appear in quilts from that time to the present day.

Pongee: True pongee is a plain woven, lightweight or medium weight fabric made from silk and cotton. Amish women used a fabric which was labeled "pongee" for dresses. This was actually a cotton fabric in a plain weave with a mercerized finish.

Heavier filling yarns than warp yarns create a fabric surface with irregular, elongated slubs. Pongee was a popular dress fabric from the 1930s onward and can be found occasionally in quilts.

Poplin: There are wool, cotton, rayon and mixed-fiber poplins. The chief characteristic of this fabric is its cord or ribbed effect, created by fine and closely spaced ribs that run across the surface of the material. Poplin was popular with Amish women for clothing and quilts, and it appears in both 19th and 20th century textiles.

Rayon: Rayon was invented in Europe in the 19th century and first exhibited at the Paris exhibition of 1889. It was not until the 20th century, however, that any wide-scale production or development of rayon materials took place.

Rayon is a generic term for fibers made from regenerated cellulose. The first rayons were called "artificial silk" and they gained quick acceptance. By 1910 American Viscose had established its first successful plant in Marcus Hook, Pennsylvania. Rayon hosiery began to appear in quantity on the market by 1912, and in 1916 the first knitted rayon fabrics for outerwear were produced. From 1925 until the appearance of nylon and polyesters, the rayon industry grew at a staggering rate, virtually supplanting the natural-fiber fabrics by the 1940s.

Fabrics made from rayon yarns are woven and finished in the same manner as natural fiber fabrics. They do have a different texture however, with a softer luster and a feel that is peculiar to rayon. Amish women used a wide variety of rayon fabrics in both quilts and clothing, particularly after the late 1920s.

Sateen: Sateen is a cotton or rayon cloth made in the sateen weave and usually mercerized. This fabric was widely used by the Amish for dresses, slips, shirts, children's clothing and quilts. It was particularly popular with midwestern Amish women from Ohio to Oklahoma. Although sateen was available in the earliest years of the 20th century, it generally appears in Amish quilts from the 1920s, 1930s and 1940s.

Serge: Serge is a twill-weave fabric that can be made of wool, worsted wool, cotton worsted and other combinations. It has a prominent diagonal line which is visible on both the front and back of the fabric. Most serge materials have a soft, smooth finish.

There are also several variations of serge based on the type of yarns used to weave the fabric. Storm serge is made of coarse yarns and is heavy with a wiry feel. French serge is woven from soft, fine yarns and has a more fluid and finer appearance. Cotton and wool serge were used by Amish women for clothing and quilts; these fabrics appear in both 19th and 20th-century quilts.

Endnotes

The Amish Church Community: Its Beginnings

1. Of particular importance are two conferences that were held in the 16th century and one in the 17th. The first took place in Schleitheim, a town on the Swiss-German border, in February of 1527. Anabaptist leaders met in secrecy to formulate the Schleitheim Articles. These Articles provided principles for the emerging groups and they are held to today by the Old Order Amish.

The second conference of the 16th century was held in Augsburg in August of 1527. This session was attended by leaders from Southern Germany, Moravia and Switzerland who met to formulate religious ideas and views; it later became known as the "Martyrs' Synod."

The third conference of importance occurred over 100 years later in 1632 in Dordrecht and was a meeting of Dutch and Old Flemish Mennonites. The "Dordrecht Confession" was developed at this meeting and then printed and widely circulated outside of the Netherlands in both French and German. Although the principles of this document are basically the same as those espoused in earlier conferences, two issues arose that were later to play an important role in the eventual schism that created the Amish — the *Meidung* or shunning, and the issue of ceremonial footwashing.
2. Hostetler, *Amish Society*, 33, 39, 40.
3. *The Mennonite Encyclopedia*, 1:90.
4. Trevor Jones, ed. *Harrap's Standard German/English Dictionary*. (London: Harrap and Co., 1974), p. 207.
5. Hostetler, *Amish Society*, 76, 77, 78.
6. Bender, "Some Early American Amish Mennonite Disciplines."
7. Reed, "The Amish — A Case Study in Accommodation and Suppression," 766–767.
8. Hostetler, *Amish Society*, 85.
9. Interviews with Amish women.

Gertrude Huntington in "Dove at the Window": "Joking about the *Ordnung* is a favorite pastime among the Amish and a feeling of camaraderie develops as each person makes a clever dig about something forbidden. One man pretends to turn on the electric light switch when someone walks into the room carrying a kerosene lamp or perhaps another teases the minister about how well he drives. They may tease one another about wearing brown shoes or buying a gold watch chain. They gently laugh at themselves for the rules they impose. They realize that the rules as such are really unimportant, but they are willing to follow it for many clearly understand that these prohibitions hold the church together" (66). "The Old Order of Amish of Ohio live in accordance to disciplines drawn up in 1568, 1688, 1838, 1865, 1917. These are published in two small booklets" (123).
10. The Amish express the gradation of strictness or rigidity of a community by referring to it as a "low church group" — the strictest — or as a "high church group," which may be affiliated with a Mennonite conference. Many gradations lie between these two extremes.
11. Author interview with Amish man in LaGrange County, Indiana.
12. *The Mennonite Encyclopedia*, 4:106.
13. The original German immigrants were former Mennonites who had been visited by Quaker missionaries in the Rhine Valley. They arrived in 1683 with Pastorius, who was the land grant agent for the Frankfort Land Company. Only one family of the original thirteen was still Mennonite, but others followed shortly, and the first Mennonite congregation was established in 1690. *The Mennonite Encyclopedia*, 3:136.
14. Swank, *Arts of the Pennsylvania Germans*, 3, 5.
15. Historical Statistics Bureau of the Census. Also Lemon, "The Best Poor Man's Country," 14. The population of the United States during this same period grew from 466,180 to 3,929,000. The first federal census was taken in 1790. Estimates from this census put the German population at 8.7% of the total United States population.
16. C. Henry Smith, *The Mennonite Immigration to Pennsylvania in the Eighteenth Century* (Norristown, PA: The Pennsylvania German Society, 1929), 240. This information is based on ship lists and tax assessment lists.
17. Lemon, "The Best Poor Man's Country," 14–15.
18. Smith, *The Mennonite Immigration to Pennsylvania*, 225–226.
19. By the 1720s the flow of Germans into Pennsylvania was so heavy that the English settlers grew alarmed and sought "protection against the foreigners." Smith, *The Mennonite Immigration to Pennsylvania*, 177. Benjamin Franklin also had a great fear of the Germanic immigration and complained in 1753, "Few of their children know English. They import many books from Germany . . . of the six printing houses in the province, two are entirely German . . . the signs on our streets have inscriptions in both languages and in some places only in German . . . they will soon so outnumber us, that all the advantages we have will be lost . . . we will no longer be able to preserve our language and even our government will become precarious." Jared Sparks, *Franklin, Works* (Boston: Tappan and Dennet, 1844), 7:66.
20. Smith, *The Mennonite Immigration to Pennsylvania*, 209.
21. Hostetler, *Amish Society*, 56, 57. Smith, *The Mennonite Immigration to Pennsylvania*, 225.
22. Smith, *The Mennonite Immigration to Pennsylvania*, 229.
23. Smith, *The Mennonite Immigration to Pennsylvania*, 205.
24. Wenger, *History of the Franconia Conference*, 399.
25. Stoltzfus, "History of the First Amish Mennonite Communities," 239.
26. Hostetler, *Amish Society*, 64.
27. Beiler, Joseph F. "Revolutionary War Records," 71.
28. MacMaster, *Land, Piety, Peoplehood*, 125–126.
29. Beiler, Joseph F., "Revolutionary War Records," 71.
30. McMaster, Horst and Ulle, *Conscience in Crisis*, 523–525.
31. Umble, "Memoirs of an Amish Bishop," 103.
32. MacMaster, *Land, Piety, Peoplehood*, 71.
33. This is also noted by Hostetler in reference to the ability of a family to hold children in the church in the 20th century. Those families that can provide their offspring with funds and farms have a much greater success in assuring their children's membership in the Amish church and community. Hostetler, *Amish Society*, 106.
34. Stoltzfus, "History of the First Amish Mennonite Communities," 239.
35. *Will Book*, Register Office of Berks County, Reading, Pennsylvania, 2:87.
36. Schmauk, "An Account of the Manners of the German Inhabitants," 63, 64.
37. Umble, "Memoirs of an Amish Bishop," 101–102.
38. Estate record of David Beiler of East Lampeter Township, Lancaster, Pennsylvania, Lancaster County Book, F:63.
39. Interviews done by David Wheatcroft and Eve Granick.
40. Lancaster County Courthouse Records, Lancaster, Pennsylvania.
41. Mifflin County Courthouse Records, Lewistown, Pennsylvania.

Amish Quilts: Their Beginnings

1. Interview done by David Wheatcroft and Eve Granick, Selinsgrove, Pennsylvania.
2. Hostetler, *Amish Society*, 65. These settlers formed communities in Butler, Stark, Wayne and Fulton counties in Ohio; Adams, Allen and Daviess counties in Indiana; Woodford and Tazewell counties in Illinois; Henry and Washington counties in Iowa; Lewis County in New York; Somerset County in Pennsylvania; and Waterloo and Perth counties in Ontario, Canada.
3. Smith, *Story of the Mennonites*, 275–292.
4. Statistics of Churches Census Bulletin, No. 131, Washington, D.C. U.S. Census of 1890.
5. Hostetler, *Amish Society*, 99. Figures are derived from Statistics of Churches, U.S. Census of 1890, *Mennonite Yearbook* and *The New American Almanac*.
6. *Mennonite Yearbook* (Scottdale, PA 1905–1967). *The New American Almanac* 1930–1979. Hostetler, *Amish Society*, 99. These figures were arrived at by a combination of information from these sources. The Amish do not keep careful numerical records of their membership beyond the number of church districts. Figures are based on a number of statistical analyses of the general trends in Amish population.
7. *The Mennonite Encyclopedia*, 1:96, 4:43.

Textiles: Their Changes from 1750–1950

1. The line of credit and goods stretched from the smallest towns to the merchants of London, but the generally slow quality of transportation and communication and the lack of any sophisticated production methods helped to keep the family farm as the chief unit of production. Lemon, "The Best Poor Man's Country," 27, 29.
2. *Cazenove Journal*, 1794.
3. Bishop, *A History of American Manufacturing*, 1:111.
4. English law forbade the export of manufacturing machinery, including models or drawings, and even the emigration of any skilled workman who might reproduce the machinery abroad. Slater left England secretly and arrived in New York in 1789. Hired by Moses Brown of Providence, Rhode Island, to set up a cotton mill, Slater built from memory the first mechanized cotton spinning spindle frames in America. Boorstein, *The Americans*, 26, 27.
5. Bishop, *A History of American Manufacturing*, 2:149.
6. Bishop, *A History of American Manufacturing*, 2:150.
7. Lancaster County Courthouse Records, Lancaster, Pennsylvania. Inventories were taken after a death by two or three men of the community. Christian Beiler's estate was appraised by two members of the Amish community, and then his possessions were sold at public sale. The extensive and detailed listing of fabric types and quantities is typical of the inventories of this era. Spellings vary widely but textiles were obviously a tremendously important asset and closely counted in inventories.
8. Bishop, *A History of American Manufacturing*, 2:453–456.
9. Wilson, *A History of Textiles*, 251.
10. Mifflin County Courthouse Records, Lewistown, Pennsylvania. Excerpts from the estate record papers of Michael Yoder, David Hartzler, Christian Zook.
11. Holmes County, Ohio, and Wayne County, Ohio, Courthouse Records. Excerpts from the estate record papers of Isaac Yoder, Sarah Schrock, John Zook.
12. Wilson, *A History of Textiles*, 255.
13. Ibid., 262.
14. Orlofsky, *Quilts in America*, 60.
15. *A History of Textiles*, 259.
16. Ibid., 281.
17. This comment was made by older Amish women in many communities. Interviews done by David Wheatcroft and Eve Granick.
18. Textile sample books can be found at: The Grace Paley Design Center, Philadelphia Textile Institute, Philadelphia, PA; Winterthur Museum Library, Wilmington, DE; Cooper Hewitt Museum, New York, NY; Metropolitan Museum of Art, New York, NY.
19. Chart is adapted from information in M.D. Potter and B.P. Corbman, *Textiles — Fiber to Fabric* (NY: McGraw Hill, 1967), 18–22.
20. Ibid., 25.
21. Edelstein, *Dye Balls and Family Colors*, 91.
22. Adrosko, *Natural Dyes and Home Dyeing*, 13.
23. Adrosko, *Natural Dyes and Home Dyeing*, 48.

24. Adrosko, *Natural Dyes and Home Dyeing*, 23.
25. Ibid., 35.
26. *The Sugarcreek Budget*, October 1915.
27. Wingate, *The Colorful Dupont Company*, 35.
28. Author interviews with Joyce Brown and William Greenburg.
29. "Remainders" are materials left over from orders placed by large-scale purchasers. For example, Sears Company will order several hundred thousand yards of denim for production of blue jeans made under their house label. Fabric left on the bolt after their order is filled is considered a remainder and sold at a much reduced cost. "Closeouts" are fabrics unsold at the close of a season. Again, the distributors are anxious to make room for new stock and sell these materials at lower costs. In both cases the materials are first quality goods. "Seconds" are materials considered slightly damaged by the manufacturer.
30. Author interview with an Amish woman in LaGrange County, Indiana.
31. Author interviews with Joyce Brown and William Greenburg.
32. *The Sugarcreek Budget*, September 1890.
33. *The Sugarcreek Budget*, May 1894.
34. *The Sugarcreek Budget*, April 1895.
35. *The Sugarcreek Budget*, August 1900.
36. *The Sugarcreek Budget*, November 1893.
37. *The Sugarcreek Budget*, November 1890.
38. *The Sugarcreek Budget*, May 1949.
39. *The Sugarcreek Budget*, 1910.
40. Author interview with the owner of Yoder's Department Store, Shipshewana, Indiana.
41. Author interview with the owner of W.L. Zimmerman's Store, Intercourse, Pennsylvania.
42. Advertising from a Rubinson Department Store flyer.
43. Emmet, Boris and Jeuck, *Catalogues and Counters*, 20.
44. Ibid.
45. *Sears and Roebuck Catalogue*, Spring 1896, 254, 315.
46. Ibid., Fall 1897.
47. Ibid., Fall 1901, 638.
48. Ibid., Fall 1901, 639.
49. Ibid., Spring 1910, 38–42.
50. Ibid., Fall 1915, 54.
51. Ibid., Fall 1915, 42.
52. Ibid., Fall/Winter 1918–1919, 375.
53. Ibid., Spring/Summer 1936, 388–390.
54. Ibid., Spring 1940, 675.
55. Interviews done by David Wheatcroft and Eve Granick in various Amish communities.

Amish Communities: Their Distinctive Quilts

1. Author interview with an Amish woman in West Union, Ohio.
2. Author interview with an Amish woman in Geauga County, Ohio.

3. Orlofsky, *Quilts in America*, 298–299.
4. Hostetler, *Amish Society*, 282.
5. Hostetler, *Amish Society*, 283. See photo on page 27 contrasting a typical Amish bonnet with the straw scoop hat worn by Nebraska Amish women. In a watercolor drawing by Lewis Miller in the collection of the Historical Society of York County, Pennsylvania, a portrait of "a Mennist woman" depicts the wearing of one of these hats.
6. *The Mennonite Encyclopedia*, 4:24–30.
7. For an in-depth reading on this subject see *The Mennonite Encyclopedia*, 4:24–30.
8. Holmes County, Ohio, Courthouse Records, Office of Deeds and Wills. Inventory of Catherine Hershberger; inventory of Barbara Hershberger.
9. Holmes County, Ohio, Courthouse Records, Office of Deeds and Wills. Inventory of Catherine Miller.
10. *The Mennonite Encyclopedia*, 4:28.
11. Gerber, "Personal Memoirs," 24–25.
12. LaGrange County, Indiana, Courthouse Records, Office of Deeds and Wills. Inventory of Joseph C. Yoder.
13. Hostetler, *Amish Society*, 99.
14. In my development of this thesis, I am indebted to conversations with David Pottinger.
15. Interviews with Amish families done by David Wheatcroft and Eve Granick.
16. Author interview with an Amish woman, Kalona, Iowa.
17. Smith, *The Story of the Mennonites*, 376–377.
18. Schlabach, *Peace, Faith, Nation*, 22.
19. Burkholder, *A Brief History of the Mennonites in Ontario*, 230–234.
20. Smith, *The Story of the Mennonites*, 409.
21. Author correspondence with David Luthy, Aylmer, Ontario.
22. Ibid.

Quiltmaking: Its Part in Amish Women's Lives

1. Author interview with an Amish woman, Loganton, Pennsylvania.
2. Author interview with an Amish woman, Nappanee, Indiana.
3. Ibid.
4. Author interview with an Amish woman, Kalona, Iowa.
5. Hostetler, *Amish Society*, 152.
6. Hostetler, *Amish Society*, 292.
7. Robert Merton, *Social Theory and Social Structure* (Glenco, IL: The Free Press, 1957), 140.
8. Hostetler, *Amish Society*, 293.
9. From a conversation between Michael Oruch and a member of a Tennessee Amish community.
10. From a conversation between David Pottinger and an Amish woman from Indiana.
11. Author conversations with Darwin Bearley contributed to the development of this thesis.
12. Author conversation with Julie Silber. Also Ferrero, Hedges, Silber, *Hearts and Hands*.

Bibliography

Textiles

Adrosko, Rita J. *Natural Dyes and Home Dyeing*. New York: Dover Publications, 1971.
American Fabrics Magazine. *The AF Encyclopedia of Textiles*. Englewood Cliffs, NJ: Prentice-Hall, 1973, 1980.
Bagnall, William. *The Textile Industry of the United States 1639–1810*. Boston: W.B. Clark and Co., 1893.
Bendure, Zelma and Gladys Pfeiffer. *America's Fabrics: Their Origin, History, Manufacture, Characteristics and Use*. New York: Macmillan Co., 1946.
Bishop, J. Leander. *A History of American Manufacturing from 1608 to 1860*. Philadelphia: E. Young, 1868. Reprint. New York: Johnson, 1967.
Edelstein, Sidney M. *Dye Balls and Family Colors — The Story of Packaged Dyes for the Home; Historical Notes on the Wet Processing Industry*. Dexter Chemical Corporation.
Emmet, Boris and John E. Jeuck. *Catalogues and Counters*. Chicago: University of Chicago Press, 1950.

Hall, A.J. *The Standard Handbook of Textiles*. England: Heywood Books, 1969.
Hess, Katherine. *Textile Fibers and Their Uses*. Chicago: J.B. Lippincott, 1936.
Hollen, Norma and Jane Saddler. *Textiles*. 3rd ed. New York: Macmillan, 1968.
Montgomery, Florence. *Textiles in America 1650–1870*. New York: W.W. Norton and Co., Winterthur/Barra Book.
Sears and Roebuck Catalogue. Chicago: Sears and Roebuck Co.
Weil, Gordon L. *Sears & Roebuck USA — The Great American Catalog Store and How It Grew*. New York: Stein and Day, 1977.
Wilson, Kax. *A History of Textiles*. Boulder, Colorado: Westview Press, 1979.
Wingate, Isabel. *Laboratory Swatch Book — Textile Fabrics and Their Selection, Some Guidelines for Examination of Fabric*.
——— *Textile Fabrics*. New York: Prentice Hall, 1935.
Wingate, P.J. *The Colorful Dupont Company*. Serendipity Press, 1982.

Author interviews with the following fabric sources for the Amish: Joyce Brown, Philadelphia, PA; William Greenburg, Philadelphia, PA; W.L. Zimmerman Store, Intercourse, PA; Yoder's Store, Shipshewana, IN.

American and Pennsylvania German History and Culture

Boorstein, Daniel. *The Americans: The Colonial Experience, The National Experience*. New York: Vintage Books, Random House, 1965.

Eshleman, H. Frank. *Historical Background and Annals of the Swiss and German Pioneer Settlers of Southeastern Pennsylvania*. Lancaster, Pa. 1917.

Fletcher, Stevenson W. *Pennsylvania Agriculture and Country Life 1840–1940*. Harrisburg: Commonwealth of Pennsylvania, Pennsylvania Historical and Museum Commission, 1955.

Geheret, Ellen J. *Rural Pennsylvania Clothing*. York, PA: Liberty Cap Books, 1976.

———— and Alan G. Keyser. *The Homespun Textile Traditions of the Pennsylvania Germans*. Harrisburg: Pennsylvania Historical and Museum Commission, 1976.

Glassie, Henry. *Patterns in Material Folk Culture of the Eastern United States*. Philadelphia: University of Pennsylvania Press, 1968.

Lemon, James T. *The Best Poor Man's Country: A Geographical Study of Early Southeastern Pennsylvania*. Baltimore: Johns Hopkins Press, 1972.

"A Record of the Journey of Theophile Cazenove Through NJ and Pennsylvania." *Cazenove Journal*, 1794.

Rosenberger, Homer T. *The Pennsylvania Germans 1891–1965*. Birdsboro, PA: Pennsylvania German Society 63, 1966.

Schantz, F.J.F. *The Domestic Life and Characteristics of the Pennsylvania German Pioneer*. Lancaster, PA: The Pennsylvania German Society 10, 1900.

Schmauk, Theodore E. *An Account of the Manners of the German Inhabitants of Pennsylvania by Benjamin Rush MD*. Notes of I.D. Rupp revised. Lancaster, PA: The Pennsylvania German Society 19, 1910.

Swank, Scott, Benno M. Forman, Frank H. Sommer, Arlene Palmer Schwind, Frederick S. Weiser, Donald H. Fennimore and Susan Burrows Swan. Hutchins, Catherine B., ed. *Arts of the Pennsylvania Germans*. New York: W.W. Norton and Co., 1983.

Amish History

Bachman, Calvin G. *The Old Order Amish Of Lancaster County*. Norristown, PA: The Pennsylvania German Society 49 (1942): 1–297.

Beachy, Alvin J. "The Amish Settlement in Somerset County, PA." *Mennonite Quarterly Review* 28, no. 4 (October 1954): 263–292.

Beller, Joseph F. "Eighteenth Century Amish in Lancaster County." *Mennonite Research Journal* 17 (October 1976).

———— "Revolutionary War Records." *The Diary* (March 1971).

Bender, Harold. "A Letter from Pennsylvania Mennonites to Holland in 1773." *Mennonite Quarterly Review* 3 (October 1929): 225–234.

———— "An Amish Bishops' Conference 1865." *Mennonite Quarterly Review* 20 (July 1946): 222–229.

———— "Some Early American Amish Mennonite Disciplines." *Mennonite Quarterly Review* 8 (April 1934): 90–98.

———— , ed. and trans. "The Minutes of the Amish Conference of 1809, Probably Held in Lancaster County, PA." *Mennonite Quarterly Review* 20 (July 1946): 239.

Burkholder, L.J. *A Brief History of the Mennonites in Ontario*. 1935. Reprint. Mennonite Historical Society of Ontario, 1986.

Collective Writing of John Beiler 1885–1937. Gordonville, PA: Pequea Publishers.

Conyngham, Redmond. "A History of the Mennonites and Aymenists or Amish." *The Register of Pennsylvania* (edited by Samuel Hazard) 7 (February 26, 1831), 7 (March 1831): 129–132, 150–153.

Cowley, W.K. "Old Order Amish Settlements: Diffusion and Growth." *Annuals of the Association of American Geographers* 68 (June 1978): 249–264.

Cross, Harold and Victor McKusick. "Amish Demography." *Social Biology* 17 (June 1970): 83–101.

Gascho, Milton. "The Amish Division 1693–1697 in Switzerland and Alsace." *Mennonite Quarterly Review* 11 (October 1937): 235–266.

Gerber, Rosina. "Personal Memoirs — The Pioneer Home." *Mennonite Historical Bulletin* 16, no. 24–25 (April 1955).

Gingerich, James N. "Ordinance or Ordering: Ordnung and Amish Ministers Meeting 1862–1879." *Mennonite Quarterly Review* 60, no. 2 (April 1986) 180–199.

Gingerich, Melvin. *Mennonite Attire Through Four Centuries*. Breinigsville, PA: The Pennsylvania German Society, 1970.

Gingerich, Orland. *The Amish of Canada*. Waterloo, Ontario: Conrad Press; Scottdale, PA: Herald Press, 1972.

Guengerich, S.D. "History of the Amish Settlement in Johnson County, Iowa." *Mennonite Quarterly Review* 3 (October 1929): 243–248.

Hostetler, John A. *Amish Society*. 3rd ed. Baltimore: The Johns Hopkins University Press, 1980.

———— "Amish Costume; Its European Origin." *The American-German Review* 22, no. 6 (August–September 1956): 11–14.

———— *Annotated Bibliography of the Amish*. Scottdale, PA: Mennonite Publishing House, 1951.

———— "The Amish Use of Symbols," *Journal of the Royal Anthropological Institute* 94, no. 1 (1963).

———— with Erickson, Eugene P., and Julia A. Erickson. "The Cultivation of Soil as a Moral Directive: Population Growth, Family Ties and the Maintenance of Community Among the Old Order Amish." *Rural Sociology* 45, no. 1 (Spring 1980): 49–68.

———— "The Life and Times of Samuel Yoder 1824–1884." *Mennonite Quarterly Review* 22 (October 1948): 226–241.

———— "The Old Order Amish on the Great Plains: A Study in Cultural Vulnerability." *Ethnicity on the Great Plains*. Edited by Fred Leubke. Lincoln: University of Nebraska Press, 1979.

———— "Old Order Amish Survival." *Mennonite Quarterly Review* 51, no. 4 (October 1977): 352–361.

———— "Old World Extinction and New World Survival of the Amish: A Study in Group Maintenance and Dissolution." *Rural Sociology* 20, nos. 3–4 (September, December, 1955): 212–219.

———— "Persistence and Change Patterns in Amish Society." *Ethnology* 3, no. 2: (April 1964): 185–198.

Huntington, Gertrude. "Dove at the Window: A Study of an Old Order Amish Community in Ohio." PhD diss., Yale University, 1956.

Kollmorgen, Walter M. "Culture of a Contemporary Rural Community; The Old Order Amish of Lancaster County, PA." *Rural Life Studies* no. 4. U.S. Department of Agriculture (September 1942).

Landing, James E. "Amish Settlement in North America." *Bulletin of the Illinois Geographical Society* 12 (December 1970).

———— "The Old Order Settlement at Nappanee Indiana; Oldest in Indiana," *Mennonite Historical Bulletin* (July 1969).

Luthy, David, *Amish Settlements Across America*. Aylmer, Ontario: Pathway Publishers, 1985.

MacMaster, Richard K. *Land, Piety, Peoplehood: The Establishment of Mennonite Communities in America 1683–1790*. The Mennonite Experience in America, vol. 1, Scottdale, PA: Herald Press, 1985.

———— with Samuel Horst, and Robert Ulle. *Conscience in Crisis: Mennonites and Other Peace Churches in America 1739–1789*. Studies in Anabaptist and Mennonite History, no. 20. Scottdale, PA: Herald Press, 1979.

The Mennonite Encyclopedia, Vols. I, II, III, IV. Hillsboro, KS: Mennonite Brethren Publishing House; Newton, KS: Mennonite Publication Office; Scottdale, PA: The Mennonite Publishing House, 1955–1959.

Mook, Maurice A. "Extinct Amish Mennonite Communities in Pennsylvania." *Mennonite Quarterly Review* 30, no. 4 (October 1956): 267–276.

———, ed. "The Changing Pattern of Pennsylvania German Culture 1855–1955." *Pennsylvania History* 23, no. 3 (July 1956): 311–340.

——— "The Amish Community of Atlantic PA." *Mennonite Quarterly Review* 28, no. 4 (October 1954): 293–301.

Nagata, Judith A. "Continuity and Change among the Old Order Amish of Illinois." Thesis, University of Illinois, 1968.

Reed, Thomas. "The Amish—A Case Study in Accommodation and Suppression." *Notre Dame Lawyer* 43 (June 1968): 764–776.

Ringenberg, William C. "Development and Division in the Mennonite Community in Allen County, Indiana." *Mennonite Quarterly Review* 50 (April 1976): 114–131.

Schlabach, Theron F. *Peace, Faith, Nation: Mennonites and Amish in Nineteenth-Century America.* The Mennonite Experience in America, vol. 2. Scottdale, PA: Herald Press, 1988.

Smith, C. Henry. *The Mennonites of America.* Goshen, Indiana, 1909.

——— *The Story of the Mennonites.* Berne, Indiana: Mennonite Book Concern, 1941.

Smith, Willard H. *Mennonites in Illinois.* Studies in Anabaptist and Mennonite History No. 24. Scottdale, PA: Herald Press, 1983.

Stoltzfus, Grant. "History of the First Amish Mennonite Communities in America." *Mennonite Quarterly Review* 28, no. 4 (October 1954): 235–262.

Stoltzfus, Victor. "Reward and Sanction: The Adaptive Continuity of Amish Life." *Mennonite Quarterly Review* 51, no. 4. (October 1977): 308–318.

The Sugarcreek Budget. Sugarcreek, Ohio: The Budget Printing Company.

Umble, John. "The Amish Mennonites of Union County PA, Social and Religious Life, Part I." *Mennonite Quarterly Review* 7, no. 2 (April 1933): 71–96.

——— "The Amish Mennonites of Union County PA, Social and Religious Life, Part II." *Mennonite Quarterly Review* 7, no. 3 (July 1933): 162–190.

———, trans. and ed. "Memoirs of an Amish Bishop." *Mennonite Quarterly Review* 22 (April 1948): 94–115.

——— "The Oak Grove-Pleasant Hill Amish Mennonite Church in Wayne County, Ohio in the 19th Century 1815–1900." *Mennonite Quarterly Review* 31, no. 3 (July 1957): 156–226.

Weber, Harry F. *Centennial History of the Mennonites of Illinois: Studies in Anabaptist and Mennonite History 1829–1929.* Scottdale, PA: The Mennonite Historical Society, Mennonite Publishing House, 1931.

Wenger, John C. *History of the Mennonites of the Franconia Conference.* Telford, PA: Franconia Mennonite Historical Society, 1937.

Yoder, Elam. "History of the Valley View Amish Mennonite Church." *Mennonite Historical Bulletin* 25 (April 1964).

Yoder, Harvey. "The Budget of Sugarcreek, Ohio 1890–1920." *Mennonite Quarterly Review* 40, no. 1 (January 1966): 27–47.

Quilts

Bishop, Robert, and Elizabeth Safanda. *A Gallery of Amish Quilts.* NY: Dutton, 1976.

Ferrero, Pat, Elaine Hedges, and Julie Silber. *Hearts and Hands: The Influence of Women and Quilts on American Society.* San Francisco: The Quilt Digest Press, 1987.

Granick, Eve W. "A Century of Old Order Amish Quiltmaking in Mifflin County." In *In the Heart of Pennsylvania, Symposium Papers,* edited by Jeanette Lasansky. Oral Traditions Projects of Union County, PA, 1986.

Hayes, Connie, and Evelyn Gleason. "Nebraskan Quilts—The Discovery of a Distinctive Style of Amish Quilts." *Antique Collecting* 2, no. 8 (January 1979).

McCauley, Daniel and Kathryn. *Decorative Arts of the Amish of Lancaster County.* Intercourse, PA: Good Books, 1988.

Orlofsky, Patsy and Myron. *Quilts in America.* NY: McGraw Hill, 1974.

Pellman, Rachel and Kenneth. *The World of Amish Quilts.* Intercourse, PA: Good Books, 1984.

——— *Amish Crib Quilts.* Intercourse, PA: Good Books, 1985.

Pottinger, David. *Quilts from the Indiana Amish.* NY: E.P. Dutton, 1983.

Author interviews with the following quilt collectors: Darwin Bearley, Rebecca Haarer, Drs. Donald and Patricia Herr, Gail Van der Hoof and Jonathan Holstein, Michael Oruch, David Pottinger and Marilyn Woodin.

Index

About the Author

Eve Granick's interest in the Amish began in the mid-1970s when she traveled throughout the Midwest with her antique dealer husband, David Wheatcroft, in search of Amish quilts. Buying and selling Amish quilts led to collecting them, and inevitably to a curiosity about the milieu in which they were produced.

For the past six years she has conducted extensive research for this book. Along the way she has lectured and written articles about the Amish and their quilts.

Eve grew up in Elkins Park, Pennsylvania, and received a B.F.A. from Washington University, St. Louis, and an M.F.A. from the University of Iowa, Iowa City. She presently lives in Lewisburg, Pennsylvania, with her husband, David, and daughter, Kate.